Does the Qur'an
(Koran) Really
Say That?

Does the Qur'an (Koran) Really Say That?

TRUTHS AND MISCONCEPTIONS ABOUT ISLAM

Naqi Elmi

ARCHWAY
PUBLISHING

Archway Publishing books may be ordered through booksellers or by contacting:

Archway Publishing
1663 Liberty Drive
Bloomington, IN 47403
www.archwaypublishing.com
1 (888) 242-5904

ISBN: 978-1-4808-7385-8 (sc)
ISBN: 978-1-4808-7383-4 (hc)
ISBN: 978-1-4808-7384-1 (e)

Library of Congress Control Number: 2019902393

Print information available on the last page.

Archway Publishing rev. date: 5/1/2019

Dedicated to those who seek the truth

Contents

So, announce the Good News to My Servants, those who listen to what is said, and follow the best thereof . . .
—The Qur'an (39:17–18)

Preface

Due to the violent events in recent years, particularly since 9/11, critics of Islam have attacked the faith and attributed violence by extremists to its holy book, the Qur'an. Many critics and people in general are uninformed about Islamic laws, concepts, and teachings, and they question how a so-called religion of peace could advocate violence. How much of what the critics and Islamic extremists claim is true? And what about the often-quoted verses from the Qur'an that seem to advocate violence?

This book attempts to answer such questions by addressing some of the myths, misrepresentations, and misunderstandings often propagated by critics who assert themselves as experts on the faith. Interestingly, this includes extremists who claim to be experts on the faith as well.

The media's tendency to sensationalize the news has had a hand in spreading false impressions of Islam. Even some western writers and scholars portray Islam as a religion of violence and radicalism. They often confuse Islamic teachings with the social and cultural practices within Muslim communities. Faith, as most of us know, is rarely practiced in a vacuum but rather under the influence of political circumstances, socioeconomics, social ranking, culture, ethnicity, and nationality. So-called experts—social scientists and scholars—should be able to draw distinctions between what a religion teaches and how these other factors drive behavior. Only when Islamic teachings and laws are studied in a scholarly manner will there be a deeper understanding of the dynamics at play within Muslim communities.

Since 9/11, there has been increasing interest in Islam, for many in the West are curious and want to learn more about the faith. Some base their understanding on what they hear in the media, particularly by uninformed critics of Islam. This is unfortunate because any hope the Christian West and the Muslim world have of transcending the misconceptions and misunderstandings require proper understanding on both sides. For we do not have a clash of civilizations, but rather a clash of perceptions. These false impressions create unnecessary hurdles to promoting peaceful coexistence in today's world, which is becoming increasingly diverse. As such, there is a greater need to understand world religions objectively and to explore common ground so we may promote solidarity and world peace. The surge in interfaith relations within the US and other Western countries is further proof that the time for religious rivalries has come to an end. Furthermore, Muslim communities recognize and appreciate the support of the many Christians, Jews, and followers of other faiths who stood by Muslims while the fingers of many were pointed at Muslim citizens who had nothing to do with these violent acts yet were blamed.

This book focuses on Islamic faith and its doctrine on the topics of violence, war, and peace based on the Qur'an (or Koran, an older spelling that does not well reflect the Arabic pronunciation) and its practical aspect, as implemented by the Prophet Muhammad (peace be upon him (PBUH)). My intention is neither to introduce Islam nor discuss general Islamic principles or the fourteen hundred years of Islamic history. There are many books and references available on these general topics. This book instead focuses on Islamic history as it relates to the life and times of the Prophet Muhammad (PBUH) in order to demonstrate Islamic principles in practice where violence, war, and peace are concerned.

Throughout this book, I have tried to take an analytical and objective approach in presenting facts and reasoning through proper meaning and interpretation of the verses. In doing so, I have relied on the Qur'anic context, the authentic prophetic traditions, and historical perspectives. Narratives reported by scholars throughout Islamic history are not relied upon as evidence or as part of the Islamic canon, because individuals have their own opinions and understandings, which may be biased. However, I draw on sample authentic narrations as historic witnesses to demonstrate the subject matter. In addition, history is often full of reports and narratives that sometimes contradict one another; hence, a thorough comparative analysis of these narratives should be made and contrasted with the Qur'anic verses. As such, I have not relied upon such reports or narratives in this work, even though some critics and extremists have done so. Since these discussions are outside of the Qur'an, I have tried to stay within the Qur'anic discussion in order to disavow any false attribution made to the Islamic holy book, which is considered the main authority on Islam.

Critics of Islam often rely on particular Qur'anic verses to depict Islam as a violent faith. The crown jewel of these verses is the abbreviated version of verse 2:191, which states "and slay them wherever you find them." This book particularly addresses misrepresentations of such verses. Cherry-picking verses or parts of verses has become a standard practice among critics of Islam whose aim is not to seek answers, but to present Islam in a different light.

Chapters 1 through 5 summarize Islamic concepts that relate to war and peace in order to raise awareness, as I hope these chapters address many, if not all, of the questions, myths, and misconceptions circulating on these topics. Chapter 6 covers the Qur'anic verses most often used by critics and extremists. A factual response to allegations and misunderstandings surrounding each verse is presented, followed by parting thoughts in chapter 7. My hope and intention behind this work is for curious readers, fair-minded critics, and extremists to read this book in its entirety as they try to reach their own informed conclusions.

Chapter 1
The Role of Religion

WHAT IS THE ROLE of religion in one's life? Generally speaking, the purpose of faith is to give guidance on how to live a righteous, peaceful life while knowing and worshiping the Creator and discovering the purpose of life on earth. In short, it is a prescription, or a manual, on how to live a happy, righteous, and prosperous life. The purpose of religion is to bring about peace and harmony to the individual and what surrounds him or her, including coexistence with other living beings and the environment should he or she choose to subscribe to it. Religion gives one a sense of purpose, gratitude in times of prosperity, and hope during hardships.

Verses in any holy book can be looked at from two different points of view: an evil or malicious point of view, or a virtuous and upright point of view, depending upon one's bias, tendencies, and agenda. As individuals, God allows us to make our decision through free will. True religion brings about goodness, hope, and righteousness; however, deviation from it brings about evil. What violent extremists do is evil, as they have no respect for the sanctity of human life and its surrounding.

A closer look at the verses of the Qur'an reveals its objective, which is to explain what is good versus what is evil (as do verses of other scriptures). It draws on many stories and events exemplifying (and warning about) the conflicts between good and evil in the past. Indeed, it is the purpose of religion to give glad tidings to mankind with the hope that good will overcome evil. Religion is supposed to give guidance on how to lead a noble life by being a good human being and how to produce a good society made up of good individuals who grow, innovate, and reach peaks of humanity, thereby making their social environment a better place to live. Unfortunately, throughout history, humans have often distorted and manipulated religion in order to gain power, wealth, and influence. This leaves many with a false perception of religion.

Some people might say they believe in God but do not follow a religion. This is where we must draw a distinction between knowing (recognizing) God and worshiping Him. Someone may gain immense knowledge regarding the existence of God, but in practice does not follow God's commands or worship Him. There are those with a negative perception of religion who say, "I believe in God but follow no religion." However, knowing God and merely acknowledging His existence makes Him an abstract being Who is hands off and has no role in managing, controlling, and sustaining the universe, including all the creations within it. From this point of view, God has no message, and it is not clear why He created all the creatures. It is as if someone goes through an elaborate scheme to build a company and a factory, with all the production people and equipment in place, ready for operation, but gives no instructions, directions, rules, plans, or production strategy and leaves the company on its own. The workers are told nothing. They can come whenever they want and do whatever they want. Then one may ask why would you create such a company?

Through religion, especially Islam, God is involved and relevant in believers' daily life. He is closer to people than they are to themselves. His revelations (through His Messenger) guide and give directions, duties, and a sense of purpose. If we created ourselves, then perhaps we would define the purpose.

In believers' minds and hearts, God created them, God sustains them, and through religion God gave them the instruction manual on how to live happy, hopeful, and righteous lives in this world, as well as in the hereafter. As such, believers worship this God and serve Him by fulfilling their duties as God intended.

Some sociologists consider religions within their historical contexts. That is, every religion corresponds to the historical events from which it came. They add that religion is not something to be placed on a shelf or understood as something abstract and without effect. For example, Islam is a summation of fourteen hundred years of history, which defines it. Christianity is defined by over two thousand years of history, not what is necessarily written in the Bible, or in the Qur'an (in the case of Islam), and everyone has a different understanding of these texts. Sociologists conclude that whatever occurred in the history of Christianity is indeed Christianity. And whatever occurred in the history of Islam comprises Islam. This narrative exists today, especially in theocracies or societies with religious overtones. Sociologists say that because of what clerics do or dictate, we have left religion, or they say, "This is the reality of Islam or Christianity (or another religion), defined by what has happened over the past centuries of their existence."

If we look at any of these histories we will see persecutions, killings, and deviations along with noble acts and liberation as well. Sociologists see human behavior as born out of religion and say religion has both positive and negative effects on a society. Many people subscribe to this point of view. They add that religious people believe in abstract and impractical concepts that exist only in books; therefore, if Islam is to be judged, it is equal to and defined by its history. Many Muslims defend the position that the horrible events of the past should not be attributed to nor blamed on Islam, and they refuse to surrender to such narratives.

The position of Muslims or the counterpoint from Muslims (and, in fact, advocates of religion) is simple and rather realistic. Firstly, as an example, if you ask a Muslim what Islam says about lying, cheating, backbiting, slander, adultery, or any social injustice, he or she will emphatically say that Islam condemns or forbids such acts. Yet, there are those who often lie, cheat, or commit any of these acts. When asked if religion told them to commit such acts, they will say no and that they are indeed acting against their religion. Why then is an act considered against one's religion attributed to that religion? How could such an act be counted as part of a religion or its teachings? By which reasoning can one accept such a narrative? Indeed, one can blame religion if someone acts according to the teachings of a religion and arrives at the wrong results.

Secondly, if we are saying that whatever happens in the history of a religion reflects that religion, then what happens to all the noble acts committed by religious men and women who have stood against injustice and lived righteous lives? Should we not count them as products of religions and their teachings? If we do so, then we are in fact combining two contradictory terms. Ultimately, Islam is saying either lie or don't lie, cheat or don't cheat, commit injustices or don't. Which is it? Islam cannot be both; it either advocates for such acts or not. Religion cannot combine both. History, however, reflects both.

Thirdly, there were events that occurred in the past, historic in nature but influenced by religion. Such events in fact were not a result of religion, but rather a symptom arising from external factors, such as political motives, foreign and economic interests, those with religious masks, and so forth. Are we to include such events as part of the religion as well?

If these are part of religion, then what criterion can researchers and scholars of religion use in order to study religion? If the religion has it all (including the contradictions), then what is there to be studied? Where is the divine guidance?

When we refer to the Qur'an and its traditions for guidance, it means we rely on it as the canon, the criterion that separates Islam and Muslims' behavior.

Chapter 2
One Religion?

ONE MIGHT ASK, "IF God is one, then why are there so many faiths?" Indeed, there is only one faith for those who believe in the oneness of God. In all monotheistic faiths, the fundamental belief is that there is only one deity worthy of worship and only one God Who is the Creator, the Lord (owner), and the sustainer. This goes back not only to all Abrahamic faiths but also to earlier faiths from Adam and Noah (peace be upon them (PBUT)) to the last messenger, Muhammad (PBUH). Oneness of God resonates as a fundamental belief in all these faiths.

While Islam is commonly known as a religion brought by Muhammad (PBUH), the definition is universal, and its all-inclusive meaning is "Peace through *submission* and *surrender* to God." The word *Islam* does not refer to any person, nation, or time, just to *submission* and *surrender*. The fundamental message of Islam is pure monotheism, and oneness of God is not new to this faith. Furthermore, Islam completes the earlier faiths as it relates to the true message of monotheism. The articles of faith in Islam include believing in one God (Allah) and worshiping Him only, believing in all His messengers (Muhammad (PBUH) and all those before him) and in all scriptures, including the Torah, scrolls, Psalms, Old Testament, New Testament, and Final Testament (the Qur'an). This also includes believing in angels, the resurrection day, and the divine destiny. Based on Qur'anic text, Muslims believe all messengers of God believed in one God,

worshiped one God, and truly *submitted* and *surrendered* to Him. As
such, they were all Muslims. As the Qur'an states,

> Verily, this brotherhood (nation) of yours is a
> single brotherhood (nation), and I am your Lord:
> therefore serve me [worship Me]. (21:92)[1]

The Islamic view is that from time to time new faiths came as reminders to different nations and generations who had deviated from
the true message (or had not heard it). These new faiths also brought
new rules and edicts based on the conditions and situations at the
time. However, the main message—oneness of God and solely worshiping and serving Him—did not change. Hence, the notion that
Muslims are somehow supposed to kill Christians and Jews wherever
they find them as so-called infidels is baseless. The Qur'an calls them
People of the Book or People of Scripture.

If there were battles in which some Christians or Jews died, it
wasn't because of their faith or refusal to accept Islam, but because
of their aggression and breaking of treaties with Muslims (more on
this later). The general Qur'anic attitude toward People of the Book
is that of an invitation.

> Say, O People of the Book! Come to common terms as
> between us and you: That we worship none but Allah; that
> we associate no partners with him; that we erect not, from
> among ourselves, Lords and patrons other than Allah. (3:64)

Chapter 3
The Islamic View

WE NOW EXAMINE ISLAMIC views on peace and war or violence in general. In this section, we briefly cover definitions regarding establishing peace, rules of engagement in war, and general attitudes of Islam toward peace and violence. In the sections to follow, we will also cover select topics whereby the critics of Islam have chosen to attack this faith with, as we clarify, the facts and historical events surrounding these topics.

3.1 The Basis of Islamic Law

According to Professor Muhammad Abdel Haleem,

> The Qur'an is the supreme authority in Islam and the primary source of Islamic Law, including the laws regulating war and peace. The second source is the hadith, the traditions of the Prophet Muhammad's acts and deeds, which can be used to confirm, explain or elaborate Qur'anic teachings, but may not contradict the Qur'an, since they derive their authority from the Qur'an itself. Together these (the Qur'an and tradition) form the basis for all other sources of Islamic law, such as *ijma'* (consensus of Muslim scholars on an opinion regarding any given subject) and

qiyas (reasoning by analogy). These and others are merely methods to reach decisions based on the texts or the spirit of the Qur'an and Hadith, as they are the only binding sources of Islamic law. Again, nothing is acceptable if it contradicts the text or the spirit of these two sources. Any opinions reached by individual scholars or schools of Islamic law are no more than opinions. The founders of these schools never laid exclusive claim to the truth or invited people to follow them over any other scholars. Western writers often take the views of this or that classical or modern Muslim writer as 'the Islamic view,' presumably based on assumptions drawn from the Christian tradition, where the views of people (priests and theologians) like St. Augustine or St. Thomas Aquinas are often cited as authorities. In Islam, however, for a scholar's view to gain credibility, it must demonstrate its textual basis in the Qur'an and authentic tradition, as well as its derivation from a sound linguistic understanding of these texts.[2]

Abdel Haleem adds:

Ijtihad (exerting one's reason to reach judgments on the basis of these two sources) is the mechanism by which Muslim scholars find solutions for the ever changing and evolving life around them. The closing of the door of ijtihad is a myth propagated by many Western scholars, some of whom imagine that 'the door' still remains closed and that Muslims have nothing to fall back on except the decisions of the schools of law and scholars of the classical period. In fact, contemporary scholars in Muslim countries reach their own decisions on laws governing all sorts of *new* situations, using the same methodology based on the

Qur'an, its traditions, and the principles derived from them without feeling bound by the conclusions of any former school of law. The fundamental sources of Islamic teachings on peace and the rules of engagement in war are in the Qur'an and its traditions.[3]

Having covered above the main sources of Islamic law, the message to the critics of Islam, as well as to the extremists, is as follows:

- The main sources of Islamic ruling on engaging with the enemy comes from the Qur'an and authentic traditions (authentic Hadith) of the Prophet Muhammad's (PBUH) conduct and implementation as described above;
- We acknowledge the unfortunate fact that many invalid reports and rulings have found their way into well-known history books and *seera* (biographies of the Prophet) that have not been verified through scholarly methodologies and chain of reports; hence, they are invalid. In fact, in some history books, such as that by Muhammad ibn Jarir al-Tabari, a disclaimer has been given that historical reports are subject to the reader's verification. Hence, one cannot rely on a single report and draw conclusions;
- A stand-alone report, translation, or narration based on some historic event or someone's conclusion cannot be considered a proven source;
- Short of scholarly research and established methodology, how can one at least gauge the validity of a report? The method used by many is to ask the following questions:
  o Does the report agree with the Qur'an and the authentic (established) tradition?
  o Has there been a similar report made by others through different chains of narrations and by whom?
  o Does the report sound rational? Islam is a faith that appeals to one's mind and reasoning. Does the report make logical sense and appeal to one's mind from a rational point of

view in terms of the people involved, timing, comparison, concurrent events, etc.?

If the answer to any of the above is no, then the report is invalid and cannot be considered a source, regardless of it being listed in any well-known book or narrated by any well-known scholar. Beyond many misrepresented and mistranslated verses of the Qur'an, many reports cited by the extremists and critics do fall into this category, as both groups want to impose certain opinions or an agenda on Qur'anic verses and reinforce their argument through these invalid reports.

An open letter written to Abu Bakr al-Baghdadi (the ISIS leader) and signed by over 120 Muslim scholars throughout the world, reiterated, "it is also forbidden in Islam to issue a *fatwa* (a legal opinion or edict) without all the necessary learning requirements. Even then the fatwa must follow Islamic legal theory as defined in the classical texts. It is also forbidden to cite a portion of a verse from the Qur'an— or part of a verse—to derive a ruling without examining everything that the Qur'an and hadith teach related to that matter. In other words, there are strict subjective and objective prerequisites for *fatawa* (rulings), and one cannot cherry-pick Qur'anic verses for legal arguments without considering the entire Qur'an and its hadith."[4].

Regarding the legal theory (*usul al-fiqh*) and the Qur'anic exegesis, the letter says, "With regards to Qur'anic exegesis, and the understanding of Hadith, and issue in legal theory in general, the methodology set forth by God in the Qur'an and the Prophet (PBUH) in the Hadith is as follows: to consider everything that has been revealed relating to a particular question in its entirety, without depending on only parts of it, and then to judge—if one is qualified—based on all available scriptural sources. God says: "What, do you believe in part of the Book, and disbelieve in part?" (2:85); "They pervert words from their contexts; and they have forgotten a portion of what they were reminded of" (5:13); "Those who have reduced the Recitation, to parts" (15:9). Once all relevant scriptural passages have been gathered, the "general" has to be distinguished from the "specific", and the 'conditional' from the 'unconditional'. Also, the "unequivocal" passages have to be distinguished from the allegorical ones. Moreover, the reasons and circumstances for revelation (*asbab al-nuzul*) for all the passages and verses, in addition to all the other hermeneutical conditions that the classical imams have specified, must be understood."[5]

The open letter also points out some of the important qualities a scholar who issues legal opinions (fatawa) must possess and disciplines he must master: "It is imperative that the mufti must be a scholar of language, for the Shari'a is [in] Arabic. . . . It is imperative that he be a scholar of syntax and parsing. . . . It is imperative that he be a scholar of the Qur'an, for the Qur'an is the basis of all rulings. . . . Knowledge of textual abrogation is indispensable; and the science of the fundamentals of jurisprudence (*usul*) is the cornerstone of the whole subject. . . . He should also know the various degrees of proofs and arguments . . . as well as their histories. [He should also know] the science of Hadith so that he can distinguish the authentic from the weak; and the acceptable from the apocryphal. . . . [He should also know] jurisprudence."[6]

3.2   Peaceful Relations

From an Islamic perspective, Abdel Haleem says, "The relationship between individuals and nations is one of peace. War is a contingency that becomes necessary at certain times and under certain conditions. Muslims learn from the Qur'an that God's objective in creating the human race as different communities was so they should relate to each other peacefully."[7] The Qur'an states:

> O mankind! We created you from a single (pair) of a male and a female, and made you into nations and tribes, that you may know [recognize] each other. Verily, the most honored of you in the sight of Allah is (he who is) the most righteous of you, And Allah has full knowledge and is well acquainted (with all things). (49:13)

The Qur'an encourages coexistence and living in peace if a society or a nation is not transgressed or violated, as the following verses demonstrate:

Except those who join a group between whom and you
there is a treaty (of peace), or those who approach you with
hearts restraining them from fighting you as well as fighting
their own people. If Allah had willed, He could have given
them power over you, and they would have fought you:
Therefore, if they withdraw from you but fight you not, and
(instead) send you (Guarantees of) peace, then Allah Hath
opened no way for you (to war against them). (4:90)

Allah forbids you not, with regard to those who fight you not
for (your) Faith nor drive you out of your homes, from dealing
kindly and justly with them: for Allah loveth those who
are just. (60:8)

Muslims, for many centuries, had active and positive trade relations with all peoples and countries that were not hostile toward them.
Islam established a form of democratic government fourteen
hundred years ago. Asghar Ali Engineer writes, "There is nothing
in the Qur'an or Islamic teachings that oppose democracy or democratic governance. The Qur'an requires even the Prophet (PBUH)
to consult his companions in all secular matters (3:159) and encourages Muslims in general to consult each other (42:38). Thus, the
Qur'an has long encouraged democratic institutions even before
the world knew of democracy. However, the pre-modern society
was not prepared for democratic governance, and Muslims eventually came under the influence of Roman and Sassanid [Persian]
institutions, and soon a monarchy developed in the Islamic world.
If one studies the Qur'an carefully and impartially, one would find
it refreshingly modern, liberal (and relevant and timeless), and humane in approach. It emphasizes human dignity (17:70), freedom
of conscience and worship (2:256), and equality of all human beings without any discrimination based on race, creed, color, language, or tribe, as these distinctions are only for identities, not
discrimination (49:13). These most modern ideals are part of the
United Nations' Universal Declaration of Human Rights (1949)."[8]

Nowhere in the Qur'an is changing people's religion given as a cause for waging war.[9]

None of the battles Prophet Muhammad (PBUH) engaged in were about forcing people to convert to Islam. The Qur'an instructs that there should be no coercion in religion (2:256). It also says the following: "Say, 'the truth is from your Lord': Let him who will, believe (it), and let him who will, reject (it)" (18:29), and "To you your religion (way), and to me mine" (109:6).

Furthermore, the Qur'an reminds us that people will remain different: "And if thy Lord had willed, He verily would have made mankind one people, but they will not cease to dispute (differ)" (11:118). In fact, God tells His Messenger that most people will not believe: "Yet most of mankind will not believe, however ardently thou do desire it" (12:103).

While this book will examine specific Qur'anic verses as they pertain to war, historical reports show that all the battles during the Prophet's (PBUH) lifetime, under the guidance of the Qur'an and the Prophet (PBUH), occurred only in self-defense or to preempt an imminent attack as is also shown in the history and the Prophet's (PBUH) biography. For more than ten years in Mecca, Muslims were persecuted, but before permission was given to fight, they were instructed to endure with patience and fortitude: "Forgive and overlook till Allah accomplish His purpose". (2:109). Or, "To those who leave their homes in the cause of Allah, after suffering oppression, We will assuredly give a goodly home in this world; but truly the reward of the Hereafter will be greater. If they only realized. (They are) those who persevere in patience, and put their trust on their Lord" (16:41–42).

After Muslims were forced from their homeland, those who remained were subjugated to even more oppression. Only then did God give His permission to fight:

To those against whom war is made, permission is given (to fight), because they are wronged; and verily, Allah is most powerful for their aid; (They are) those who have been expelled (driven) from their homes in defiance of right, (for no cause) except that they say, 'our Lord is Allah'. Did not Allah check one set of people by means of another, there would surely have been pulled down monasteries, churches, synagogues, and mosques, in which the name of Allah is commemorated in abundant measure. Allah will certainly aid those who aid his (cause); for verily Allah is full of Strength, Exalted in Might, (able to enforce His Will);- (They are) those who, if We establish them in the land, (they will) establish regular prayer and give regular charity, enjoin the right and forbid wrong: with Allah rests the end (and decision) of (all) affairs. (22:39–41)

According to Abdel Haleem, "Here war is seen as justifiable and necessary to defend people's rights to their own beliefs, and once the believers have been given victory they should not become triumphant or arrogant or have a sense of being a superpower because of the promise of help given above. The rewards are for those who do not seek to exalt themselves on earth or to spread corruption."[10] The Qur'an states:

That Home of the Hereafter We shall give to those who intend not high-handedness [exalt themselves], or mischief on earth, and the end is (best) for the righteous. (28:83)

Abdel Haleem adds:

Righteous intention is an essential condition. When fighting occurs, it should be *Fee Sabil Allah*—In the way (path) of God—as is repeated often in the Qur'an. His way is prescribed in the Qur'an as the way of truth and justice, including all the teachings it gives on the justifications and the conditions for conducting war. The Prophet (PBUH) was asked about those who fight for the spoils of war and those who fight out of self-aggrandizement or the desire to be seen as a hero. He said that none of these were in the path of God. The one who fights in the path of God, is he who fights so that the word of God is uppermost

(Bukhari). This expression of the word of God being "uppermost" was misunderstood by some to mean that Islam should gain political power over other religions. However, if we use the principle that "different verses of the Qur'an interpret each other," we find in verse 9:40 that by simply concealing the Prophet (PBUH) in a cave from his enemies after he had narrowly escaped an attempt to murder him, God made His word "uppermost", and the word of the wrongdoers "lowered." This could not be described as gaining military victory or political power.[11]

The Qur'an states:

If you help not (your leader), (it is no matter): for Allah did indeed help him, when the Unbelievers drove him out: he had no more than one companion; they two were in the cave, and he said to his companion, 'Have no grief, for Allah is with us': then Allah sent down His peace upon him, and strengthened him with forces which you saw not, and He made the word of the unbelievers the lowest, and the Word of Allah is the highest, for Allah is Exalted in might, Wise. (9:40)

3.3   Jihad

Another term often misunderstood, misrepresented, and even mistranslated is *jihad*.

Islam's critics claim that Muslims and the politically correct continuously repeat that jihad means only "striving to be a good Muslim." This is not entirely true. Early in Islamic history, jihad came to mean fighting against unbelievers in order to expand the territory under Muslim rule. And that Islamic history is full of leaders declaring jihad against their enemies. This claim has elements of truth. The term has been used (or misused) in such context in a few Islamic writings and by a few religious leaders, especially those who abused religion for political gains. The term had been used incorrectly and frivolously by many Muslim leaders in order to galvanize the masses for what they considered was a just cause.

Firstly, jihad does not mean holy war as it is portrayed in some books and in the media. As pointed out on the website IslamiCity. org and elsewhere, holy war does not exist as a term in Arabic, and its translation into Arabic sounds alien. Secondly, the term that is specifically used in the Qur'an for physical fighting or combat is *qital,* not jihad. Holy war doesn't even exist in the Qur'an. It is a word commonly used during the Crusades (the holy wars). Indeed, even some Muslims had been misled by this interpretation for nearly a millennium. After 9/11, Muslims were forced to take another careful look at the meaning of this word, and they found it to be entirely different.

Jihad is often associated with violence and is misunderstood to mean bloodshed, while jihad literally means "struggle" or "strive" to the best of one's ability, to make the utmost effort to spread goodness (what the Qur'an calls *ma'ruf*) and can be carried out by logical argumentation (25:52) or by giving financial help. It must start in people's hearts and emerge into the real world through their actions. It is a general, overarching term to mean struggle or strive, part of which of course could mean a physical struggle or fight. However, based on the use of the term in the Qur'an and tradition, the more important aspect of it is about self-purification and striving to do better. Today, an example of jihad for a Muslim is to educate the masses about Islam and to eliminate any misunderstandings, misconceptions, and stereotypes. Jihad is always described in the Qur'an as *fee sabil Allah* (in the path of Allah). The biggest jihad is against oneself and one's desires, and striving to purify oneself. Confirming this meaning, the Qur'an ascribes jihad to strayed parents who *strive* to persuade their son to idolatry as it says: "But if they strive to make you join in worship with Me things (partners) of which you have no knowledge, do not obey them; yet bear them company in this life with justice (and consideration)" (31:15).

In other chapters jihad means to strive and make the best effort: "And if any strive (with might), they do so for their own soul: for Allah is free of all needs from all creation" (29:6).

According to Mustafa Huseini Tabatabai, in this verse, the aim of jihad is to strive to increase one's faith and to improve oneself or "jihad for self or struggle for self." However, some scholars have interpreted jihad in this verse to mean "fighting enemies," which is an unlikely interpretation since this is a Meccan chapter (a chapter revealed in Mecca before the migration), and during the Meccan period there were no battles with enemies. Muslims' struggle (jihad) during that period was for self-improvement, an invitation to others of monotheistic faiths, and to tolerate the idolaters' persecution. Even at the end of this chapter there is a mention of a similar struggle: "And those who strive in Our (cause), we will certainly guide them to our Paths: For verily Allah is with those who do right" (29:69). This refers to "striving within," and the result of that striving is mentioned as "guidance to His Path." This result is closer to seeking knowledge and striving for self than fighting enemies. Nevertheless, Muhammad ibn Jarir al-Tabari, the Muslim scholar of Qur'anic exegesis, has interpreted the word "strive" to mean "fight" (as in combat) with the enemy.[12]

Another verse, in which scholars (of exegesis) all agree and that indicates strive to educate, states:

Therefore, listen not to the Unbelievers, but strive against them
with the utmost strenuousness, with the (Qur'an). (25:52)

The reason commentators have not been able to associate this verse with physical fighting is the word *behee* (or "with it"), a preposition and pronoun which returns (or refers) to the Qur'an, which in this verse means to start the great striving by inviting to faith with the Qur'an. As even al-Tabari says, "Engage with them in great striving with this Qur'an."[13]

From this verse we realize striving to educate takes priority over striving in combat, as is confirmed by studying the biography of the Prophet (PBUH) [14] (such as *The Life of Muhammad* by Ibn Ishaq) and history books by al-Tabari and Ibn al-Athir.[15] The Messenger of God invited people to Islam for several years, but when unbelievers started persecuting Muslims and became determined to kill him, he was forced to migrate and to defend Muslims, which is mentioned explicitly in the Qur'an, as it speaks about the reason for his effort to engage in the battle: "To those against whom war is made, permission is given (to fight), because they are wronged; and verily, Allah is most powerful for their aid. (They are) those who have been driven from their homes unjustly only because they said: Our Lord is Allah" (22:39–40). Note the term *qital* is used here to mean an explicit physical fight.

To conclude, the main duty of Muslims is to offer an invitation and an enunciation (or "strive to educate"), and if those who reject or oppose the invitation become hostile and war against Muslims, thus preventing them from practicing their faith or inviting to God's path, permission to defend has been given to Muslims. However, when called to a truce, Muslims must accept, according to explicit words in the Qur'an: "But if the enemy incline towards peace, do you (also) incline towards peace, and trust in Allah: for He is One that hears, and knows (all things)" (8:61). This was demonstrated by the Prophet's (PBUH) conduct during the Hudaybiyyah peace treaty.

Tabatabai adds, however, that in our times, those who cannot debate and reason or confront today's social and political challenges peacefully, arm themselves and resort to murder, kidnappings, suicide bombings, and destruction. They call it jihad or the Islamic struggle. Whereas the noble Messenger of God (PBUH), long before engaging in any war with oppressors and aggressors, invited people to Islam for several years, an invitation based on wisdom and fair exhortation with high-level reasoning, as revealed in the Qur'an:

> Invite (all) to the Way of thy Lord with wisdom and
> beautiful preaching (fair exhortation); and argue with
> them in ways that are best and most gracious: for thy Lord
> knows best, who have strayed from His Path. (16:125)

Islamic history tells us that when early Muslims seized Samarqand (a region in present-day Uzbekistan), the people of Samarqand went to a Muslim judge to complain that a Muslim army had entered and seized their town without first inviting them to Islam! The fair-minded judge ordered the Muslim army to leave Samarqand. The army obeyed and left the city. When the people of Samarqand saw the equity and justice in Muslims' attitudes, they embraced Islam and according to history, "This was the reason for their surrender."[16] Indeed, an invitation cannot be accompanied with tyranny and injustice, as one cannot give a gift with an empty hand.

The main goal of inviting people to Islam is to give them a path to greater happiness and blessings in this world and the hereafter. This goal is reached by propagating Islamic culture and education, not coercion and bloodshed. But war in the Muslim world is often adventitious and unavoidable and is mainly prescribed to establish justice and to prevent sedition and corruption, as the Qur'an indicates in its philosophy of war: "And if Allah did not check [repel] some people by means of another, the earth would indeed be full of mischief. But Allah is full of bounty to all [creatures] of the worlds" (2:251).[17]

Indeed, if war, in and of itself, cannot prevent tyranny and corruption, it will become the cause of tyranny and corruption, as we have seen happen with the majority of wars throughout history.

According to Abdel Haleem,

> When there is a just cause for qital (battle), with righteous intention, it becomes an obligation to defend religious freedom (22:39–41) for self-defense (2:190) and to defend the weak and oppressed—men, women, and children who cry for help (4:75). It is the duty of the Muslims to help the oppressed, except against a people with whom the Muslims have a treaty (8:72). These are the only valid justifications for war we find in the Qur'an. Even when war becomes necessary, there is no "conscription" in the Qur'an. The Prophet (PBUH) is instructed only to "urge on the believers." The Qur'an (and the hadith at greater length) urge on the Muslim fighters (those who are defending themselves or the oppressed) in the strongest way to show justice in their cause, the bad conduct of the enemy,

and promising great rewards in the afterlife for those
who are prepared to sacrifice their lives and property
for such a good cause (3:169–172, 9:120–121).[18]

Even the treaties can be implicit or explicit. Today there is an
implicit peace agreement among most nations around the world, and
one cannot start a war against another nation without just cause or
provocation. Empire building or taking land is not a valid reason to
justify war in Islam.

There is another aspect of jihad that is often exploited or misunderstood. While jihad promotes the betterment of individuals and
society through striving, it is also about unity of the *Ummah*—the
entire Muslim community—when it comes to helping and defending
each other and the oppressed. For instance, if a small Muslim community is suffering great injustice, especially for the sole reason of
being Muslim, it is then the duty of every Muslim to come to their
aid; however, if this is not feasible, it then becomes the duty of every
Muslim nation to fulfill this duty through various means, which is
unfortunately absent among many Muslim nations today; hence, jihad, in this sense, does not exist today.

Although many Muslim speakers, writers, and scholars have repeatedly attempted to awaken Muslim communities and nations from
this deep sleep and apathy, they've been unsuccessful for the most part.
In fact, there are numerous instances where more aid arrived through
the help of international communities rather than through Muslim
communities. The war in Bosnia is a prime example of international
communities, rather than Muslim nations, who helped Bosnia.

Asghar Ali Engineer describes that the Qur'an, in fact, repeatedly
enjoins Muslims to embrace four essential values: justice or equity (*adl*
or *qist*), benevolence (*ihsan*), compassion (*rahmah*), and wisdom (*hikmah*).
Therefore, a good Muslim should be just, benevolent (for humanity),
compassionate, and wise. One must constantly strive to establish these
values. That is the real jihad. The Prophet (PBUH) is reported to have
said that the real jihad is to speak the truth in the face of a tyrant, and
he also is reported to have said that to fight with the sword is the "small

jihad" and to control one's desires is the "great jihad." One should also bear in mind that in any religious tradition, there is no single trend but rather multiple trends, and one should not cite an example of one particular trend and generalize it. For example, to cite the actions of a few extremists among Muslims and then generalize it for all Muslims is an unfair and unscientific method. It is true that a few Muslims use violence and justify it in the name of jihad, but it is wrong to say all Muslims agree with such an untenable position.[19]

While some Muslims may share the same political views about the state of Muslim nations, there is an insurmountable difference of opinion between the Muslim majority and the extremists on how to deal with such disparities, grievances, and oppression in Muslim societies and nations as a whole.

3.4   Qital and the Ground Rules for Battle

In Islam, there are many factors that must be taken into consideration before engaging in a physical fight or war. One must understand the conditions and limits that permit engaging in a war. What are the alternatives to a conflict? Who is to be fought? What is the intention? How to cease fighting and what to do with the prisoners of war? One must keep in mind that qital is the last resort and a defensive measure when unavoidable.

We first briefly discuss two verses in the Qur'an which are often quoted by those who are eager to criticize Qur'anic teachings on war: "Slay them wherever you find them" (2:191), and the verse that is often labeled as the "sword verse" (9:5). Both verses have been misinterpreted and misrepresented. The first verse 2:191 says:[20]

And slay them wherever you find them, and drive
them out of where they drove you out. (2:191)[21]

Critics often take this verse out of context and claim that it applies to any non-Muslim. However, when we look at the preceding verse, 2:190, which begins this passage, the Qur'an defines clearly who is to be fought:

> Fight in the cause of Allah those who fight [against] you, but do not transgress limits. For Allah loves not the transgressor. (2:190)

We already discussed what some sociologists consider religions within their historical contexts in Chapter 1, and that when we refer to the Qur'an and its traditions for guidance, it means we rely on it as the canon, the criterion that separates Islam and Muslims' behavior.

There are three key points to consider about verses 2:190–191:

1. Middle Eastern studies scholars have suggested Muslim wars were fought to gain spoils, where in fact these were incidental or adventitious.
2. "Those who fight against you" means actual fighters or those who attacked you, not those who merely differ in faith.
3. "Those who fight against you" also means protecting civilians. This was evident by the actions of the Prophet (PBUH) and his immediate successors. When they sent out an army, they gave specific instructions not to attack civilians—women, children, the elderly, and religious people engaged in worship—nor to destroy crops or harm animals. These are considered acts of transgression as the verse says: "God loves not the transgressor."

These limits must be strictly observed. Only the combatant enemies are to be fought, and no more harm should come to them than they have caused as indicated within the same passage:

> If then, anyone transgresses the prohibition against you,
> Transgress you likewise against him. But fear Allah and know
> that Allah is with those who restrain themselves. (2:194)

Therefore, the Qur'an, its traditions, and the actions of the Prophet

(PBUH), which are the only binding authorities in Islamic law, do not support wars and weapons of mass destruction that kill civilians and destroy communities. Abdel Haleem describes that the prohibition is regularly reinforced by the phrase "Do not transgress" and "God loves not the transgressor." Transgression has been interpreted by Qur'anic exegetes to mean "initiation of fighting or offense," which includes fighting those with whom a treaty has been signed, surprising the enemy without first inviting them to make peace, destroying crops, or killing those who should be protected (see commentaries written on verse 2:190-191, in chapter 6, as well as others.)

The directives are always expressed in restraining language with much repetition of warnings, such as *"do not transgress," "God does not love the transgressors," "He loves those who are conscious of Him,"* and *"Those who restrain themselves"* or *"Be careful of your duty towards God."* These are instructions given to those who should have the intention of acting "in the path of God" from the very beginning.

Linguistically, the verses in this passage always restrict actions by limiting what is permissible, which appeals strongly to a Muslim's conscience. In six verses (2:190–195), we find three prohibitions (*"do not"*), six restrictions or conditions (two *"until,"* two *"if,"* two *"who attack you"*), as well as caution signs, such as *"in the path of God," "be conscious of God," "God does not like aggressors," "God is with those who are conscious of Him," "with those who do good deeds,"* and *"God is Forgiving, Merciful."* In treating the theme of war (as with many other themes), the Qur'an gives the reasons and justifications for any action it demands.[22] For example, verse 2:191 begins: "And slay them wherever you find them, and drive them out of where they drove you out; persecution [fitna] is worse than killing."

Who does "them" refer to? The answer is found in the preceding verse: *"those who fight (attack) you."* In some articles, the reference to "them" is removed from its context. *"Wherever you find them"* is also misunderstood; Muslims were apprehensive that if their enemies attacked them in Mecca's Sacred Mosque (which is a sanctuary) and they retaliated, they would be breaking the law. Thus, the Qur'an simply gave the Muslims permission to fight those enemies, whether inside or outside the mosque in Mecca, and assured them that persecutions committed by the unbelievers against them for believing in God was more sinful than killing those who attacked them, whether in the Sacred Mosque or elsewhere. Finally, it must be pointed out that the entire passage (2:190–195) is given within the context of fighting those who barred Muslims from reaching the Sacred Mosque at Mecca for their pilgrimage. This is evident in the preceding verse (189) and verse 196 after the passage. In the same way another verse giving permission to fight occurs in the Qur'an, also in the context of barring Muslims from reaching the mosque to perform the pilgrimage (2:217).[23] There is also the fact their persecution was aimed at forcing Muslims to renounce their monotheistic faith (More details on this verse in chapter 6)

Another verse much referred to but notoriously misinterpreted and taken out of context is known as the "sword verse":

So, when the Sacred Months (months of grace) have passed, slay the idolaters wherever you find them, and take them (captive), and besiege them, and prepare for them each ambush. But if they repent and establish worship and pay the poor-due, then open the way for them. Lo! Allah is Forgiving, Merciful. (9:5)[24]

However, even if the enemy seeks asylum:

If one amongst the Pagans [idolaters] ask you for asylum, grant it to him, so that he may hear the word of Allah; and then escort him to where he can be secure. That is because they are men without knowledge. (9:6)

Several points to note here regarding verse 9:5 (a full explanation of this verse is in chapter 6):

1. Not all directives mentioned must be performed. The situation, time, and place relative to idolaters must first be considered, then one or two of the actions are chosen accordingly.

For example, if besieging and capturing stops the aggression, then that is the appropriate way; otherwise, they are permitted to slay.

2. *"Wherever you find them"* is mentioned because idolaters used to attack, kill, and pillage anytime and anywhere they could, and then run back to their place of safety. They intended to kill Muslims anywhere they found them, hence wipe out the Muslim community.

3. However, the rest of verse 9:5 says if these idolaters who murdered, pillaged, and broke treaties repent and embrace Islam, showing sincerity with acts of worship such as prayer and paying *zakat* (an obligatory payment to support the poor), then Muslims must let them go, and God's mercy will be upon them.

4. The next verse (9:6) refers to if they seek asylum, they must be given protection and escorted to their place of safety, even if they do not wish to join the Muslims' camp or become Muslims.

At some point, the hostility of the idolaters and their persecution (fitna) of Muslims grew so great that the unbelievers were determined to convert Muslims back to idolatry or finish them off, and hence repeatedly broke their treaties.

Even with such an enemy, Muslims were not simply ordered to pounce on them and reciprocate by breaking the treaty themselves. Instead, Muslims gave the idolaters a four-month grace period (not the four Sacred Months) to decide whether they wanted to stop their hostile activities and end their twenty-two years of animosity and paganism and join the community, or face war.

The main clause of the sentence *"slay idolaters"* is singled out by some scholars or critics to misrepresent the Islamic attitude toward war. Even some Muslims take this view and allege this verse abrogates other verses on war. This is pure myth, isolating and taking a portion of the sentence out of context. The full picture is given in the passage that contains verses 9:1–15 and gives many reasons for the directive to fight such polytheists. They continuously broke their agreements and aided others against the Muslims. They started hostilities against the Muslims, barred others from becoming Muslims, expelled Muslims from the Sacred Mosque, and even from their own homes. At least eight times the passage mentions their misdeeds against Muslims.

Consistent with restrictions on war elsewhere in the Qur'an, the immediate context of the sword verse (9:5) excludes polytheists who did not break their peace agreements with Muslims, as indicated in verse 9:7, which states "except those with whom you made a treaty near the Sacred Mosque." These include enemies seeking safe conduct and refuge who should be protected and delivered to their place of safety: "If one amongst the idolaters ask thee for asylum, grant it to him, so that he may hear the word of Allah; and then escort him to where he can be secure" (9:6). The reason to engage in war was not due to their polytheistic beliefs, but rather their aggression and the breaking of treaties. Nevertheless, the entire context of verses 9:1–15 (with all its restrictions) is ignored by those who simply isolate one part of the verse or passage to support their theory of war or justification of violence in Islam on what is termed the sword verse, even though the word for "sword" does not appear anywhere in the Qur'an.

Asghar Ali Engineer says that another aspect of the Qur'an, which even some Muslim scholars (ulama) are often unaware of, is the transcendent aspect in Qur'anic teachings. The Qur'an takes a realistic attitude toward a given situation but does not confine itself to it and goes beyond the given in order to create an ideal based on higher values. If it asks Muslims to defend themselves when attacked, it also requires Muslims to establish justice and peace so that humanity can flourish.[25]

What about the cessation of hostilities? Once the aggression from the enemy ceases, Muslims must stop fighting: "But if they cease, Let there be no hostility except to those who practice oppression" (2:193), and "But if the enemy incline towards peace, you (also) incline towards peace, and trust in Allah . . . should they intend to deceive you, verily Allah is sufficient for you" (8:61–62).

Abdel Haleem explains that when the war is over, the Qur'an

and tradition give instructions on how to treat the captives and how to establish a new relationship with non–Muslims. In Islam, war certainly is not seen as a mean to convert people from their religions or to fight them because of their religion. The often-quoted division of the world into *dar al-kufr* or *dar al-harb* (abode of disbelief or abode of war) and *dar al-Islam* (abode of Islam) is seen nowhere in the Qur'an or tradition, which are the only authoritative sources on Islam. The scholars who used these expressions were referring to warring enemies in countries surrounding Muslim lands.[26] Even for such scholars, it was not a choice between two but three, with a third division, *dar al-salam* (abode of peace), meaning the lands with which the Muslims made a way or had peace treaty obligations.

The Qur'an and tradition talk about different situations that might exist between a Muslim state and a neighboring enemy at war. It mentions a state of defensive war within the prescriptions and limits specified above, the state of a peace treaty for a limited or unlimited period, the state of a truce, and the state in which a member of a hostile camp can enter a Muslim land for special purposes and under safe conduct.[27]

Nowhere in the Qur'an do we find a verse that advocates engaging in a war for the purpose of converting people to Islam, nor ceasing a war with the condition that they convert to Islam. There are verses about having people hear the word of God, which is considered part of an invitation to the Islamic faith.

Regarding prisoners of war, Muslims in general did not keep many captives, as they were mostly either freed or ransomed. Abdel Haleem adds that there is nothing in the Qur'an or tradition to prevent Muslims from following the contemporary, international humanitarian conventions on war or prisoners of war. There is nothing in the Qur'an to say that prisoners of war must be held captive, but since this was the practice at the time and there was no international body to oversee prisoner exchange, the Qur'an states:[28]

When you have thoroughly subdued them [overcome the enemy], bind a bond firmly (on them): thereafter (is the time) either generosity [set them free] by an act of grace or ransom. (47:4)

Grace is suggested before ransom. Even when some were not set free for one reason or another, they were (according to the Qur'an and tradition) treated most graciously (76:8–9, 9:60, 2:177). As a result, many prisoners embraced Islam, gained their freedom, and served Islam afterwards.

In the Bible, where fighting is mentioned, we find a different picture of how defeated people were treated.

> When you march up to attack a city, make its people an offer of peace. If they accept and open their gates, all the people in it shall be subject to forced labor and shall work for you. If they refuse to make peace and they engage you in battle, lay siege to that city. When the Lord, your God delivers it into your hand, put to the sword all the men in it. As for the women, the children, the livestock and everything else in the city, you may take these as plunder for yourselves. And you may use the plunder the Lord your God gives you from your enemies. This is how you are to treat all the cities that are at a distance from you and do not belong to the nations nearby. However, in the cities of the nations the Lord your God is giving you as an inheritance, do not leave alive anything that breathes. Completely destroy them—the Hittites, Amorites, Canaanites, Perizzites, Hivites and Jebusites—as the Lord your God has commanded you. Otherwise, they will teach you to follow all the detestable things they do in worshiping their gods, and you will sin against the Lord your God. (Deuteronomy 20:10–18)[29]

Finally, Islam always resumed peaceful relations postwar while establishing justice and protection, as verse 22:41 confirms: "Establish worship and pay the poor-due and enjoin what is good and forbid iniquity."

To that extent, when the Muslim army was victorious over the enemy, any of the defeated people who wished to remain in the land could do so under a guarantee of protection for their lives, religion, and freedom. If they wished to leave, they could do so safely. If they chose to stay among the Muslims, they could become members of the Muslim community. If they wished to remain in their faith, they had the right to do so and were offered security. Today, many remaining followers and houses of worship from other faiths in Muslim countries attest to this fact. Their only obligation was to pay *jizya* (tribute), which is explained in the next section.

3.5   Jizya (Tribute Tax)

Jizya refers to a tax exempting a non-Muslim person from military service and from paying zakat (payment for the poor), which Muslims must pay (a tax considerably more than jizya). Neither had the option of refusing to pay, but in return the non-Muslims were given protection by the state. Jizya was not a poll tax, and it was not charged to the elderly, poor people, women, or children. Muslims paid zakat to the Islamic government; however, because zakat is considered to be an Islamic act of worship, it is not required of non-Muslims.

Muslim scholars have written many books about jizya (such as *Ahkam Ahli Zimmah* by Ibn Qayyum) in which rules and conditions for jizya are discussed in detail. In *al-Kharaj*, an old text by Abu Yusuf from the Harun al-Rashid period, the author writes: "Jizya is required by men only, not women or children" and explicitly excludes men who are old, poor, blind, jobless, and men in monasteries.[30] Those who pay jizya are not required to enlist and go to war. If the Islamic government cannot protect them, it is a requirement that their jizya be returned, as famous Near East scholar Thomas Arnold acknowledged and praised in his book, *The Preaching of Islam*.[31]

According to Tabatabai, Muslim radicals and extremists whose rules are precarious have no right to collect jizya from religious minorities. Arnold writes, "Abu Ubaidah, one of the Prophet's companions, announced to people of a conquered Syrian town, 'We will return all that we have collected from you because we have received the news that enemy's strong army is advancing toward us and we may not be able to protect your town.'"[32] Indeed, during the early Muslim period, the Islamic government collected jizya under the condition (and to the extent) they were able to protect their territory and not just when it was threatened. This is the true meaning of justice and gives a sense of duty with Muslims of yesterday.[33]

3.6   The Treaty of Hudaybiyyah

Of all the treaties, one of the most prominent and famous was the treaty of Hudaybiyyah, which occurred in the sixth year of hijra (emigration) at a time when the entire Medina region was under Muslim control. In Islam, faithfulness to a treaty is considered the most serious obligation relentlessly emphasized in the Qur'an and tradition:

O you who believe, fulfil (all) obligations . . . (5:1)

Fulfill the Covenant of Allah, when you have entered it, and break not your oaths after they have been confirmed them [by swearing in His Name], indeed ye have made Allah your surety. (16:91)

Even defending a Muslim minority living within the non-Muslim camp is not allowed if Muslims have a treaty with them.

Through crucial diplomacy, the Prophet (PBUH) had warded off several potential acts of aggression by signing multiple peace treaties with warring tribes and factions, thus securing safe passage for the caravans. As such, the presence of Muslims was felt throughout the region and to the extent news of this transformation reached two neighboring superpowers (the Persian and Eastern Roman Empires). It was under such conditions that the Prophet (PBUH) decided to make a pilgrimage to Mecca after he had a dream in which he saw himself visiting the Sacred Mosque and performing *hajj* (a pilgrimage to the Sacred Mosque in Mecca as part of five pillars of worship). As the verse in the Qur'an states, "Truly did Allah fulfill the vision for His Messenger: you shall enter the Sacred Mosque, if Allah wills, with minds secure, heads shaved, hair cut short, and without fear. For He knew what you knew not, and He granted, besides this, a speedy victory" (48:27). The Prophet's (PBUH) decision had the following implications:

1. The decision came at a time when pilgrims from all parts of Arabia visited Mecca, and the Muslims' presence could impact the public perception of Muslims and negate all the negative propaganda spread by the Quraysh tribe. It would also show that Muslims did not have any hostility toward the beliefs of others and even their traditions of pilgrimage.
2. The timing was important because the Prophet (PBUH) was going on pilgrimage during the sacred months, which all Arab tribes observed. Having been in several victorious battles, the Prophet (PBUH) and his companions were in a position to approach any enemies and propose peace and goodwill from a position of strength, thus potentially removing any animosities.
3. The Sacred Mosque belonged to all Arabs and tribes, including Muslims. The Quraysh, a mercantile Arab tribe, were merely the custodians. Hence, Muslims, especially from their position of strength, assumed they should be able to enter Mecca in order to perform their rites without any disturbance.
4. It had been six years since the Prophet (PBUH) and the Muhajereen (Emigrants) had visited their homeland; therefore, they looked forward to visiting Mecca, especially the Muslim minority in Mecca whom the Quraysh had not allowed to leave.

Considering the above, the Prophet (PBUH) invited all the people of Medina to exercise their religious rights and accompany him to Mecca (if they wished to perform pilgrimage). The invitation to include non-Muslims was a clever strategy because it would potentially prevent an attack by the Quraysh, and even if they did attack, certainly the other tribes would not support them and would perhaps support Muslims instead. It was also a key opportunity to promote the message of Islam.

Therefore, the Prophet (PBUH), along with Muslims (Muhajereen and Ansar, the Muslims who were native to Medina) and a few non-Muslims who joined him, left Medina to perform the pilgrimage. Their numbers reached one thousand four hundred. In order to show peaceful intentions, the Muslims did not take any arms other than a few for protection during their travel.[34]

The news of the Prophet's (PBUH) departure from Medina, along with one thousand four hundred men for pilgrimage, reached Mecca. Given the events of the past, the Quraysh worried and didn't believe the Muslims intended only to perform a pilgrimage. Even though the news of the Prophet's (PBUH) entrance into *ihram* (a sacred state a Muslim must enter in order to perform the pilgrimage) had spread throughout the land, the Quraysh still did not believe it; hence, they sent an army, under the leadership of Khalid ibn Walid and Ekramat ibn Abi Jahl, to intercept and block the Prophet (PBUH) from entering Mecca. When the Prophet (PBUH) heard this news, he ordered a detour around Mecca in order to avoid meeting the Quraysh army and to prevent any violence from breaking out during the sacred month. A man by the name of Aslam guided the Muslims' caravan through difficult terrain until they reached Hudaybiyyah, some twenty-two kilometers outside of Mecca, where they camped.[35]

Once the Quraysh army was notified, they returned to Mecca and took up their position to defend the city, in case the Muslims decided to attack. After a while, the Quraysh decided to send emissaries to the Prophet (PBUH) in order to persuade him to turn around and return to Medina. The emissaries—named Budail ibn Warqa', Mekraz ibn Hafs, Hulayse ibn Alqamh, and Urwat ibn Mas'oud Thaqafi—each visited the Prophet (PBUH), one after the other, and each was convinced the Prophet (PBUH) and his companions were visiting Mecca for the sole purpose of a pilgrimage. Nevertheless, the Quraysh leaders refused to accept this possibility. Days passed, but no conclusion was reached. Finally, the Prophet (PBUH) sent his emissary, Kharrash ibn Umaya, to the Quraysh with a clear message explaining their intention. The Quraysh reacted with violence, killing his camel and pursuing him with the intention to kill him, but he escaped. There was now a rumor about the possibility of a war, but the Prophet's (PBUH) strategy was to be patient and to control the situation through peaceful means; hence, he ordered the release of the Quraysh men who had been disturbing and throwing stones at the Muslims' camp.[36]

According to several reports in *Sahih Bukhari* and *al-Maghazi*, the Prophet (PBUH) decided to send another emissary to Mecca. This time he sent Uthman and told him that after he convened with the Quraysh leaders, he was to visit Muslim families in Mecca and reassure them about the future. Although the Quraysh had sworn not to allow Muslims into Mecca, they now seemed willing to negotiate. Due to Uthman's delayed return, however, the Prophet (PBUH) grew worried, and a rumor spread through the Muslim camps that the Quraysh had killed him. As a result, the Prophet (PBUH) indicated that if the rumor were true, Muslims must go forth and fight the Quraysh. So, he gathered everyone to take an oath of allegiance for the support of war.

At this point, the following verse was revealed: "Allah's pleasure was on the Believers when they swore Fealty to thee under the tree: He knew what was in their hearts, and He sent down tranquility to them; and He rewarded them with a speedy Victory" (48:18). However, before long, it became clear the rumor was false when Uthman returned to the camp. Negotiations continued through several emissaries on both sides, which at times was frustrating. The Prophet (PBUH) dictated a letter to Ali ibn Abi Talib and had Suhail ibn Amr, the Quraysh representative, read it. Suhail objected multiple times, and each time the Prophet (PBUH) yielded and asked Ali to change the letter. Upon agreement from both sides, the final draft included the following major concessions:[37]

1. The Prophet (PBUH) and his companions will return home and not enter Mecca this year; however, next year they are

free to visit Mecca and perform Hajj, provided they stay no more than three days and their swords remain sheathed.

2. The Quraysh and the Muslims committed not to engage in any war against each other for ten years.

3. Any tribe(s) may enter into the agreement with the Muslims or the Quraysh and as a result they will be bound by this agreement as well.

4. If any Muslim in Mecca leaves without permission from his guardian and joins the Muslims in Medina, he must be returned to Mecca and not be killed; however, any Muslim from Medina who joins the Quraysh will not be returned.

5. Hereby forbearance and pardon are established between both sides so that neither side questions the other about past wars.

Two copies of the agreement were written and signed by several Quraysh leaders. Suhail took one copy and the Prophet (PBUH) kept the other. The Muslims were not pleased about what appeared to be a one-sided agreement in the Quraysh's favor; however, the Prophet (PBUH) invited them to be patient and to consider the agreement as progress for Muslims in the long run. For example, according to the agreement, a Muslim could join the Quraysh, and Muslims would have no need for that individual; but if a Quraysh joined the Muslims, he would be returned to the Quraysh only to promote Islam within the Quraysh tribe. This was a reality that Muslims as well as the Quraysh did not fully realize at the time, but the Prophet (PBUH) foresaw such a turn of events. As a result, during this peaceful period the Prophet's (PBUH) followers increased from one thousand four hundred (at Hudaybiyyah) to ten thousand.[38] Eventually, however, the Quraysh broke the terms of the treaty.

3.7   The Rights of Disbelievers

Islam grants specific rights to combatant and noncombatant unbelievers, most of whom were idolaters (*mushrekeen*) and enemies of Islam. The rights presented here reject the notion that Muslims were sanctioned to kill any and all non-Muslims, an assertion based on the verse "slay them wherever you find them." The following are examples of rights granted to all unbelievers:

1. Security is provided to those who seek refuge and who want to hear the message of God. Muslims are commanded to give them protection and escort them to safety after they hear the message, so they are protected from their brethren who might think they are deserters and hence kill them. The Qur'an states: "If one amongst the idolaters ask thee for asylum, grant it to him, so that he may hear the word of Allah; and then escort him to where he can be secure" (9:6). Note this verse was revealed in one of the last chapters of revelation, and it could have been revealed differently (given the state of war at the time), commanding Muslims to let the enemy who seeks refuge hear the message and if he accepts it, he joins the fight against his brethren, and if he does not join kill him. But Islam says to let the soldier hear the word, and regardless of his decision, escort him to safety.

2. Muslims are commanded not to revile or defame unbelievers or their gods, as it says: "Revile not you those whom they call upon besides Allah, lest they out of spite revile Allah in their ignorance" (6:108).

3. Unbelievers have the right to justice. "O ye who believe! stand out firmly for Allah, as witnesses to fair dealing, and let not the hatred of others to you make you swerve to wrong and depart from justice. Be just" (5:8). Muslims are commanded to deal justly with anyone who may be considered an enemy, or anyone who is of another faith or a polytheist.

4. Even idolaters who have persecuted Muslims for several years are protected, once a treaty or oath is signed. Muslims must respect it as long as the enemy does so, for the Qur'an says: "How can there be a league [treaty], before Allah and His Messenger, with the idolaters, except those with whom you made a treaty near the Sacred Mosque? As long as they stand

true to you, stand you true to them: for Allah does love the righteous" (9:7).

5. If the enemy is inclined toward peace, even if it may be from a position of deceit or weakness, Muslims are instructed to accept this tendency. "But if the enemy incline towards peace, do thou incline towards peace, and trust in Allah" (8:61).

6. Even during periods of retribution, equality and patience in retaliation must be observed: "And if you punish them (take your turn), then retaliate with the like of that with which you were afflicted; but if you are patient, it will certainly be best for those who are patient" (16:126).[39]

7. Treachery is forgiven of those with whom Muslims had a pact but who continued their treachery. The Qur'an says: "nor will thou cease to find them—barring a few—ever bent on (new) deceits: but forgive them, and overlook (their misdeeds): for Allah loveth those who are kind" (5:13). This verse was re- vealed during the peak of the Prophet's (PBUH) sovereignty.

8. Muslims are instructed to give alms to those whose heart is to be won (to belief), as the Qur'an reveals: "Alms are for the poor and the needy, those employed to administer the (funds); and for those whose hearts have been (recently) reconciled (to Truth)" (9:60).

Of course, the above rights are mere examples of what Islam con- siders the rights of unbelievers and were granted at a time when most were considered combatant idolaters. Given these rights are still ob- served today, does this sound like a religion that promotes violence and war?

3.8   How to Get Along with Others

As to international relations within the context of war and peace, Abdel Haleem points out that there is nothing in the Qur'an or tra- dition that prevents Muslims from signing peace and cooperation agreements in accordance with modern international conventions;

in fact, there is much in the Qur'an and tradition that modern international law could benefit from. The Prophet Muhammad (PBUH) honored the alliances he witnessed between some chiefs of Mecca to protect the poor and weak against oppression before the call for his prophethood. Islam fosters peaceful, amicable, and positive relations with other nations as reflected in the Qur'anic injunction, referring to members of other faiths:

> Allah does not forbid you to be kind and to act justly to those who have neither made war on your religion nor driven you from your homes. God loves those who are just. (60:8)

This includes participation in international peacemaking and peacekeeping efforts. The rules of arbitration in violent disputes between groups of Muslims is given in the Qur'an:

> If two parties among the Believers fall into a quarrel [fight], make peace between them: but if one of them transgresses beyond bounds against the other, then fight you (all) against the one that transgresses until it complies [they comply] with the command of Allah; but if it complies [they comply], then make peace between them with justice, and be fair: for Allah loves those who are fair (and just). (49:9)

This could, in agreement with rules of Islamic jurisprudence, be applied more generally to disputes within the international community. For this reason, Muslims participate in arbitration disputes by international bodies such as the United Nations.[40]

Modern international organizations and the ease of modern travel do make it easier for different nations to "get to know one another" (59:13) and aid one another in accordance with Qur'anic teachings—"Help you one another in righteousness and piety (warding off evil), but help you not one another in sin and transgression" (5:2)—and to live in peace as the Qur'an affirms: "In most of their secret talks there is no good [virtue]: But if one exhorts to a deed of charity or justice or conciliation between men (secrecy is permissible), To him who does this, seeking the good pleasure of Allah, We shall soon give a reward of the highest (value)" (4:114).

Paul Findley, a former US congressman, reiterates, "To those who may be troubled by the declaration that links the principles of governance set forth in the Qur'an with those expressed in the US constitution, I ask them to consider whether hundreds of thousands of Muslims in foreign countries would seek American citizenship if they believed structure of US government to be in serious conflict with the basic principles of the ideal Islamic state. By undertaking the long, challenging journey to obtain US citizenship, great number of Muslims have, in fact, voted for America. I conclude that many, perhaps most of them believe America has a governmental structure that is closer to the idealism of Islam than other forms of government. The largest most sustained flow of Muslim emigration is to American shores. Why the attraction to the United States, a non-Muslim country whose governmental structure is among the most secular in the world and where Muslims number less than 3 percent of the total population? One might reasonably assume that they chose America as a place of economic opportunity, as well as a good place to rear their families and practice their religion. Before moving here, all must have received some indication of America's longstanding, rigorous efforts to protect freedom of religion, and its commitment to tolerance and human rights."[41]

3.9   Terrorism

Terrorism, as defined by the Oxford Dictionaries, is "The unlawful use of violence and intimidation, especially against civilians, in the pursuit of political aims." While the word is predominantly used to identify extremist groups, it can be applied, according to the definition, to any group with a political agenda regardless of their religious affiliation.

In recent years, many people have been injured and died in the bombings in Europe, US and other regions many of which were unfortunately reported as acts of terror committed by Muslims.

Following these events were backlashes against Muslims and their places of worship. These "blind" bombings indiscriminately killed and injured people, causing families to suffer in the same way that backlashes indiscriminately killed or injured innocent Muslims, damaged their property, and their places of worship, even though they had no role in the bombings. These acts of terror have similarities in that innocent people died or suffered injuries and property was damaged. In the meantime, some of the perpetrators walked away without harm. Furthermore, mostly innocent Muslims have fallen victim to these acts of terror directly or indirectly within Muslim countries as well. The intention here is not to address who committed these crimes and why, but rather to answer the question: Does Islam condone or condemn such acts, and does Islam fundamentally condemn any form of surprise killings or assassinations?

The holy Qur'an, which is the most binding, authentic, and authoritative book for Muslims, explicitly states that a surprise killing, or an act of terror, is the method used by evildoers or rebellious wrongdoers who, in the name of God and faith, become allies to subdue those who oppose them:

There were in the city nine men of a family, who made mischief in the land, and would not reform, they said 'Let's swear a mutual oath by Allah that we shall make a secret night attack on him and his people, and that we shall then say to his heir (when he seeks vengeance): We were not present at the slaughter of his people, and we are positively telling the truth.' (27:48–49)

The Qur'an considers scheming with malice and deceit criminal behavior, as described immediately in the next verse:

They plotted and planned, but We too planned, even while they perceived it not. Then see what was the end of their plot! - this, that We destroyed them and their people all (of them). (27:50–51)

More than fourteen hundred years ago a similar plot unfolded when a few men made a surprise visit to Prophet Muhammad's (PBUH) house in an attempt to murder him; however, the Messenger of God had been informed earlier, and the Prophet (PBUH) left the city so the plot failed.

In another example, the Qur'an states that if your enemies stop fighting you, and you are in an implicit or explicit state of peace with them, then you have no way (by God) to fight them.

> Therefore, if they withdraw from you, and wage no war against you, and (instead) send you (guarantees of) peace, then Allah has opened no way for you (to war against them). (4:90)

With this explicit directive, no one has the right to wage war or commit any act of violence against an opponent while in a state of implicit or explicit peace, much less engage in acts of terror or surprise attacks. Any bombing (suicide or otherwise) or blind killing carried out by anyone who kills or injures innocent people is considered a great injustice. The Qur'an warns Muslims "and let not hatred of any people make you swerve to wrong and depart from justice, be just: that is next to piety" (5:8).

Furthermore, the Prophet's (PBUH) teachings affirm that acts of terror are explicitly forbidden. In historic writings by famous scholars such as al-Tabari and Ahmad ibn Hanbal, the Messenger of God (PBUH) said, "Faith (iman) prevents surprise attack (and terror), and no believer commits such acts." [42] This narration has been repeated in multiple reports. Another well-known ancient scholar, Abu Dawood, recounts the following story: One day, during his rule, Mu'awiyah traveled from Syria to Medina to visit the home of the Prophet (PBUH). A'isha, the wife of the Prophet (PBUH), asked in jest, "Aren't you afraid that I might have someone hidden behind the curtain who might jump out and kill or assassinate you?" Mu'awiyah replied, "No, because I heard the Prophet said that faith prevents one from committing any act of terror; hence, no faithful believer would commit such an act." [43]

Even when war became necessary, the Messenger of God

instructed his men to move forth in the name of God and in the path of God, to follow the creed of His Messenger (PBUH) and to not transgress and kill any civilians—including old men, women, and children—but to do good because God loves the good doers. Such a leader would never direct his followers to commit acts of terror and indiscriminately kill or injure innocent people. If he sentenced someone to death, it would only be for a criminal act and carried out through the courts by a judge or head of state, similar to what is routinely done today in many countries and presided over by elected judges or officials.

During war, if there were a chance that civilians and innocents would die, the Prophet (PBUH) would avoid such encounters as the Qur'an indicates. A prime example was the migration to Medina. The enemy idolaters of Mecca not only persecuted the remaining Muslims in Mecca, but they often raided Muslim camps in and around Medina. Although the Prophet (PBUH) could have potentially mobilized his men toward Mecca and seized the city; he did not do so to avoid the deaths of many innocent people—both Muslims and non-Muslims. The Qur'an reminds Muslims of the following: "Had there not been believing men and believing women whom you did not know, that you were trampling down and on whose account a crime would have accrued to you without (your) knowledge" (48:25). However, the Messenger of God (PBUH) later conquered Mecca without bloodshed and, as reported by historians, after performing the Islamic (mono-theistic) ritual, pardoned all Meccans in an important speech. This included the Quraysh enemy tribe. He then said, "My treatment of you today is similar to that of Joseph with his brothers" and then recited: "He (Joseph) said: Have no fear this day! May Allah forgive you, and He is the Most Merciful of those who show mercy" (12:92). Would such a Prophet (PBUH) and his faith allow his followers to commit acts of terror? Never!

Chapter 4
The Qur'an and Leniency

THERE ARE MANY VERSES in the Qur'an about mercy and forgiveness. Verse 3:159 of the Qur'an states:

> It is part of the Mercy of Allah that you dealt gently (leniently)
> with them, had you been harsh or hard-hearted, they would
> have broken away from you: so pardon them, and ask for
> (Allah's) forgiveness for them; and consult them in affairs (of
> moment). Then, when you have taken a decision put your trust
> in Allah. For Allah loves those who put their trust (in Him).[44]

According to Tabatabai, in this verse, an important point to consider is that had the Prophet (PBUH) been harsh, rigid, and hard-hearted, even at the height of his sovereignty, his followers would have surely deserted him and dispersed, leaving a vacuum for despots to gather people and to establish their rule through force and violence.[45]

The Qur'an also states "And consult them in affairs (of the moment). Then, when you have taken a decision put thy trust in Allah," meaning when, after a consultation, the majority has a different opinion (from yours), O Prophet, follow the majority vote and put your trust in God. Historically, there were several occasions when this occurred. During the Battle of Uhud, between the early Muslims and their Meccan enemies, in AD 624, is one example where the Prophet (PBUH) consulted beforehand with his companions.

Another verse tells us about the Prophet's (PBUH) mercy and compassion toward the believers: "Now has come unto you a messenger from amongst yourselves: it grieves him that you should perish: ardently anxious is he over you: to the believers is he most kind and merciful" (9:128).

Addressing Prophet Muhammad (PBUH), the Qur'an says, "We sent you not, but as a Mercy for all people of the world" (21:107). It must be noted this verse does not say we sent you as a mercy; rather it says "not, but as a mercy." Therefore, his prophetic mission never accepts violence as the prevailing rule, for violence in this religion is considered adventitious and motivated by necessity. Mercy for mankind is for *all people*, including those who agree and those who do not, as reflected in the examples of the Prophet's (PBUH) life. But first, we need to start with the Qur'an and learn how the Prophet of Islam (PBUH) praised and emphasized forgiveness, tolerance, and leniency, and then refer to history and biographies to understand the Prophet's (PBUH) behavior toward friend and foe.

The Qur'an does not limit the Prophet's (PBUH) forgiveness and kind treatment to merely believers. Indeed, it enjoins him to treat even his most treacherous enemies with grace and forgiveness as it says of the Jewish enemies in Medina:

> But because of their breach of their covenant, we cursed them, and made their hearts grow hard; they change the words from their (right) places and forget a good part of the message that was sent to them, nor will you cease to find them—barring a few—ever bent on (new) deceits: but forgive them, and overlook (their misdeeds): for Allah loves those who are kind. (5:13)

We note two points here: firstly, this verse was revealed toward the end of the Prophet's (PBUH) life, during the peak of his sovereignty. Secondly, in addition to enjoining forgiveness, *sfah* mentioned, literally means removing blame that drives forgiveness to perfection.

Raghib al-Isfahani, an eleventh-century Muslim scholar and the author of *al-Mufradat*, wrote: "*Sfah* means leaving the reproach and is considered more eloquent than forgiveness."[46]

Above and beyond this directive, the Qur'an at times commands the Prophet (PBUH) to return the vileness of people with goodness and to transform their enmity into goodwill:

> Nor can goodness and Evil be equal. Repel (Evil) with
> what is better: Then will he between whom and you was
> hatred, become as it were thy friend and intimate! (41:34).

Of course, this teaching is not exclusive to the noble Prophet (PBUH) but is given to his true followers as well. The Qur'an refers to them with rewards in the following verses:

> Those who patiently persevere, seeking the countenance
> of their Lord; establish regular prayers; spend, out of (the
> gifts) we have bestowed for their sustenance, secretly and
> openly; and turn off [repel] evil with good: for such there
> is the final attainment of the (eternal) home. (13:22)

> Let not those among you who are endowed with grace and
> amplitude of means resolve by oath against helping their kinsmen,
> those in want [need], and those who have left their homes in Allah's
> cause: let them forgive and overlook, do you not wish that Allah
> should forgive you? for Allah is oft-forgiving, most merciful. (24:22)

The Qur'an commands the Prophet (PBUH) to continue in the same manner and to treat captives of war gently, with consolation, even those who had killed Muslims in combat, as reflected in verse 8:70: "O Prophet! say to those who are captives in your hands: If God finds any good in your hearts, he will give you something better than what has been taken from you, and he will forgive you: for Allah is Oft-forgiving, Most Merciful." Ironically, some of these captives were from tribes that had tortured and killed Muslims in the past.[47]

Verses exulting such high qualities and excellence are not limited to those mentioned above; however, we suffice here and proceed with the books of history and the Prophet's (PBUH) biography so we may render examples of his graceful treatment of others, especially his enemies. There are many other verses throughout the Qur'an that refer to mercy and leniency. We will review a few more in upcoming sections as we address different aspects of how the Qur'an suggests dealing with enemies.

Chapter 5
The Prophet's Treatment of His Enemies

ACCORDING TO TABATABAI, RADICAL revolutions around the world have often been followed by horrific bloodshed after victory. Intense, widespread violence and vendettas unfolded during and after the Russian and French revolutions. For example, David Shub, in his book *Lenin: A Biography*, notes that despite the abdication of Emperor Nicholai II after the Russian Revolution, he and his family were executed, including his young son, and their bodies immersed in a pool of sulfuric acid and dumped into a deep well.[48]

During the great revolution of Muhammad (PBUH), which reached its peak by conquering Mecca, people expected it to be accompanied by horrific bloodshed to recompense for the crimes committed by the Quraysh idolaters and for their killings in the Battle of Uhud. According to the report of Waqidi in *Kitab al-Maghazi*, chief Sa'd ibn Ubade Khazraji, upon his entrance to Mecca, shouted, "Today is the day of bloodshed, today forbidden becomes permitted, today Quraysh is humiliated by God."[49]

But when the Prophet (PBUH) heard this, he announced, "Today is the day of mercy, today God will honor Quraysh."[50] He immediately discharged Sa'd from leading the army corps and gave the leadership to someone else.[51] The Prophet (PBUH) then stood next to the Ka'ba, addressing the people of Quraysh: "O people of Quraysh, starting today God has taken away the magnification of the ignorance era and taken away boasting about lineage from amongst you. All men were created from Adam, and Adam was created from clay."[52] He then recited verse 49:13: "O mankind! We created you from a single (pair) of a male and a female, and made you into nations and tribes, that you may know [recognize] each other. Verily the most honored of you in the sight of God is (he who is) the most righteous of you, And Allah has full knowledge and is well acquainted (with all things)."

The Prophet (PBUH) then asked: "O people of Quraysh, what do you suppose I shall do with you?" They replied, "You will treat us well as you are a magnanimous brother." The Prophet (PBUH) said, "Go, you are all free."[53] It is important to note the Prophet (PBUH) did not make acceptance of Islam a condition of his pardon and their freedom.

Waqidi narrates in his book *Kitab al-Maghazi*: "The Messenger of God came upon the people who were sitting tightly next to each other and around Ka'ba, and said, 'Thanks and glory to the Lord whose promise came true and helped his servant, and he alone defeated confederates of enemy. What do you say (about my treatment towards you)? And what do you think?' The people of Mecca replied: 'We have well thoughts about you as you are our magnanimous brother who has come to power.'"[54] The Prophet (PBUH) said, 'I will tell you what my brother Yusuf (Joseph) said (to his brothers who mistreated him)'[55] and then recited the following verse: 'He said: this day let no reproach be (cast) on you, Allah will forgive you, and he is the most merciful of those who show mercy!' (12:92)." He then spoke what was mentioned earlier from Ibn Hisham's *al-Seerat al-Nabawiyyah*.

Is this loving and benevolent treatment comparable to the violence perpetrated by revolutionists around the world after their victory? Did Lenin and those alike follow up with mercy and forgiveness after their victory, or did they order mass killings with extreme brutality, thus trampling decency and humanity? Are the Muslims of today who bomb and slaughter minorities and their own brothers, including innocent families, following in the footsteps of the Prophet (PBUH) or the likes of Lenin and Hitler? What creed do suicide bombers subscribe to?[56]

Upon his victory over the Meccans, the Prophet (PBUH) pardoned the enemy leader Abu Sufiyan. He even pardoned Wahshi ibn Harb, the killer of his beloved Uncle Hamza. He pardoned those who had remorse with the exception of a few individuals who had committed cowardly acts, such as the murderer Ibn Khatel. He was sent by the Prophet (PBUH) to collect the obligatory alms (for the poor) and regular charity, with a man from Banu Khuza'a to assist him. Ibn Khatel ordered the man to prepare some food for him and went to sleep. When he awoke, he saw the man sleeping and killed him out of anger because he had not prepared his meal. He then took the charity collection and joined the enemy idolaters of Mecca. He composed a few poems as songs in mockery of the Messenger of God and gave them to two of his women slaves. He taught them to sing the poems during his wine-drinking gatherings. After Mecca was conquered, he was sentenced to death in retribution for his crimes.[57]

These examples indeed show a Prophet (PBUH) of mercy who did not forget justice and kindness even when he was victorious over his enemies. Similarly, in the face of defeat, he did not shy away from benevolence toward his enemies or wishing them well. According to Ayaz Maqhrebi's books, *Kitab al-Shifa* and *Sahih Muslim,* the Prophet (PBUH) was once urged by his followers to curse the idolaters who had injured his face and teeth during the Battle of Uhud.[58] The Prophet (PBUH), who was not ready to curse them, said, "I was not sent to curse, I was not sent but as mercy to people." In fact, according to al-Ghazali in *Ahya al-Uloumuddin*, the Prophet (PBUH) also said, "O Allah, guide my people as they do not know."[59]

In *Fath al-Mubdi*, Muslim scholar al-Sharqawi writes that when Thamamat ibn Ethal, who was from Yamama (an ancient historical region in present-day Saudia Arabia), arrived in Medina and embraced Islam, he swore he would not sell his wheat to the Meccans unless the Prophet (PBUH) ordered him to do so. He then returned to Yamama. The people of Mecca wrote to the Prophet (PBUH) and requested that he ask Thamamat not to stop his shipment of wheat to Mecca. Despite their animosity toward the Prophet (PBUH), especially during the Battle of Uhud (where his close companions were killed, and he was injured), the Prophet (PBUH) wrote to Thamamat ordering him not to refuse sending his shipment of wheat to Mecca, so Thamamat complied.[60]

The Prophet (PBUH) forbade the assassination of his adversaries. He did not allow murder or surprise attacks on individuals, according to explicit reports in the Prophetic traditions, which are direct sayings of the Prophet Muhammad (PBUH). As head of state, if he ordered an execution, it would only be because someone intentionally murdered a Muslim or, like Ka'b ibn Ashraf, encouraged the enemy and conspired with enemy tribes to engage in a fight against the Prophet (PBUH) and their blockade of Medina.[61] All of this would be considered a declaration of war on the Prophet (PBUH) and the Muslim state.

Al-Tabari, in his book of history, reported the Prophet (PBUH) saying "belief will dissuade man from murder, and no believer will kill through murder or ambush."[62] This teaching agrees with the explicit Qur'anic text, which indicates that if the enemies of Islam have no fight with Muslims, God has left no way for Muslims to justify and commit aggression against them:

Except those who join a nation between whom and you there is a treaty (of peace), or those who approach you with hearts restraining them from fighting you as well as fighting their own people. If Allah had pleased, he could have given them power over you, and they would have fought you: Therefore, if they withdraw from you and do not fight you, and (instead) send you (guarantees of) peace, then Allah has opened no way for you (to war against them). (4:90)

There is not a single verse in the Qur'an that gives Muslims license to kill people because of their beliefs. All Qur'anic verses referring to punishment for unbelievers (kuffar) are about their punishment by God in the next life after the Day of Judgment, not a punishment carried out by Muslims in this world.

In Tarikh al-Ya'qubi, a well-known classical Islamic book older than al-Tabari's, there is mention of Arab tribes (such as Banu Mudalij,

Banu Zamrah, and Banu Dayel) who said they had no quarrels with Muslims and told the Prophet, "We are not with you and we are not against you." The Prophet (PBUH) prohibited fighting any of them.[63]

This prohibition was in accordance with the above verse (4:90). Therefore, Islam's fight was with those who initiated fights with Muslims, as the Qur'an explicitly refers to in verse 9:13. Nevertheless, when the enemy was inclined toward peace, the Prophet (PBUH) was commissioned to make peace and welcomed it. He showed that he was merely concerned with defending his people and was not a warmonger. As the Qur'an states, "But if the enemy incline towards peace, do thou (also) incline towards peace, and trust in Allah: for He is All hearing and All knowing" (8:61).

Therefore, Islamic history tells us that when the Prophet (PBUH) signed a peace treaty at Hudaybiyyah with the idolaters of Mecca, he urged Muslim refugees who came to Medina to return to their families in Mecca.[64] However, according to the books of traditions, when any group fought with the Prophet (PBUH) and he sent his army toward them, he enjoined his men to "move forward in the name of God and his religion and put your trust in him, and do not kill the elder, women, and children. Do not betray each other in the booty, but rather share it. Seek reform and do good deeds as God loves the good doers."[65]

After fighting and winning a victory over the combatant enemy, the Prophet (PBUH) often freed the prisoners of war or held them for ransom, as explicitly stated in the Qur'an: "When you have thoroughly subdued them, bind a bond firmly (on them): thereafter (is the time for) either free them by generosity [grace] or ransom: Until the war lays down its burdens [terminates]" (47:4). The number of prisoners of war pardoned by the Messenger of God (PBUH) was so many that their mention is beyond the scope of this text. As an example, according to Ibn Hisham's biography of the Prophet (PBUH), during the Battle of Hawazin, six thousand prisoners were freed by the Prophet (PBUH), as is also mentioned in other books of history and biographies.[66] Also, according to verse 47:4, it is evident that accepting Islam was not a condition of their freedom; the only condition was a promise that they would not return and fight against Muslims.

According to Abu Dawood's collection of traditions, as reported by Abdullah ibn Abbas, the Prophet (PBUH) enjoined compassion even toward animals and forbade dogfights and cockfights.[67]

Tabatabai asks how then could such a noble Prophet (PBUH) condone hostility or violence? As historic witnesses noted from the Qur'an and tradition, war in Islam becomes a matter of necessity when an enemy initiates and carries out acts of aggression against God's religion and its followers. Some Christian and Jewish scholars portray Islam as a religion of violence and war. It is as though (without any due diligence) they believe their own creed has been free of violence.[68]

Of course, as a faith, Islam is confined to the Qur'an and to the traditions of the Prophet (PBUH). What despotic rulers did after the Prophet's (PBUH) time is a matter of history and can only be legitimate (from an Islamic perspective) if their actions complied with the rulings in the Qur'an.

For thirteen years in Mecca, the Prophet (PBUH) and his companions invited people to monotheism and forbade them from engaging in polytheism, superstitions, and female infanticide—all in a peaceful manner. It was also during this period that Muslims suffered persecution, torture, and death at the hands of idolaters. Such events are recorded in the oldest known biography of the Prophet's (PBUH) life, *Life of Muhammad* by historian Ibn Ishaq, as well as in books by al-Tabari and in *al-Kamil fi al-Tarikh* by Ali ibn al-Athir and others that describe the tortures in detail. During this period, the Prophet (PBUH) and his companions never armed themselves and tolerated various inflictions to the point that many of the Muslims were forced to flee to Medina, formerly known as Yathrib. Finally, the idolaters decided to kill the Prophet (PBUH); hence he was forced to leave his home during the night and escape to Medina. However, the Quraysh idolaters did not cease their hostilities and wrote a threatening letter to the people of Medina warning them that if they did not kill or banish the Prophet (PBUH) from their land, they would have to fight them, as is recounted in Abdurazzaq San'ani's historic book *al-Musannaf*:

You have received our fellow citizen Muhammad in your town and you are the majority in Medina and we swear to God if you do not kill him or banish him from your land, we will seek assistance from Arab tribes against you and will rally towards you, and we (will) kill your fighters and allow your women for ourselves.[69]

It was under these circumstances that permission to fight and defend was given to Muslims as the Qur'an states: "To those against whom war is made, permission is given (to fight), because they are wronged;—and verily, Allah is most powerful for their aid, those who have been driven from their homes in defiance of right [unjustly],—(for no cause) except that they say, 'Our Lord is Allah'" (22:39–40).

All of the Muslims' battles with the Quraysh (which concluded with a victory over Mecca) went through the same stages and were defensive battles. As mentioned previously, after victory over Mecca, the Prophet (PBUH) issued amnesty to the Quraysh and ordered all combatant enemies to be freed. There are many biography and history books available for further details.

Chapter 6
Responses to Allegations, Misconceptions, and Misrepresentations

As MENTIONED EARLIER, ISLAM advocates peace as do other faiths. However, some of its followers do not, which is also the case with followers of other faiths. Unfortunately, regarding war and violence, the uninformed rely on many misconceptions and misunderstandings of Islam, while its critics perpetuate plenty of allegations and misrepresentations. We also acknowledge that misunderstandings and misrepresentations among some Muslims emanate from inauthentic narrations and sources, some of which have found their way into major books of history, narrations (*ahadith*), or even wrong explanations (exegesis) of the Qur'an. Interestingly, the critics of Islam and extremists have a lot in common in their understanding (or misunderstanding) and misrepresentation of Islam.

As a religion, the nature of Islam is to draw distinctions between truth and falsehood, or good and evil, while enjoining communities to establish peace and justice; however, there are times when conflicts become unavoidable. When the hostility turns to violence and aggression, the advocates of truth and justice must defend their lives, faith, and community. By the way, we must clarify one common definition that is often misquoted or misunderstood. We often see or hear "Islam is a religion of peace." Some misunderstand it to mean Islam is a pacifist faith, which is not a complete definition. Islam advocates peace and calls on all nations to be peaceful. There is a difference between the two. Advocating peace means Islam and its followers stand for peace and justice. If Muslims see injustice anywhere (especially when there is call for help), they must stand up and defend against injustice and make their best to establish peace. That is; Islam is about being at peace with the peaceful (those who want love and peace). At the same time, Muslims should be ready to stand up against injustice, corruption, and destruction.

According to Tabatabai, there are those who oppose violence with no exceptions and under any circumstances, such as Tolstoy, who, toward the end of his life, came to such beliefs. The credo of Jesus Christ (PBUH) echoes this teaching, as stated in Matthew 5:39: "But I tell you, do not resist an evil person. If anyone slaps you on the right cheek, turn to them the other cheek also."[70]

Tolstoy's commentary on the command "Do not resist an evil person" means never resist and do not respond to violence with violence; in other words, never do anything that is incompatible with kindness, and if you are insulted, tolerate it and do not resort to force.[71] Jesus (PBUH) gives the high ideal that if someone hits you on one cheek, you should turn the other cheek.[72] Leniency and forgiveness of the individual is also highly recommended in the Qur'an:

Nor can goodness and Evil be equal. Repel (Evil) with what is better, Then will he between whom and you was hatred become as it were your friend and intimate!, And no one will be granted such goodness except those who exercise patience and self-restraint,— none but persons of the greatest good fortune. (41:34–35)

Tell those who believe, to forgive those who do not look forward to the Days of Allah: It is for Him to recompense (for good or ill) each People according to what they have earned. (45:14)

But when places of worship are destroyed, the helpless, including old men, women, and children, are persecuted, and unbelievers try to force believers to renounce their religion, the Qur'an considers it total dereliction of the duty of the Muslim state not to oppose such oppression and to defend what is right. It becomes a matter of justice and liberty which is what no religion or men and women of faith can tolerate.

Tabatabai adds Tolstoy accepted this teaching in general and in absolute terms and considered it the only way to save humanity. However, it is clear that excess acceptance of oppression and forbearance is not always liberating because generalizing it in absolute terms would mean not holding criminals and oppressors accountable and allowing them to continue their aggressions. This in and of itself becomes self-defeating and takes away the rights of the oppressed and the innocent, eventually promoting violence.

For this reason, other thinkers in the West have opposed generalizing this rule. In Jean-Jacques Rousseau's book, *The Social Contract*, he refers to this and similar teachings: "Christianity is a religion of complete spirituality, which speaks about heavenly matters, and its content is not about this world."[73] It can be said that the Gospel of Matthew has fallen to exaggeration and has not reported Christ's teachings accurately. In any case, if forbearance in the extreme is not socially permissible, then unjustified violence is far worse than extreme forbearance, because violence is most destructive to an individual's character and has a more harmful impact on society.

From an Islamic perspective, mercy and leniency are essential elements in building a peaceful and compassionate society. This is not to say all punitive laws are suspended, because just punishment of a criminal (properly applied) *is* considered a mercy to the society; therefore, mercy and justice are not in contradiction to each other.[74]

There are numerous examples in the Qur'an and in the traditions of the great Prophet (PBUH) of his forgiveness, compassion, and clemency toward friends and foes, while condemning force and violence as the only way to provide security for a society.

Famous Western legislators have also endorsed defensive wars. As an example, Montesquieu, the famous French lawyer and political philosopher who lived during the Age of Enlightenment, in his book *The Spirit of the Law*, says, "Nations have the right in order to fight to protect themselves, because protecting any nation and its people is like protecting any other nation and its people that have attacked it."[75]

The notion by some Middle Eastern studies scholars that war is forbidden in the creed of Christianity or Judaism is completely false and is considered contradictory to narratives in their holy books. In the Torah, for example, there are explicit mentions of wars Abraham (PBUH) and Moses (PBUH) had with their enemies. Genesis 14:14–16 says

> When Abram heard that his relative (Lot) had been taken captive, he called out the 318 trained men born in his household and went in pursuit as far as Dan. During the night Abram divided his men to attack them and he overpowered them, pursuing them as far as Hobah, north of Damascus. He recovered all the goods and brought back his relative Lot and his possessions, together with the women and the other people.

And the battle between Moses (PBUH) and the Midianites and the Amalekites is mentioned in Deuteronomy 31:7–8: "Then Moses summoned Joshua and said to him in the presence of all Israel, 'Be strong and courageous, for you must go with this people into the land that the Lord swore to their ancestors to give them, and you must divide it among them as their inheritance.'"

Also, from Exodus 17: 8–13, we learn the following:

> The Amalekites came and attacked the Israelites at Rephidim. Moses said to Joshua, 'Choose some of our men and go out to fight the Amalekites. Tomorrow I will stand on top of the hill with the staff of God in my hands. So Joshua fought the Amalekites as Moses had ordered, and Moses, Aaron and Hur went to the top of the hill. As long as Moses held up his hands, the Israelites were winning, but whenever he lowered his

hands, the Amalekites were winning. When Moses' hands grew tired, they took a stone and put it under him and he sat on it. Aaron and Hur held his hands up—one on one side, one on the other—so that his hands remained steady till sunset. So Joshua overcame the Amalekite army with the sword.[76]

Jesus (PBUH) had no reservations about a defensive war when he ordered his companions to prepare arms, as indicated in Luke 22:36–38: "He said to them, But now if you have a purse, take it, and also a bag; and if you don't have a sword, sell your cloak and buy one. It is written: 'And he was numbered with the transgressors'; and I tell you that this must be fulfilled in me. Yes, what is written about me is reaching its fulfillment. The disciples said, 'See, Lord, here are two swords.' 'That's enough!' he replied." Although the disciples did not get a chance to use them because they were outnumbered, nevertheless they armed themselves with swords ready to fight; however, Jesus (PBUH) anticipated a fight between his disciples and their close relatives in the near future and therefore said, "Do not suppose that I have come to bring peace to the earth. I did not come to bring peace, but a sword" (Mathew 10:34), and then explained how belief in him and rejection of him will turn the closest relatives against each other (which will potentially end up in altercations and fights).

Therefore, we observe that Christians of old considered the Crusades as holy wars. Thousands participated in these wars and massacred many Muslims. Pope Urban II ruled the Crusades legitimate and encouraged people to participate.[77] One might argue Pope Urban II's ruling and the participation of Christians in the Crusades have no relevance to the teachings of Jesus (PBUH) and should not be considered a part of the Christian faith. Likewise, we argue that tyrannical wars perpetrated by oppressive Arab or non-Arab kings and despotic leaders in the Muslim world today and in the past, and the violent behavior of a few unbridled lone Muslims, have no relevance to Islam and the teachings of its compassionate Prophet (PBUH). The Prophet (PBUH) never initiated a war but he did sign peace treaties with combatant idolaters to prevent war. However, in the holy books of Judaism, Christianity, and Islam, we witness verses that clearly deal with aggression, and the response to aggression with physical fighting is a defensive measure and a last resort.

Another clarification regarding terminology used in the Qur'an is the term *kufr* or *kafir*. Kufr has multiple meanings, but its literal translation means "to cover" as in covering the truth or rejecting the truth; it is also used to express ingratitude for a favor. One who covers or rejects the truth is called a *kafir*. The term *mushrekeen* is used throughout the Qur'an and exclusively refers to idolaters or polytheists. Yet another term, *ahlul kitab*, literally translates as People of the Book or people of earlier revelations (Christians and Jews). These were the groups of people mentioned in the Qur'an as the People of the Book who existed when Islam was introduced. Each of these groups was divided into those who were hostile toward Muslims and those who were not (or those with whom there were peace treaties). Muslims had to defend their existence against those who were hostile toward them. The Qur'an categorically separates these groups based on their enmity, not their faith. The term *infidel*, often mentioned by those who are unaware of its meaning or by critics of Islam, does not exist in the Qur'an or the Arabic language, so it will be discussed separately.

One of the major misunderstandings or misrepresentations is that Muslims regard all non-Muslims as kafir(s) and hate them and want to either convert them or kill them. This is an absolute falsehood. It is unfair to quote some of the Qur'anic verses to this effect without understanding their contexts. The Qur'an clearly distinguishes between combative and noncombative kafir and advises Muslims to live in peace with the latter. Not only that, it requires Muslims to fulfill a covenant with unbelievers and to never renege on the covenant unless they renege. To honor a covenant with unbelievers is a must for Muslims, as verse 9:4 makes clear they must honor the covenant with polytheists: "(But the treaties are) not dissolved with those idolaters with whom you have entered into alliance and who have not subsequently failed you in way, nor aided any one against you. So fulfill your engagements with them to the end of their term: for Allah loveth the righteous." This verse and others clarify that Muslims must keep their agreements with idolaters as long as they do.

In light of this verse, who can say the Qur'an wants to impose Islamic beliefs with coercion when its basic doctrine is freedom of conscience, as is pointed out in verse 2:256? Faith and freedom go together; one cannot separate one from the other. And, in fact, there can be no real faith without genuine freedom. Faith is a matter of conviction, and conviction cannot be imposed with coercion; it can be acquired only by exercising one's freedom. This is why the Qur'an stresses the importance of freedom of faith. Chapter 109 of the Qur'an makes freedom of faith quite clear. The *kafereen* (unbelievers or re-jecters) are free to follow their religion just as Muslims are to follow their own. It is a clear declaration of harmonious coexistence with anyone, whatever their belief. And even if one calls someone to the path of Allah, it must be done not only in peace, but also in the best possible manner and with wisdom, for as the Qur'an says:

"Invite (all) to the Way of thy Lord with wisdom and beautiful preaching [goodly exhortation]; and argue with them in ways that are best and most gracious: for thy Lord knows best, who have strayed from His Path, and who receive guidance" (16:125).

In this chapter, we will address some of the allegations critics of Islam have made, including the verses they cite as evidence of violence in Islam. The sources for these claims, compiled by critics of Islam, are taken from various articles, books, and websites. We will attempt to address most claims, but not all, as they will become too tedious and repetitive. Our hope is that once impartial readers learn about Islam from the previous sections and the sections to follow, they will review the allegations, misrepresentations, and misinterpretations, compare them with what was presented thus far, along with our responses to individual allegations, and they can then judge for themselves where the truth lies. As for advocates of truth, they should be armed with the logic and reasoning presented here so they can lead their own campaign to educate the masses and respond to any further allegations and comments made by such critics or extremists.

6.1 "Qur'an Has More Verses on Violence"

Critics of Islam have said that while other books of faith contain verses of violence, the Qur'an contains more. It is not clear how this conclusion was reached, nor the criteria followed; however, investigating whether the Qur'an actually is more violent than its Judeo-Christian counterparts, software engineer Tom Anderson processed the text of all three holy books to find which contained verses with the most violence. He summarized: "Killing and destruction are referenced slightly more often in the New Testament (2.8 percent) than in the Qur'an (2.1 percent), but the Old Testament clearly leads—more than twice that of the Qur'an—in mentions of destruction and killing (5.3 percent)."[78] Going beyond numbers, here are additional facts to consider:

1. When noting the inception and duration of each faith, the establishment of Islam and the Muslim state were on a different track from that of Christianity and Judaism. While Islam, like Judaism and Christianity, began with just a few followers, it established itself as a state with many followers in a lawless area where there were no established territories. Many tribes inhabited these territories and were often at war with each other. As a state, it had to adopt policies that governed a nation that included Muslims and non-Muslims. It had allies and enemies outside its borders as well as within; it also had peace treaties and conflicts that ended in war. There are verses in the Qur'an associated with each of these conflicts that regulate how to deal with the enemy and that remind Muslims not to transgress the rules of engagement, as mentioned in earlier sections.

2. Unlike Muslims, Christians and Jews did not form a state at the inception of their faiths. Neither Moses nor Jesus (PBUT)

became head of the state. The mission of Moses (PBUH) was to free the Israelites and relocate them to the promised land; however, they never establish a state during the lifetime of Moses (PBUH). During his life among people, Jesus (PBUH) had a limited number of disciples and followers who did not establish a state either. How would these two noble Prophets (PBUT) react had they eventually established a state and were to rule as Prophet Muhammad (PBUH) had? Nevertheless, the verses and instructions within their holy books are clear on how to deal with violent hostilities and oppression.

3.   Islam came into existence during one of the most violent periods in history, and Prophet Muhammad (PBUH) had to face brutal opposition. It was not easy to establish peace in such a society. The primary aim of Islam was to establish a just and compassionate society, but Muslims also had to respond to the given violence of the times. The Qur'an nowhere glorifies violence but permits it reluctantly in defensive situations. It makes it clear to Muslims not to be tempted and become aggressors, as God does not love aggressors (2:190). Also, the Qur'an requires Muslims to fight to liberate oppressed men, women, and children who are helpless (4:75). Indeed, Prophet Muhammad (PBUH) was not only a Messenger of God, but also a statesman over a Muslim and a non-Muslim nation. In Michael H. Hart's book, *The 100: A Ranking of the Most Influential Persons in History*, Prophet Muhammad (PBUH) is ranked first on the list as the most influential person in history who contributed to the benefit and upliftment of mankind. Hart wrote, "My choice of Muhammad to lead the list of the world's most influential persons may surprise some readers and may be questioned by others, but he was the only man in history who was supremely successful on both the religious and secular levels."[79]

Alphonse de Lamartine, an eighteenth-century French writer, poet, and politician, wrote, "If greatness of purpose, smallness of means and astounding results are the three criteria of human genius, who could dare to compare any great man in modern history with Muhammad? . . . A Philosopher, orator, apostle, legislator, warrior, conqueror of ideas, restorer of rational dogmas, of a cult without images, the founder of twenty terrestrial empires and of one spiritual empire, that is Muhammad."[80]

4. The Qur'an never permitted a war of aggression and never allowed Muslims to kill a single soul, as it would mean killing the whole of humanity. He taught them saving one innocent life amounts to saving all of humanity:"If anyone slew a person—unless it be for murder or for spreading mischief in the land—it would be as if he slew the whole people [all mankind]: and if any one saved a life, it would be as if he saved the life of whole people [all mankind]" (5:32).

   Had Muslims of later years followed this Qur'anic teaching, they would have been great examples of peace and symbols of nonviolence. Similarly, the Qur'an requires Muslims to fight in self-defense when necessary, and to work for justice and peace so the world becomes violence-free. The situation in the Arab society at the time was such that it was not possible to stop violence, so war was permitted in that context, but the ultimate goal was always to establish peace—an ideal condition. In other words, violence is existential, and peace is transcendent. The Prophet of Islam (PBUH) and his companions endured persecution for over ten years and Qur'anic verses about war were revealed after their migration to Medina. Had there been no threat and no animosity from the Meccans, there would be no migration, nor the need to fight in order to defend their faith, life, and existence. Qur'anic commands include accepting the offer of peace from the enemy even if it does not seem sincere.

5. It is true that there has been an abundant use of violence in Muslim history, but that is because Muslims rarely followed the Qur'anic ideals in their lives. This happens with the followers of all religions. Many of us claim adherence to the

ideals of our religion or quote them to prove its superiority but struggle to follow them on a daily basis. The Christians stress love and compassion, but their history is full of violence as well. The problem is that we wrongly compare the history of one religion with the ideals of another.

6. Even ignoring the above arguments, the number of verses about violence do not reflect how peaceful a faith is or is not. According to critics of Islam who claim Christianity has fewer verses about war and violence, we say (even if that were true), history reflects that numbers are irrelevant. Christianity's history of wars, such as the Crusades, the Spanish Inquisition, and many others, attest to this. No one can deny the historical facts. Readers should keep this in mind as we later discuss the number of Qur'anic verses in the critics' list about violence, and their conclusions that Islam is a religion of violence (as they seem to keep scores on the terminology) while they ignore the meaning, historical context, and significance related to each verse.

6.2   Critic: "Like Today's Extremists, Muhammad Could Not Tolerate Christians and Jews."

Some critics claim Islam is not a religion of peace. If they were objective and fair-minded according to the teachings of Jesus Christ (PBUH) and studied the Qur'an and Islamic history, they would never make such a statement. With even slight diligence, they would find the word *Islam* comes from the root word *slm* or "peace"; thus, *Islam* means "submission and surrender." The complete definition is "peace through submission and surrender to God." Of course as mentioned in the beginning of this chapter, some do quote "Islam is a religion of peace," which is often misunderstood to mean Islam is a pacifist faith, which is not a complete definition. Islam advocates peace and calls on all nations to be peaceful. Advocating peace means Islam and its followers stand for peace and justice. If Muslims see injustice anywhere (especially when there is call for help), they must stand up and defend against injustice and do their best to establish peace. That is, Islam is about being at peace with the peaceful (those who want love and peace). At the same time, Muslims should be ready to stand up against injustice, corruption and destruction

If the critics dug even deeper into history, they would learn that the Prophet of Islam (PBUH), in a location called Hudaybiyyah (current Arabia), signed a peace treaty with the enemy (as discussed in earlier sections and by other historians). Unfortunately, some critics of Islam give strong, yet uninformed opinions based on very little information on important issues; these same critics, especially those with a bias, trust rumors and conjectures more than facts.

Furthermore, when discussing violence within Islam, critics often bring up the violent acts perpetrated in the name of Christianity, which undeniably includes the Crusades. However, Christ (PBUH) never entered into a war during his lifetime and he never promoted violence in his sermons, whereas these critics claim the Qur'an says Muhammad was a warrior who promoted violence in his sermons. Those who make such claims have read neither the Qur'an nor the Bible, properly. As mentioned earlier in this chapter, in the Gospel of Matthew, Jesus (PBUH) said, "Do not suppose that I have come to bring peace to the earth. I did not come to bring peace, but a sword" (Matthew 10:34). He then explains that believing in him separates kinfolk and makes them enemies of one another. Of course, enmity can lead to altercations and wars, which is why Christ (PBUH) mentions the sword as a symbol of war. But why didn't Christ himself participate in a war? Because during his time, with few followers, he had no army prepared for battle. His story is similar to when Muhammad (PBUH) was in Mecca and did not fight his enemies for thirteen years, but God protected him (through his migration from enemy's harm). Whereas Christ (PBUH), according to Christians, before he could escape from his enemies, was arrested, thus ending his mission.

But the notion that Christ (PBUH) was against defensive wars is an unduly claim and not in agreement with his order to his disciples to buy swords, as reported in the Gospel of Luke: "But now if you have a purse, take it, and also a bag; and if you don't have a sword,

sell your cloak and buy one" (22:36). Furthermore, Christians believe in the entire content of the holy Bible, which contains not only
the New Testament but also the Old Testament and recalls explicitly
the battles of Moses (PBUH) in Exodus 17 and Number 31. Can a
Christian claim Moses (PBUH) was not a prophet of God because
he fought the Midianites and Amalekites? How odd these critics ac-
cuse Muhammad (PBUH), who conducted defensive wars and often
pardoned his enemies post-victory, of being violent and the founder
of the most violent religion in history. However, they accept Moses
(PBUH) as a prophet while the holy book states:

> The Lord said to Moses, "Take vengeance on the
> Midianites for the Israelites. After that, you will be
> gathered to your people." So Moses said to the peo-
> ple, "Arm some of your men to go to war against
> the Midianites so that they may carry out the Lord's
> vengeance on them. Send into battle a thousand men
> from each of the tribes of Israel." So twelve thousand
> men armed for battle, a thousand from each tribe,
> were supplied from the clans of Israel. Moses sent
> them into battle, a thousand from each tribe, along
> with Phinehas son of Eleazar, the priest, who took
> with him articles from the sanctuary and the trumpets
> for signaling. They fought against Midian, as the Lord
> commanded Moses, and killed every man. Among
> their victims were Evi, Rekem, Zur, Hur and Reba—
> the five kings of Midian. They also killed Balaam
> son of Beor with the sword. The Israelites captured
> the Midianite women and children and took all the
> Midianite herds, flocks and goods as plunder. They
> burned all the towns where the Midianites had set-
> tled, as well as all their camps. They took all the plun-
> der and spoils, including the people and animals, and
> brought the captives, spoils and plunder to Moses and
> Eleazar the priest and the Israelite assembly at their

camp on the plains of Moab, by the Jordan across from Jericho. Moses, Eleazar the priest and all the leaders of the community went to meet them outside the camp. Moses was angry with the officers of the army—the commanders of thousands and commanders of hundreds—who returned from the battle. "Have you allowed all the women to live?" he asked them. "They were the ones who followed Balaam's advice and enticed the Israelites to be unfaithful to the Lord in the Peor incident, so that a plague struck the Lord's people. Now kill all the boys. And kill every woman who has slept with a man, but save for yourselves every girl who has never slept with a man (Numbers 31:1–18).

Similar words are mentioned in Exodus 17.

We can compare the commands in the above verses with those given to Prophet Muhammad (PBUH) about war, so we gain a better understanding about the difference between leniency and religious violence. As presented earlier, Prophet Muhammad (PBUH) and his companions did not make any effort to initiate wars as long as they were not threatened with persecution, violence, and death. We read in history that Salam ibn Meshkam, a Jewish leader, said to the Jewish people about the Prophet (PBUH), "This is the man that unless they grab him by the collar [neck], he would not turn to war and I swear to God this is an admirable attitude."[81] When the Prophet (PBUH) decided to mount a defense, he would summon his companions and advise them: "Act in the name of God, rely on God and act by the creed of his messenger and do not kill any old man, the women and children, and do not commit treachery with the spoils and share them with each other. Work toward amending the matters and do good deeds as God loves good doers."[82]

As quoted in the above verses, we realize that women and young boys were killed during battles waged by Jews and accepted by Christians, while the Prophet of Islam (PBUH) forbade committing such crimes. Nevertheless, critics refer to Islam as a religion of violence! Their error does not end here; they mainly protest the Prophet's (PBUH) attitude toward Christians and Jews by alleging: "Just like today's Muslim extremists, Muhammad could not tolerate Christians and Jews." One who has not read the history may pontificate as such; however, if one studies the history one will realize that when Muhammad (PBUH) entered Medina, he treated Jews peacefully and signed several peace and cooperation treaties with them. When the Jews saw his influence and power increase, they became fearful and broke their treaties, thus aligning themselves with the Meccan idolaters and claiming polytheism is better than monotheism; hence, the Prophet's (PBUH) relation with them was strained. Nevertheless, in chapter 5 of the Qur'an (which contains final verses revealed toward the end of the Prophet's life), there is mention of forbearance and forgiveness toward Jews:

> But because of their breach of their covenant, We cursed them, and made their hearts grow hard; they change the words from their (right) places and forget a good part of the message that was sent them, nor wilt thou cease to find them– barring a few – ever bent on (new) deceits: but forgive them, and overlook (their misdeeds): for Allah loveth those who are kind. (5:13)

The Jews' betrayal and collusion with the Meccan idolaters was not only reported in the Qur'an (4:155), but fair-minded Jews have also concurred and reproached their coreligionists. Among them, the famous Israeli historian and researcher Dr. Israel Wolfensohn, who, in his book *Tarikh al-Yahud fi Bilad al-Arab* (History of Jews in Arab Territory), writes: "It was obligatory for Jews not to make such a grave mistake and not openly say worshiping the idols is better than Islamic monotheism in front of Quraysh leaders."[83]

Recognition of Jewish rights, which were formalized in a treaty and recorded during the early Medina period, can be seen in the oldest Muslim books. Ibn Hisham (an early biographer who edited the biography of the Prophet Muhammad by Ibn Ishaq) has reported this treaty in his book of prophetic tradition called *al-Seerat al-Nabawiyyah*

(Biography of the Prophet), in which he writes, "Jews onto their faith and Muslims onto theirs. In this decree, Jewish confederates and Muslims are equal unless someone commits aggression (and treachery)."[84] Again, in the same treaty it says:

> Jews and Muslims each are responsible for their expenses in wars and as members of this treaty, they must defend and help each other against anyone who fights either member. Muslims and Jews must have pure intention and goodwill toward each other (no evil or misdeed), and no one allows misdeed (treachery) toward his confederate.[85]

This strong record has been mentioned in well-established historical documents by scholars such as al-Bukhari, al-Tirmizi, Abu Dawood, Ibn Majjah, and in Ahmad ibn Hanbal's *Musnad* (Traditions of the Prophet). Also, Ibn Sa'd, al-Tabari, Bilazari, and al-Maqrizi have recalled parts of this information as well, all showing the Prophet of Islam (PBUH) had the utmost intention of making sure the rights of others were respected, and the Jews' breach of the treaty alone was the reason for breaking off the relationship. This topic is addressed further in section 6.3.4.

Regarding Christians, we recall during the Prophet's (PBUH) time a peace treaty was signed between Muslims and the Christian community in Najran, as the Qur'an says: "And nearest among them in love to the believers [who love the believers (Muslims)] thou find those who say, 'We are Christians'" (5:82).[86] In the same chapter, Muslims are given permission to visit the houses of the People of the Book (meaning Christians and Jews), eat their food, and marry their virtuous women, as the Qur'an illustrates in the following verses:

> The food of the People of the Book is lawful unto you and yours is lawful unto them. (Lawful unto you in marriage) are (not only) chaste women who are believers, but chaste women among the People of the Book, revealed before

your time,- when ye give them their due dowers, and
desire chastity, not lewdness, nor secret intrigues (5:5)

And dispute you not with the People of the Book, except with
means better (than mere disputation), [in good manner] unless
it be with those of them who inflict wrong (and injury): but
say, "We believe in the revelation which has come down to
us and in that which came down to you; Our Allah and your
Allah is one; and it is to Him we bow (in Islam)." (29:46)

6.3   Were All Battles Defensive?

Some critics assert that Muslims claim all the Prophet's (PBUH) battles were defensive, which is incorrect. In some cases, they initiated
preemptive wars, such as the Battle of Badr. One should examine
more closely what was considered a "defensive" war at that time.
If we examine the root cause of each of the Prophet's battles, there
is substantiation for each. Of course, defense can take many forms,
from protecting lives and property to defending faithful warriors and
those who are being persecuted. For instance, we know the Battle
of Badr occurred after a period in which Muslims were persecuted,
tortured, and killed by the idolaters, forcing some to leave Mecca as
their home and possessions were seized and expropriated. As a result,
many Muslims migrated to Medina, as the Qur'an recalls: "(Some part
is due) to the indigent Muhajirs [Migrants], those who were expelled
from their homes and their property" (59:8) and "Those who have
left their homes, or been driven out therefrom, or suffered harm in
My Cause, or fought or been slain,- verily, I will blot out from them
their iniquities, and admit them into Gardens" (3:195).

Therefore, the war of aggression against Muslims started in Mecca
long before their migration to Medina. During those thirteen years,
Muslims tolerated their persecution as they did not have permission
to respond accordingly. The Battle of Badr was the first defensive
measure against the enemy, as Muslims were not safe even after their
migration. Idolaters instigated and demanded their banishment from

Medina. As discussed in earlier sections, this topic will be revisited again in upcoming sections and will include a section on the events leading up the Battle of Badr.

6.3.1 "Fight for Plunder"?

Did Muslims fight to acquire the spoils of war, as some critics claim? This could not be further from the truth. Had these critics analyzed the concepts of justice and liberty in Islam, they would have understood that Islam condemns gaining possessions through force and violence. Qital (physical fight) or jihad (struggle) in the path of God is considered a form of worship in Islam; as such, the intention behind it should be to get close to God, not to plunder or amass wealth. Any novice of Islam easily understands this tenet, as specified in the Qur'an: "Fight in the way [cause] of Allah" (2:190).

The Prophet (PBUH) was once asked, "Is it possible for someone to fight heroically and courageously in order to gain fame and the spoils of war, who can be said is also fighting for the cause of God?" The Messenger of God replied, "One who fights until God's word is victorious is fighting for God's cause," which refers to defending God's word and the faith. [87]

However, fighting to gain wealth, fame, and women are actions the Qur'an deems unfitting. As the Prophet (PBUH) said, "Deeds are related to intentions, one receives according to his intention. Therefore, anyone who emigrates for the sake of gaining wealth or spouse, his migration is considered toward such cause accordingly."[88] Even when some Muslims lapsed and left their posts to gather the spoils in the Battle of Uhud, the Qur'an analyzes the reasons for the Muslims' defeat in that battle and reproaches them: "Among you are some that hanker after this world" (3:152), and as such, since they disobeyed, they were defeated. How then could the Qur'an fundamentally sanction war for the purposes of gaining the spoils or more territory? If critics reviewed the Islamic law regarding the conditions and limits for qital or jihad, they would never make such an absurd claim. The verse considered to be the first verse for qital (fight in a battle) in the Qur'an says, "To those against whom war is made, permission is given (to fight), because they are wronged" (22:39). We note qital in this verse is mentioned not as a directive but as a permission. Fighting is sanctioned only if a Muslim has been wronged. The next verse explains how that might happen: "(They are) those who have been expelled from their homes in defiance of right [unjustly],- (for no cause) except that they say, 'our Lord is Allah'" (22:40). The fight itself is a defensive measure, as the language attests. The verb *yuqatalun* is given in the passive form to mean the believers are put in a position that requires them to fight and defend themselves, which is why permission is given to them.

Indeed, as mentioned earlier, the primary reason Muslims engaged in war was to counter oppression and to open the way to practice their faith and invite others to God's word; however, the oppressors conspired, schemed, threatened, forced, and caused bloodshed in order to stop the Muslims and those who pursued the guiding light. It was upon Muslims to stand up to this persecution and violence as the Qur'an points out explicitly multiple times: "Nor will they cease fighting you until they turn you back from your faith if they can" (2:217) and "those who reject Allah and hinder (men) from the Path of Allah,— Allah will render their deeds astray (from their mark)" (47:1).

Profiting from the spoils of war was never the impetus for struggling or fighting in the path of God, and if Muslims took any spoils from the Quraysh, this action was adventitious and hardly a compensation for what the Quraysh had seized and expropriated from the Muslims in Mecca, just as the Qur'an says: "(Some part is due) to the poor emigrants who were expelled from their homes and their possession" (59:8).

6.3.2 A "Caravan Attack"?

Some critics claim the Prophet (PBUH) attacked caravans in order to seize their goods. This is a generalized statement without any basis of truth. The two events most commonly mentioned are Sariyah Nakhlah led by Abdullah ibn Jahesh, and the other an event that occurred before the Battle of Badr, both of which we will review in this section and the next.

According to history books, news of a Quraysh caravan traveling to Syria led by Amr ibn Hazrami reached the Prophet (PBUH).[89] According to al-Waqidi, this event occurred during the sacred month of Rajab, when fighting is not allowed. In a letter, the Prophet (PBUH) dispatched Abdullah ibn Jahesh and eight to twelve others on a scouting mission to the Nakhlah region between Mecca and Ta'if (the event is called Sariyah Nakhlah, named after the location), and to wait for the Quraysh. Ibn Jahesh was also instructed not to force any of his companions to go with him, as it might be a dangerous mission. Ibn Jahesh read the letter and said, "I obey" and conveyed to his companions what the Prophet (PBUH) had written to him. They asked to accompany him anyway. As indicated, the historians have clearly reported that the Prophet (PBUH) neither approved nor ordered any attack on any caravan.

Once they arrived at Nakhlah, they set up camp. After a while, the Quraysh caravan from Yemen passed through. The Muslims debated whether they should fight them or not (because it was a sacred month in which Arab Muslims and non-Muslims did not fight). Ibn Jahesh and his companions remembered all the persecution and torture by the Quraysh and, after a long discussion, decided to disregard the Prophet's (PBUH) directive and attack the caravan. They shot an arrow into the caravan, killing one person and capturing two along with some of their possessions. According to Ibn Hisham, when they returned to Medina, the Prophet (PBUH) was presented with a done deed, of which he did not approve, and he reproached Ibn Jahesh and his companions, as did the rest of the Muslims. The Prophet (PBUH) refused to take the seized goods and held the prisoners until he later released them both. One embraced Islam and the other returned to the Quraysh. However, this event gave the Quraysh in Mecca and the Jews in Medina an excuse to step up their negative campaigns against Muslims. Furthermore, under such conditions and after this event, a Qur'anic verse was revealed condemning this action: "They ask you concerning fighting in the prohibited (Sacred) Month. Say:

'Fighting therein is a grave (sin) but graver in the sight of Allah is to prevent access to the path of God, to deny him, to prevent access to the Sacred Mosque'" (2:217). The verse not only condemns fighting during the sacred month, but also the actions of those who prevented Muslims from visiting the Sacred Mosque. How could critics make such absurd claims regarding the Prophet (PBUH) and Muslims sanctioning an attack on the caravan? As confirmed through many historical accounts, we know the Prophet (PBUH), in his letter to Ibn Jahesh, made certain the objective of the mission was clear and furthermore instructed him not to force anyone to accompany him. If he had intended to attack, why did he not send some brave fighters to accompany Ibn Jahesh to make sure the mission was successful?[90]

6.3.3 Events Leading to the First Battle (Battle of Badr)

Historic accounts relate multiple events that occurred prior to the Battle of Badr, which provide the background for this first battle. A well-known fact is that after his migration, the Prophet (PBUH) was wary of Muslims' safety from attacks and pillage by the Quraysh. He was also aware of the Quraysh's influence on other Arab tribes and that they could leverage this influence to turn other tribes against Muslims and prevent them from practicing their faith and living peacefully. Hence, he followed and monitored the Quraysh's movements and activities, and let them know they were on the alert. These activities have been recorded in numerous history books.

Scholars Waqidi, al-Tabari, Ibn Hisham, and others have written that after Sariyah Nakhlah, Kurzubn Jaber Fehri, who was connected with the Quraysh, raided the herds from Medina and the Prophet (PBUH) chased him but could not catch him.[91] Eleven months after his migration to Medina, the Prophet (PBUH) followed a Quraysh caravan to Abwa' until he reached Waddan, and without any encounter with the Quraysh, he signed a treaty with the Banu Zamrah tribe so that they would not help the Quraysh against Muslims. The treaty itself is also listed in history books. Another time the Prophet (PBUH) dispatched Ubaidah ibn Harith along with sixty to eighty men from the Muhajereen (Emigrants) to follow a Qurayshi caravan led by Abu Sufiyan. They met the Quraysh in a valley called Rabiq but no encounter occurred. Also, during the sixteenth month of his migration, the Prophet (PBUH) followed another caravan from Quraysh to the Suqiya vicinity, and there he signed a treaty with the Banu Mudalij tribe and returned to Medina without any encounter with the Quraysh.[92]

From this, we gather that by following these tribes, the Prophet (PBUH) wanted to let the Quraysh know that the Muslims were on the alert and that, by establishing treaties with other tribes, they were preventing the Quraysh from creating alliances with other tribes and preventing these tribes from harming and pillaging Muslims in Mecca, while somewhat isolating the Quraysh who were the main and most hostile enemy. Despite these efforts, the Quraysh made no attempts at peace, so the Muslims felt their threat of aggression. The Quraysh alliance was strong and could muster a large, well-equipped army. As a result, Muslims had to be cautious. As reported in *al-Musannaf* by Abdul Razzaq San'ani, a very early book of the Hadith, before the Battle of Badr, unbelievers from the Quraysh wrote a letter to various groups in Medina:

> You have allowed our fellow Meccan (Muhammad) to your town and you are the majority in Medina. We swear to God that if you don't kill him or banish him from your town, we will seek assistance from all Arab tribes against you, then we will mobilize our forces to kill all your fighters and allow your women for ourselves.[93]

Hence, Muslims showed their presence in and around where the Quraysh caravans traveled, in hopes that they would understand the Muslim's wariness and perhaps stop their intimidation and hostility. Unfortunately, the Quraysh were not interested in peace and co-existence. They continued their hostile tactics toward Medina and persecuted the remaining Muslims in Mecca, thus preventing them from leaving.[94]

It was at this point the Qur'an allowed Muslims to fight in order to defend their faith, lives, and existence:

Verily Allah will defend (from ill) those who believe: verily, God loves not any that is a traitor to faith, or show ingratitude. To those against whom war is made, permission is given (to fight), because they are wronged;- and verily, Allah is most powerful for their aid. (They are) those who have been expelled from their homes in defiance of right[unjustly],- (for no cause) except that they say, "our Lord is Allah".' Had Allah not repelled some people by the means of others, the monasteries and churches, the synagogues and mosques in which the Name of Allah is commemorated in abundant measure would have been destroyed. (22:38–40)

And why should ye not fight in the cause of Allah and of those who, being weak, are ill-treated (and oppressed)?- Men, women, and children, whose cry is: "Our Lord! Rescue us from this town, whose people are oppressors; and raise for us from thee one who will protect. (4:75)

Prior to the Battle of Badr, in his second year of migration, the Prophet (PBUH) and two hundred men left Medina to sign peace treaties with a few tribes in the region. News arrived of a large caravan leaving Mecca, so the Prophet (PBUH), as part of his strategy, decided to change his route in order to follow the caravan, as mentioned above. But the caravan escaped their reach; hence, after signing a peace treaty with tribes in A'shira, the Prophet (PBUH) returned to Medina with the intention of reaching the caravan on its return from Syria. When news of its return reached the Prophet (PBUH), he dispatched a few men to gather news, and, once confirmed, Muslims left Medina in order to reach the caravan.[95]

According to reports, the caravan was carrying a large supply of valuable commodities, partly invested by those who were hostile to Muslims. Their goal was to utilize its proceeds to finance an all-out war against Muslims. Abu Sufiyan personally led a group of seventy heavily armed men to accompany the caravan.[96] Historical reports indicate Muslims took precaution and prepared themselves in the event of an encounter with the Quraysh or other enemies on the way. On the other hand, Abu Sufiyan and the Meccan caravan were notified (most likely by hypocrites in Medina) that Muslims might be waiting for them; hence they decided to avoid the major crossroad and instead took a fast detour to Mecca. At the same time, Abu Sufiyan dispatched someone to Mecca asking for help in case they encountered Muslims. In the end, no attack occurred on either side.

An alternate view analyzes what occurred before the Battle of Badr based on chronology and evidence from the Qur'an.[97] This view refutes the Muslims' initial motivation for meeting the Quraysh caravan, and says the Prophet (PBUH) never intended to follow or intercept the caravan; his main reason, according to this viewpoint, was to mobilize the three hundred men to defeat the Quraysh army led by Abu Sufiyan (who had already left Mecca), as the Muslims would outnumber Sufiyan's small army for the following reasons:[98]

1. The Quraysh had already written a letter to the people of Medina, threatening them that if they did not kill or banish the Prophet (PBUH), they would mobilize a large army and kill their men and take their women for themselves. They had also sent a message to the Muslims of Medina earlier saying: "We can come and destroy you in Medina." To Muslims, this could mean that Abu Sufiyan and his men did not leave Mecca only to protect the caravan.

2. Anticipating the probability of an attack by Abu Sufiyan, the Prophet (PBUH) wanted Muslims to be prepared and to mobilize for a possible encounter. However, some of the Muslims were inclined to intercept the caravan and claim what was rightfully theirs. Verse 8:7 attests to this: "Behold! Allah promised you one of the two (enemy) parties, that it should be yours: You wished that the one unarmed should be yours, but Allah willed to justify the Truth according to His

word." And it shows that the Prophet's (PBUH) intention was that of God's, which was to stop the enemy's army.

3. Verse 8:5, which states, "Just as your Lord caused you to leave your home with the truth, even though a party among the Believers disliked it," illustrates the Prophet (PBUH) left Medina with the intention of encountering and defending against Abu Sufiyan and his army, which is why he summoned the Muslims, even though some were reluctant. This verse demonstrates his intention was not to intercept or even follow the caravan.

4. As the caravan passed through without any trouble, the Quraysh army would naturally return to Mecca (had the intention been to protect the caravan and not to fight). This means that Abu Jahl, based on Abu Sufiyan's suggestion, would turn around and go back to Mecca. However, instead, he said, "We will teach Muslims a lesson, so they would always be in fear of us." Biographers have reported the Quraysh idolaters joyfully mobilized an army of over one thousand men with all the necessary provisions and means to fight the Muslims. The term *batara* (meaning "boastfully and joyfully") refers to their state of mind, as revealed in verse 8:47: "Do not be like those who left their homes elated with insolence and boastfully to be seen of men, and to hinder (men) from the Path of Allah," which shows their elation and determination in barring others from the path of God.

Considering the facts above, regardless of initial motivation, there were no attacks on any caravan at any time by a Muslim army, except the one instance mentioned in the last section in Sariyah Nakhlah led by Abdullah ibn Jahesh, who acted on his own and was reproached for his action by the Prophet (PBUH) and other Muslims. The subsequent events prior to the Battle of Badr are pivotal and worth noting:

1. Once Abu Sufiyan's courier delivered the message, the Quraysh and their allies prepared an army of one thousand

three hundred men with weapons, horses, and provisions under the leadership of Abu Jahl. They brought all that was necessary to clinch a victory and to celebrate afterwards.

2. According to historical records in *Kitab al-Jihad Bab al-Imdad*,
   once Abu Sufiyan felt secure about the caravan's safe arrival
   in Mecca, he sent another courier to inform the Quraysh that
   there was no need for additional men to rescue the caravan
   and that Abu Jahl and his army should return to Mecca. But
   Abu Jahl did not accept this recommendation saying, "We
   will teach the Muslims a lesson, so they will always fear us."
   Nevertheless, some of his men returned to Mecca, thus re-
   ducing his army to one thousand men.[99]

About halfway to Badr, the Prophet (PBUH) and his companions
of three hundred men were informed that the Quraysh had mobilized
in Mecca for the purpose of fighting them. The Prophet (PBUH)
made a supplication that revealed the condition of his companions
on this journey: "O Lord, these are barefooted: mount them on rides
and clothe them. They are hungry: feed them."[100] This supplication
illustrates the vast difference between the two armies—the Muslims'
condition compared to that of Quraysh's in terms of equipment and
provisions. Naturally, once the Muslims received the news of the
Quraysh, they were worried that if they returned to Medina, the
Quraysh would pursue them, and the encounter in Medina would
be worse as the Qur'an illustrates in verse 8:5–6: "Just as your Lord
caused you to leave your home with the truth, even though a party
among the Believers disliked it. Disputing with you concerning the
truth after it was made manifest, as if they were being driven to death
and they (actually) saw it."

Under such conditions, the Prophet (PBUH) consoled them and
assured them of God's wisdom and that God must have a higher purpose for them, as the Qur'an explains in verse 8:7: "Behold! Allah
promised you one of the two (enemy) parties, that it should be yours:
Ye wished that the one unarmed should be yours, but Allah willed
to justify the Truth according to His words and to cut off the roots of

the Unbelievers." This refers to the Muslims' original expectation of encountering a smaller army led by Abu Sufyan (which accompanied the caravan), as opposed to the thousand-strong army led by Abu Jahl.

Nevertheless, the Prophet (PBUH) was worried and called a meeting to consult with his companions to seek their opinions. In this meeting, Miqdad ibn Aswad, who represented the Muhajereen, quoted the Qur'an: "They said: 'O Moses! while they remain there, never shall we be able to enter, to the end of time. Go thou, and thy Lord, and fight you two, while we sit here (and watch)" (5:24). With that, Sa'd ibn Mu'az from the Ansar (the Muslim inhabitants of Medina who helped the Prophet (PBUH)) added, "O Messenger of God, we have believed in you, and know that your message is the truth, if you enter the sea we will enter with you, and we will persevere in war."[101] The Prophet (PBUH) was pleased to hear these sentiments. But he exempted Hazifat ibn Yaman and his father from war because they had been captured and released earlier by the Quraysh and had promised not to join the Muslims to fight against them. The Prophet (PBUH) told them they must act on their promise and return to Medina.[102] Finally, the two armies engaged in the battle at Badr, and according to biography books (seerat) and historical accounts, it concluded with a decisive victory for the Muslims. Here are other points to consider:[103]

1. In the beginning, upon the Prophet's directive, Muslims camped in a sandy area. Hubab ibn Munzar asked, "Messenger of God, did you order to camp here based on God's direction, or based on your own opinion?" The Prophet (PBUH) replied, "It was based on my own tactical decision." Hubab said, "Then I think we should move, and I suggest getting closer to the enemy position where the water source is, so we build a water basin and fill up our water pools." The Prophet (PBUH) accepted and proceeded with his suggestion.[104] This clearly shows that Muslims drew a distinction between God's revelation and the Prophet's (PBUH) own opinion, and that in cases where God's revelation (directive) was not involved,

the Prophet (PBUH) consulted with others and proceeded accordingly.

2. One of the factors contributing to a Muslim victory was that idolaters saw some of their own relatives in the Muslim army fighting against them. For example, Abu Bakr's son was in the Quraysh army, while Abu Bakr himself, the Prophet's (PBUH) longtime friend, was by his side fighting the idolaters. This condition introduced some doubts in the minds of the Quraysh fighters, and in addition many of them were from the Banu Hashim tribe and were reluctant to fight Muhammad (PBUH).

3. Right before the battle broke out, the Prophet (PBUH) ordered his companions not to attack and to keep their swords in their sheaths. This they did until Mehja, the freed slave of Umar, was struck and killed by a Quraysh arrow. After that a Quraysh man pulled his sword out and rushed to the Muslims' water reservoir in order to drink and destroy it, and he was met by the Prophet's (PBUH) Uncle Hamza.[105] This is how the first Battle of Badr began and ended with the idolaters' defeat.

Nevertheless, prior to the battle, the Prophet (PBUH) made every attempt to prevent it through graceful efforts, reasoning, and warnings, according to the Waqidi reports. He dispatched Umar ibn al-Khattab to meet with the Quraysh and tell them to return [to Mecca]. Abu Jahl, the Quraysh leader, responded, "We swear to God who has put this task on us we will not return."[106] Of course, once initiated, this battle (as well as any other battle with the Quraysh) was not about collecting the spoils, but about crushing the Quraysh's splendor and oppressive rule so they could no longer threaten and impose their policies on other tribes in order to engage in hostile activities against Muslims. This is why the Qur'an shows that prior to the Battle of Badr, some Muslims were inclined to skirmish small groups of fighters and collect the spoils, because they believed the Quraysh had capitalized on their migration to Medina by expropriating the wealth Muslims were forced to leave behind. Nonetheless, fighting for the spoils of war is condemned by the Qur'an, as God wanted to prepare Muslims to fight against their oppressors and defeat their false glory. In addition, Muslims are advised to purify their intentions away from worldly goods and to strive toward divine goals and the rewards of the Hereafter, as is reiterated in the same chapter: "You look for the temporal goods of this world; but Allah looketh to the Hereafter" (8:67).

This is the essence of the Qur'an's teachings regarding war and its spoils. Those who have spent their lives accruing worldly possessions would not comprehend the divine goals set by the Qur'an when it comes to engaging in war. Indeed, the Prophet (PBUH), in his years leading the Muslims, demonstrated that if there is no force, threat, or torture, and if there is freedom of expression, Islam, before any other faith, would choose peace over war; in fact, Islam would flourish under such conditions because it appeals to reason while also penetrating the heart. Among the evidence is the Prophet's (PBUH) peace treaty of Hudaybiyyah with the idolaters of Mecca (including the Quraysh), and his forgiveness of all Meccans as he conquered Mecca.

6.3.4 "Killing the Men of (the) Jewish tribe"?

Some critics have said Muslims killed men from the Jewish tribes in Medina. These critics do not wish to conduct a scholarly analysis, nor do they bother to at least read well-known books of history and biography. Historians report that after his arrival in Medina, the Prophet (PBUH) wrote a covenant to be agreed upon and signed by Muslims, Jews, and even the idolaters of Medina. It was to form a strategic alliance regardless of their respective faiths.

This covenant was based on mutual respect and peaceful coexistence. Its main goal was to establish peace within Medina and to unite all parties against potential enemy attacks on Medina, as well as to share the cost of defending the city. This was a brilliant plan from a brilliant statesman. It ensured that people of different faiths could live together in peace and cooperation, which is worthy of praise because prior to the Prophet's (PBUH) migration many of these tribes were at war with each other. It also demonstrates Islam's broadmindedness and peaceful attitude compared to other faiths, which is worthy of consideration by those who advocate human rights and freedom of thought and expression.

The covenant was recorded by Ibn Hisham in ancient history books as well as in Abu Ubaid's book *al-Amwal*, *Uyoun al-Athar* by Ibn Sayyad al-Nas, and in other narrations by al-Bukhari, al-Tabari, Abdul Razzaq, and Ahmad ibn Hanbal.[107]

The covenant reads:

> Jews to their faith and Muslims to theirs. All equal with all groups, unless someone commits injustice or a betrayal . . . Jews and Muslims each are responsible for their own expenses in a war, and they must cooperate and help each other against those who fight with tribes mentioned in this covenant. Muslims and Jews must establish goodwill among each other, not evil deeds and ill intentions toward other members of this covenant.

After signing this covenant, the relationship between Jews and Muslims was based on justice, peace, and goodwill, as the Qur'an enjoins: "Allah forbids you not, with regard to those who fight you not for (your) religion nor drive you out of your homes, from dealing kindly and justly with them: for Allah loves those who are just" (60:8).

However, when the Jews witnessed the Muslims' increasing power and influence, instead of maintaining their good relationship and supporting them as they had done in the past, they started antagonizing the Prophet (PBUH), opposing the Muslims, and betraying the people of Medina. First, they strengthened their relationship with the hypocrites and secured their commitment to cooperate. Then, they colluded with the Muslims' enemies in evil plots against Islam and Muslims. Their decision was to fight Muslims with deceit from within Medina, such as the group who came to the Prophet (PBUH) pretending to have embraced Islam, but instead left Islam in order to influence Muslims' spirit and morale, in hopes of turning them away from Islam. However, the noble Qur'an exposed their scheme and disgraced them, as verse 3:72 says: "A section of the People of the Book say: 'Believe in the morning what is revealed to the believers, but reject it at the end of the day; perchance they may turn back.'"

The Jews stepped up their opposition and schemes as their leaders, Ka'b ibn Ashraf and Hoyy ibn Akhtab, along with their companions, went to Mecca and encouraged the Quraysh to fight the Messenger of God and the Muslims. They swore to help the Quraysh in this fight. The idolaters of Mecca replied, "You are People of the Book and your creed is closer to the creed of Muhammad, hence we are aware of your schemes and not assured of your intentions, hence prove your sincerity by prostrating to our idols." The Jews, in hopes of gaining the Meccans' assurance against the Muslims, complied and prostrated to their idols along with their acknowledgment, as the Qur'an admonished their action: "Have you not seen those to whom a portion of the Book was given believing in idols and false deities, and how they say of those (idolaters) who disbelieve: "These are more rightly guided than those who believe?"[108](4:51) Inside Medina they rehashed the old grievances between the Awus and Khazraj tribes in order to rekindle fights between Muslims. They also gave the Jews who embraced Islam a difficult time.

The Jews, however, did not stop their sedition. They started insulting Muslims in public and even slandering their women, as historians have reported: "An Arab woman from Medina who had married a man from her own tribe came to Banu Qaynuqa market to buy jewelry from a jewelry store. A man from Banu Qaynuqa arrived and went behind her and tied her long dress from the back in such a way that when she got up her lower body was exposed, and the Jewish men all laughed. A Muslim man got up and followed the Jewish man and killed him. Thereafter, in retaliation, the Jewish men of Banu Qaynuqa gathered and attacked the Muslim man and killed him. They then broke their treaty with the Prophet (PBUH) as they declared war against Muslims."[109] Indeed, the Jews of Banu Qaynuqa, instead of defusing the situation by offering apologies, shut down their market, retreated to their citadels, and declared war. Their arrogance had deceived them so much that they thought breaking the treaty and declaring war would result to their advantage, allowing them to defeat the Muslims.[110]

Before the Prophet's migration, the Jews had few a victories against their tribal enemies; as such they were conceited and deluded about their ability to defeat the Prophet (PBUH) and the Muslims. Hence, they were not afraid to break the peace treaty. They continued colluding with the Prophet's (PBUH) enemies and declared war against him. Once, when the Prophet (PBUH) was visiting the Banu Nadir's fort, they attempted to kill him. Another time, according to historians, when various Arab tribes had surrounded Medina, the Jews of Banu Qurayza sent a message of solidarity to the idolaters and then officially waged war against the Prophet (PBUH) and Muslims. The non-Muslim historians, as well as the orientalists, have concurred as well. The fair-minded Jews also protested such behavior and considered their actions against the laws in the Torah. Israel Wolfensohn, a Jewish writer and historian, in his book, *Tarikh al-Yahud fi Bilad al-Arab* (History of Jews in Arab Territory), writes:

> It was essential that the Jews not make such grave mistake by acknowledging to the Quraysh elite that worshipping the idols is better than worshipping one God, furthermore seeking refuge with idolaters, hence going to war against their own beliefs and against the teachings of the Torah.[111]

In spite of all this, because the Prophet (PBUH) exiled a group of Jews from Banu Qaynuqa and Banu Nadir to Syria, and then defeated another group (Banu Qurayza), there is an uproar and he is taunted. What holy book or any rational thinker says that a Messenger of God should not protect his followers from broken treaties and treacheries and instead subject them to persecution and aggression? If that is the case, then why would these critics, whether Christians or Jews, have not adhered to such peaceful teachings? If we were to be indifferent to broken peace treaties and betrayals, how then could any society live in peace?

At the peak of his power, the Prophet (PBUH) honored all peace treaties, and verses were revealed enjoining Muslims to honor their treaties, even with idolaters, as part of God- consciousness. "(But the treaties are) not dissolved with those Pagans [idolaters] with whom you have entered into alliance and who have not subsequently failed you in aught [any ay all], nor aided any one against you. So fulfill your engagements with them to the end of their term: for Allah loves the righteous" (9:4).

There were other non-Muslim tribes (some of whom were even idolaters) who had peace treaties with the Muslims and lived in peace with them. The Jews could have been part of these communities as they were in the beginning, but when they instigated sedition and conspired against the Prophet (PBUH), the Muslims, their allies, and the Messenger of God (PBUH), who was also a statesman, had no choice but to respond.

6.3.5 Engaging the Banu Qurayza

As reported by biographers and historians, after the altercation with Banu Qaynuqa and in the period between the battles of Badr and Uhud, given the mischief created by Ka'b ibn Ashraf and his follow-ers, the Prophet (PBUH) signed another treaty with the Jews (beyond the original one signed at the time of his entrance to Medina), just to make sure they did not follow in Ka'b's footsteps.[112] The Jews ac-knowledged and recorded in the treaty that in the event they colluded with the Muslims' enemy and endangered Medina as a whole, their lives and blood would be wasted, and they would be killed or taken captive and their possessions expropriated.[113] In fact, even in the first treaty, the essence of the language was captured as part of the consti-tution of Medina (which was listed earlier).

There are multiple unsubstantiated reports on the number of Jewish fighters killed during the Banu Qurayza's upheaval. Some claim four hundred, six hundred, or seven hundred, while others claim up to one thousand. None of these numbers are aligned with the detailed events and other related reports. For example, according to some biographers, after the men of Banu Qurayza surrendered, they were brought to the home of an Ansar woman named Kais bint Harith, to be imprisoned before they were killed. Her house surely could not have been large enough to accommodate four hundred men, much less six hundred or seven hundred. Even if we assume four hundred were killed, that would have created such fear and concern among the remaining Jews that they would have immediately left Medina as a result. We know that after the Banu Qurayza's upheaval ended and Medina was calm, the Jewish tribes continued with their businesses and trades for quite some time without any disturbance. Furthermore, Prophet Muhammad (PBUH), who would not kill anyone unless forced (as he graciously demonstrated after conquering Mecca), it is highly unlikely he would approve killing all these men.[114] Therefore, the reported mass killing by some biographers is likely a story developed by Jewish descendants (who perhaps pretentiously converted to Islam), but reported by Muslim writers who did not make due diligence to validate these reports through multiple sources and events.

The Banu Qurayza upheaval, based on further research and analysis of accounts, along with the Qur'anic verses (and without conjectures), revolves around the following facts:

The Jews of Banu Qurayza broke their treaty of peace and cooperation with the Muslims. When the enemy attacked Medina, they betrayed the Muslims and the rest of the community by colluding with the enemy to the point it could destroy the new Muslim community. In so doing, they knowingly signed their own death warrant (considering the second treaty). However, their greed and arrogance, along with provocations from the Banu Nadir's exiled Jews, caused them to sell out their Muslim allies in hopes of gaining victory over the Muslims and overtaking the leadership of Medina.

As the Ahzab army retreated, hence the defeat of the Jewish conspirators from Banu Nadir and Khaybar, the Jews of Banu Qurayza, along with the leader of the conspirators, Ibn Akhtab, retreated to their citadels and apparently thought that through resistance they could eventually achieve victory and continue with treachery.[115]

However, considering past experiences, the Prophet (PBUH) saw the Banu Qurayza as an imminent threat to the Muslim community, one whose treacheries and continued treaty violations could not be ignored; therefore, he mobilized his men toward their fort. As Salam ibn Mishkam, a Jewish man from Khaybar, said, "He (Muhammad) is a man who will not fight unless he is being strangled." Furthermore, the Muslims could not leave the Banu Qurayza issue unresolved, as they were wary the Banu Qurayza would join other Jewish tribes in alliance with the Quraysh, whose leader, Abu Sufiyan, had already threatened Muslims to return to Medina with a larger army than that of Uhud.[116]

1. As Muslims surrounded the fort, a cold war ensued as both sides exchanged accusations. Before long, arrows and stones were shot from the fort above and arrows shot from below by Muslims. Even at this point, if the Banu Qurayza had shown remorse about breaking the treaties and igniting upheaval and expressed a genuine intention to stop and mend their ways, they would not have ended up defeated as they did.

2. Eventually the Banu Qurayza stopped and surrendered, as the Qur'an says: "And those of the People of the Book who aided them—Allah did take them down from their strongholds and cast terror into their hearts. (So that) some you slew, and some you made prisoners" (33:26). *"Some you slew"* refers to those who were killed in the battle, although some reports have said it refers to those who were executed. Even if this were the case, the ruling was issued by a mutually agreed arbitrator, Sa'd ibn Mu'az, and the Prophet (PBUH) had no role in such a ruling.

3. Perhaps it can be concluded that a limited few, such as Ibn Khatab, along with several conspirators, were killed or executed according to Sa'd ibn Mu'az's ruling (who was chosen to be the arbitrator, as requested by the Banu Qurayza's).[117] As

Tabari also brings in his commentary of verse 33:26, according to Sa'd ibn Mu'az, those found guilty were executed and those found innocent were freed.

4. Regarding the captives, there is no reason, why the Prophet (PBUH) would not act, as stated in verse 47:4, which says, "Bind a bond firmly (on them): thereafter (is the time for) either set them free by generosity or ransom: until the war lays down its burdens." In addition, according to the Waqidi report, the Prophet (PBUH) freed some of the captives and put others to work.[118]

Beyond the above points, there have been many contemporary scholars and historians who, through research, examination of existing reports, references, and the Qur'anic verses, have concluded that considering the typical population of those days, especially parties involved in this event, the magnitude of the reported killings (from four hundred to one thousand men) does not align with the event, nor the exposure given to this killing; hence, According to Tabatabai, it does not make sense and raises many valid questions, such as the following:

1. Not all of the Banu Qurayza men conspired and were at fault. What about the older men (as the original report says all men of this tribe were killed)?

2. What about Qur'anic verse 33:26, which states, "Some you killed and others you took captive"? This clearly refers to those who were killed and captured in the battle; otherwise, if it were not during the battle, either all would have been killed, or all would have been captured.

3. What about the home of the Ansar woman, which was supposed to house over four hundred men?

4. Even if this were not the Prophet's ruling, with his mercy, as demonstrated throughout his life, how could he agree to a ruling of mass executions?

5. Wouldn't such killings be reflected with more points and reminders in the Qur'an as well as in authentic reports as was

done in the Battle of Badr, where only seventy Quraysh men were killed?

In the end, neither the number nor the claim that these men were killed because they did not accept Islam can be true. There were other Jews who coexisted with the Muslims peacefully. They were never coerced to accept Islam nor killed for being Jews.[119]

6.4   "And fight them on until there is no more oppression" (2:193)

Sections 6.4 through 6.44 address the comments and questions raised by critics of Islam about some of the most commonly used Qur'anic verses. Each verse is explained, and its historical context is given.[120] Key phrases from verses are also used as titles for each section and in the table of contents. The comments by critics who question Islam as a religion of peace are general in nature and have been raised in various books, articles, and websites.[121]

It is astonishing how critics, who have no real knowledge of the history nor any in-depth familiarity with the Qur'an, presumptuously give opinions about Islam and their disdain for it. In order to prove violence in Islam, the critics attempt to bring evidence from the Qur'an but fail to present proof. For instance, in verse 2:193, which says "And fight them on until there is no more Tumult or oppression, and there prevail faith in Allah; but if they cease, Let there be no hostility except to those who practice oppression [wrong doers]," they present an erroneous English translation: "Fight with them until Polytheism is destroyed and God's religion encompasses, but if they ceased, fight the followers of Satan."

With this erroneous translation, the verse's ending refers to Satan and his followers (implying any non-Muslim); whereas in the correct translation, it refers to those who oppress and persecute, hence "Let there be no hostility except against those who practice oppression." Furthermore, the term *fitna* has multiple meanings in the Qur'an, and here it does refer to polytheism and coercion of Muslims (by idolaters) to idol worshiping for the reason shown in a few verses thereafter:

"Nor will they cease fighting you until they turn you back from your faith if they can. And if any of you turns back from his faith and die in unbelief, their works will bear no fruit in this life and in the Hereafter" (2:217). The verse also talks about fighting a war not murder. Fighting (a war) is between two sides; hence, the verse refers to fighting with those who came to fight them and to force them back to polytheism with the sword. Can we say that under such conditions, actions of Muslims defending themselves constitute offensive violence in Islam?

The circumstance in which this verse was revealed also confirms the condition, as commentators have discussed how seditious the idolaters of Quraysh were. Obviously if provocation of the enemy were removed, meaning coercion to idolatry was eliminated, monotheism would prevail, which is in the meaning of "and faith [religion] is for Allah"; that is, an environment where there is freedom of religion for all to practice their own faith does not mean fight them until everyone becomes Muslim because the Qur'an says: "And if they (unbelievers) incline to peace, incline thou also to it" (8:61), which was also demonstrated by the treaty of Hudaybiyyah. In societies where there is no coercion in religion, Islam will flourish, as is evident by its rapid growth in the West.

6.5   "Slay them wherever you find them" (2:191; 9:5)

We introduced and explained both verses in chapter 3, which we suggest readers review before continuing. In this section, we will address additional allegations.

Critics of Islam say extremists refer to these verses or similar verses and act on them to justify their violence. While this may be true, these critics (as well as extremists) should first read the earlier verses in chapter 9 of the Qur'an, where it says, "A (declaration) of immunity from Allah and His Messenger, to those of the Pagans [Idolaters] with whom you have contracted mutual alliances" (9:1), and "(But the treaties are) not dissolved with those Pagans [Idolators] with whom you have entered into alliance and who have not subsequently failed you in aught [anything at all], nor aided any one against you" (9:4). And again, in the same passage, it says, "How can there be a league[treaty], before Allah and His Messenger, with the Pagans[idolaters] except those with whom you made a treaty near the Sacred Mosque? As long as these stand true to you, stand you true to them" (9:7). Of course, those who have chosen to read selectively and who close their eyes and minds to the verses before and after, thus missing the context and the full picture, can reach any desired conclusion and not just with the Qur'an. However, this is not a method used by seekers of truth. This is a method used by those who want to take the matter in the direction of their own preconceived notions and agenda. We first discuss verse 2:191 which says,

> And slay them wherever you find them, and drive them
> out of where they drove you out, for oppression is worse
> than slaughter. And do not fight with them in the Sacred
> Mosque until they first fight you there.[122] (2:191)

In this verse, the pronoun *hum* (meaning "them") in *waqtuluhum* ("fight them") refers to *"those who fight you"* mentioned in the preceding verse "Fight in the cause of Allah those who fight you" (2:190), which is a sanction to defend against aggression, but not because they have a different faith (idolatry). If they entered Muslims' homes or places of safety (as they did in Mecca) and drove them out, Muslims can drive them out of Medina. It follows that their *fitna* (oppression) is worse than slaughter, because by *fitna* the verse is referring to the fact they wanted to force Muslims back to polytheism and keep their rule with sword (2:217). However, as Muslims are instructed to defend, the verse concludes with: "and do not exceed the limits, surely Allah does not love the aggressors" (2:190). Verses 190-191 underscore the following facts about Islam:

1. True fighting in the cause of God is merely to defend against aggression, oppression and injustice and establishing peace which is what God has intended for man on earth not to gain

power, position, spoils and territory (as erroneously suggested by some Western writers)

2. Fight only those who those who fought against you, not those who merely differ in faith

3. "Those who fight against you" also means protecting civilians. Neither the fighting against women, children and the elder (of even the enemy camp), nor pillage, destruction of property, crops and harming animals are allowed. These are considered acts of transgression as the verse says: "God loves not the aggressors."

As to verse 9:5, it specifically mentions the idolaters in "But, when the sacred months (months of grace) are past, slay the idolaters wherever you find them," where *al* ("the") in the term *al-mushrekeen* ("the idolaters") linguistically refers to certain idolaters. There are two contexts given for the timeline of this verse. Some commentators claim it belongs to the period of the treaty of Hudaybiyyah, in the sixth year of migration, when the Banu Bakr tribe (an ally of the Quraysh) and members of the Quraysh tribe attacked the Banu Khuza'a tribe (a Muslim ally), hence breaking the treaty, which ended up with Muslims conquering Mecca. The majority of commentators however have said that these verses relate to the period after Mecca was conquered in the eighth year of migration. At that point, most Meccans, including the Quraysh, were given general amnesty and embraced Islam while some remained idolaters, but also were true to the treaty and stood by their pledge. However, there were remaining groups of idolaters who either reneged on their covenant or those who did not have any treaties; both of these groups continued their campaigns against Muslims, ambushing and pillaging the caravans entering and leaving Mecca. Muslims gave a four-month grace period (not during the four sacred months) to these idolaters so they could decide whether to stop their activities and end their twenty-two years of animosity or face the war (more on this topic later in this chapter).

It is perplexing how a group who identify themselves as followers of the Qur'an generalize their interpretation and ignore all the exceptions and specificities mentioned in the verse, as well as the verses before and after. How do these verses extend to any non-Muslim at any time? Is this not an opinion-based interpretation and betrayal of the Qur'an? These verses were not about forcing idolaters to become Muslims or fighting against them because they were of a different faith.

Some say extremists act according to a narration from the Prophet (PBUH), as reported by Abu Hurairah that says, "I am commended to fight people until they say: there is no deity except Allah, and whosoever said it, he is safe, and his possessions protected, and accountability of his deeds is with God." Firstly, this is a very general statement and taken as such would contradict the Qur'anic verse "Let there be no compulsion in religion" (2:256). There are many other verses from the Qur'an, such as 9:29, which allow non-Muslims to keep their faith, but if they live under Islamic rule, they are required to pay jizya (tribute). Secondly, Muslims are permitted to invite People of the Book (Jews and Christians) to their homes, share meals, and marry their virtuous women. Therefore *people*, as mentioned in the narration above by Abu Hurairah, could not mean People of the Book.

Thirdly, verses 9:4 and 9:7 specify that idolaters who had an intact peace treaty with Muslims were excluded. Hence, by *people,* who is this quote referring to? Quoting the above report by Abu Hurairah, or any like it as a general statement, is invalid and in contradiction to the Qur'an and the conduct of the Prophet (PBUH). However, some critics refer to Abu Hurairah's narration and say it justifies "offensive jihad" against non-Muslims abroad. There is no such thing as offensive jihad or an offensive physical fight in Islam. However, if by offensive jihad, one means introducing Islam, propagating Islam, and preaching Islam through peaceful means of education, then yes, these forms of jihad exist in Islam (which is also commonly done by Christians). This is evident by the letters the Prophet (PBUH) wrote to a Persian king, a Roman emperor, and to other leaders inviting them to Islam with no further expectations. The choice is then left up to them to accept or decline. Muslims would have no way to pursue this further and certainly not by means of force or violence.

Therefore, we can conclude that those with an insufficient

understanding of the Qur'an will not benefit much from *fiqh al-hadith* (comprehensive studies of tradition) either. In addition, ironically, extremist groups are usually at war with those who *do* declare that there is no deity except Allah (that is, Muslims); hence, the above narration from Abu Hurairah is actually against them and presents an argument for those who oppose extremists. Muslims form the biggest group who fall victim to the extremists' actions. The extremists carry on with such brutal and criminal acts against Muslims under *their* blanket pretext of jihad. What they do not know, or choose to ignore, is that there is no such thing as jihad against Muslims, and such acts are strictly forbidden by Islam. Nonetheless, when it comes to violence, the extremists do not discriminate and target Muslims and non-Muslims alike at any time and any place.[123]

Another claim critics make is that all the verses that enjoin leniency and forgiveness in the Qur'an were abrogated by verses of violence in chapter 9, which is the last chapter revealed. The answer is, even if we assume chapter 9 was the last chapter, what about verses 9:1, 9:4, and 9:7? Are they not explicit enough about whom Muslims should *not* fight? Do they not exclude those who are not hostile toward Muslims or those who have peace treaties with Muslims? Even with combatant idolaters engaged in fighting Muslims, the Qur'an says, "If one amongst the Pagans [idolaters] ask you for asylum, grant it to him, so that he may hear the word of Allah; and then escort him to where he can be secure. That is because they are men without knowledge" (9:6). This verse refers to combatant idolaters who had doubts about fighting Muslims or perhaps wanted to hear the message of Islam (but were not allowed) and are given the right to seek refuge with Muslims and hear the words of God. If they accept, they have the option to stay with Muslims and live under their protection. And, if they do not accept, Muslims are obligated to escort them to their place of safety so no harm comes to them from their own people.

It is interesting that extremists, in order to justify their actions, are similarly misrepresenting (as critics of Islam do) the verses of mercy and violence. Today's extremists, in the name of Islam, have attacked not just non-Muslims, but Muslims—killing men, women, and children under the pretext of wanting to revive Islam and establishing jihad for God's cause. They have no basis for such claims. The Qur'an says, "Therefore if they withdraw from you and fight you not, and (instead) send you (Guarantees of) peace, then Allah Has opened no way for you (to war against them)" (4:90). This is the way to treat unbelievers who do not wish to fight Muslims, much less Muslims, who share the same faith, but, unfortunately, make up the majority of their victims. One may ask what is their thought process? Do they have any source above the Qur'an that allows them to kill innocent Muslim men, women, and children?[124]

Other critics sometimes say that in general, those verses of the Qur'an that enjoin forgiveness and compassion were revealed earlier in Mecca, but others revealed in Medina talk about fighting the unbelievers, which abrogate the Meccan verses, and we must act on the later verses, not the abrogated. Firstly, this claim is illogical and proves deficient reading and understanding of the Qur'an and is invalid because there are also verses revealed in Medina that enjoin forgiveness and compassion toward believers and unbelievers. For instance, regarding believers, as referred to in "Let them forgive and overlook" (24:22) and unbelievers in "but forgive them and overlook (their misdeeds)" (5:13), both of which were revealed in Medina, according to consensus among commentators. Secondly, the Prophet's (PBUH) life in practice should be a paragon for every Muslim, as suggested in Qur'anic verse 33:21: "You have indeed in the Messenger of Allah a fine pattern (of conduct) for any one whose hope is in Allah and the Final Day." He had compassion and forgiveness toward the unbelievers in Medina, as well as toward the believers. His compassionate attitude was reflected after his victory over Mecca and in the Battle of Hunayn, as well as at other times.

Thirdly, compassion and forgiveness are considered noble and generous acts of morality; noble acts cannot be abrogated, because the ultimate objective of faith is to attain such qualities. As such, the Prophet (PBUH) said, "I was sent to carry noble conduct to perfection." This narration in Imam Malik ibn Anas's book *al-Muwatta* has been reported and translated as "I was sent to carry the best of conduct to perfection,"[125] and in Imam Ahmad's book *al-Musnad* as "I was sent to carry virtuous conduct to perfection,"[126] both of which give the same understanding.

Fourthly, a side note on abrogation. One must remember that Islam appeared at a time to a backward society void of any feelings and regard toward human life, as they buried alive their young girls and there was always fighting between tribes over trivial disputes. They were also void of intellect, as they worshiped idols they had created themselves from wood and stone. Therefore, any new law (which also had to last till the end of time) would need to be presented to them carefully and gradually. A society that was immersed in ignorance, superstition, and lawlessness had to be educated in steps. Customs such as gambling, drinking, and slavery that were entrenched in their culture had to be abolished gradually as we witness, for example, with prohibition of intoxicants in the Qur'an. There are very few verses that allude to abrogation and are mainly regarding personal matters and acts of worship such as changing the direction of prayer (*qiblah*) from Jerusalem to Mecca in verses 2:144 and 2:150. Regarding abrogation the Qur'an says: "None of Our revelations do We abrogate or cause to be forgotten, but We substitute something better or similar" (2:106), which is also the only verse in the Qur'an using the term *abrogate*. Based on the above, the points raised by the critics regarding any form of abrogation of aforementioned verses in chapter 9 are not valid.

Seeking such excuses to justify violence are the products of twisted minds, not from any evidence within the canon or any established reference that can be attributed to Islam. Extremist groups believe there are no more than two regions in the world: the "abode of Islam" and the "abode of unbelief," and they say that those of us who live in the abode of Islam must fight those in the abode of unbelief.

The answer, as we indicated earlier, is that in this division, they dropped the "abode of peace," which is the third and largest region.

Tabatabai adds that the Prophet of God (PBUH) must be the example for all to follow. He signed the peace treaty with idolaters in Hudaybiyyah and as long as they did not breach it, he did not protest. Today, many non-Muslim nations live in peace along with Muslims and have not declared any wars against Muslim nations. They have trade relations with these nations. Muslim children are freely studying and gaining higher education in non-Muslim countries; however, the extremists will not cease sending their agents to these countries to attack noncombatant innocents on streets, bridges, trains, shops, and so forth, or by planting bombs in populated places to blow up innocent passersby, even though in addition to non-Muslims some of those killed have been Muslims or women and children whom the Messenger of God forbade killing (even if they were the women and children of a combatant enemy). Is this the meaning of forming an "Islamic basis" and "reinstating *khalafa*" (Muslim Leadership)?

Extremists often cite the violence of some of the Prophet's companions and consider them as their leaders, although the true leader for all Muslims is the one God himself called the "Mercy to mankind" in the Qur'an, and the reference for all Muslims (after the Qur'an) is the Prophet's (PBUH) tradition and his conduct, not the conduct of others. Have the extremists not read the following verse in the Qur'an: "You have indeed in the Messenger of Allah a fine pattern (of conduct) for any one whose hope is in Allah and the Final Day" (33:21)? Have they not seen in historical sources that when the famous companion Khalid ibn al-Walid, despite his service to Islam, mistreated the Banu Jazeyma tribe and harmed them, the Messenger of God (PBUH) raised his hand toward the sky and said three times, "O God, I declare, that I am averse to what Khalid ibn al-Walid did"? He then sent Ali ibn Abi Talib to the Banu Jazeyma with some material goods as compensation. Therefore, the unjustified violent act of any companion of the Prophet (PBUH) cannot legitimize any act of violence, and we must be averse to it. This is a prescript that must be observed for all events in Islamic history, which also enables Muslims to answer the objections of those who oppose Islam.[127]

Another critic made misleading comments regarding verse 9:5, which says "So, when the Sacred Months (months of grace) have passed, slay the idolaters wherever you find them, and take them (captive), and besiege them, and prepare for them each ambush. But if they repent and establish worship and pay the poor-due, then open the way for them for Allah is Forgiving, Merciful."[128]

This critic says that because the verse mentions acts of worship—prayer (salat) and the alms-giving (zakat)—the best way to be safe from Muslims' violence during the time of Muhammad was to convert to Islam. The critic also says this passage challenges the claim of self-defense because the Muslims to whom it was revealed were not under attack. Had they been under attack, according to the critic, there would have been no waiting period. The historical context refers to a period in Mecca after the idolaters were subjugated by Muhammad (PBUH) and posed no threat. The critic adds that when Muslims gained power, they violently expelled those who would not accept Islam. Other critics assert that the phrase "wherever you find them" refers to attacking unbelievers who are not on the battlefield and that the Islamic State referred to this verse urging the faithful to commit terrorist attacks on or off the battlefield.[129]

We will discuss verse 9:5 in detail, and we will also respond to this critic and to those who have given much publicity to this verse—all of which emanates from confusion and misunderstanding of the text. Our hope is that one who seeks the truth would spend the time to read the explanation of the verse and gain the knowledge to answer any related questions about 9:5. However, first we will address statements made by this critic and then refer to the details in the explanation of verse 9:5.

To the critic's assertion that the best way to stay safe from Muslims' violence at the time of Muhammad was to convert to Islam, here is another perspective:

First of all, in the span of twenty-three years since the inception of Islam (and during Muhammad's (PBUH) lifetime), there was never any unjustified violence initiated or perpetrated by Muslims, as we have discussed and cited from multiple sources (the Qur'an, biographies, and history books) in this section and earlier ones. Secondly, this passage refers only to fighting idolaters who had reneged on their treaties, which did not include all idolaters. The prior verse supports this point. Had the goal been to convert them, then the verse would not be specific to a certain group. In addition, *"al-Mushrekeen"* refers to specific groups. Furthermore, the historical accounts and the timing show that besides a few isolated encounters, there were no major battles in Arabia after Mecca was conquered. This verse played more as a warning role to these groups in order to stop their treachery.

Thirdly, the verse says if they repent and decide on their own to accept Islam and do so by observing acts of worship, such as prayer and alms-giving, then Muslims must open their way to them. This did not mean forcing anyone to convert to Islam. Verse 9:6 says they can even seek amnesty with Muslims *without* converting to Islam (and Muslims must give them protection and escort them to their place of safety).

Fourthly, the Prophet (PBUH) and his companions never forced anyone to convert, as this would have been contradictory to the teachings of Islam and the Qur'an. Furthermore, history has shown when it comes to faith, coercion has never worked and never will whether through force of violence or financial enticement. Christian missionaries tried it in India and Algeria, and the number of Christians in such places today attests that even with financial, medical aid, and other enticements, one cannot convert people. Islam requires people to submit with love and sincerity in their hearts and minds, as doing so transforms their attitudes through noble deeds, not merely a declaration of the tongue. Had idolaters or followers of any other faith been forced to convert to Islam, they would have reverted to their original faith after the threat was removed or by the generations to follow. This is true not just of the idolaters of Arabia, but how the rest of the world embraced Islam generation after generation. Readers are encouraged to read *The Preaching of Islam: A History of the Propagation of Muslim Faith* by Sir Thomas Walker Arnold, or other sources available on this topic.

The critic also asserts that this passage challenges the claim that the Qur'an addresses violence within the context of self-defense, because the Muslims to whom the passage was revealed were not under attack at the time. Had they been under attack, according to the critic, there would have been no waiting period.

To begin with, the Qur'an never inspired violence. It permits fighting only in situations of self-defense in order to preserve the faith, the community, and the freedom of religion and its propagation. Muslims were constantly under attack for twenty-three years, even after Mecca was conquered (which is the context of the verse) and the enemy retreated, but continued scheming, attacking, and pillaging caravans entering and leaving Mecca. The four-month grace period was for those idolaters who had no peace treaties with the Muslims and the few who had broken their treaties and continued their intolerable criminal behavior. The sacred months mentioned earlier are not to be confused with this four-month grace period given to those specific idolaters to stop their violence.

To the critic's claim that the historical context refers to a period in Mecca after the idolaters were subjugated by Muhammad and posed no threat and that once Muslims gained power they violently expelled those who would not accept Islam, we counter with the following explanations:

The context is after Mecca was conquered; however, the violence against Muslim individuals in various forms continued by those who had no obligations under any treaties. This critic does not cite any references as to where he obtained this information that unbelievers were no threat and that they were violently evicted because they did not convert. If it were about converting unbelievers, then having a treaty (or not) would be irrelevant; hence, the preceding verse 9:4—"Except those of the idolaters with whom you (Muslims) have a treaty, and who have since abated nothing of your right nor have supported anyone against you"—would be irrelevant. This means there were in fact idolaters with no treaty who opposed Muslims and supported others against them, underscoring the fact that the reason to engage in war was not due to their polytheistic beliefs, rather their aggression and breaking of treaties. Nevertheless, the entire context of verses 9:1–15, with all its restrictions, is ignored by critics who simply isolate one part of the verse or passage to support their theory of war in Islam with the sword verse, even though the word for sword does not appear anywhere in the Qur'an.

We now continue with a detailed explanation of verse 9:5:

To understand the full picture, we must first understand the entire passage beginning with verse 1, which clarifies the sequence of
events and the meaning of each event and the verse that corresponds
to it. The timing, of course, is after Mecca was conquered and most
Meccans, including the Quraysh idolaters, had embraced Islam. These
verses provide a framework demarcating the relationship between
the Muslim community, now well established in Medina and the
Arabian Peninsula, and the unbelievers in Arabia who chose not to
accept Islam. Relations were thus regulated with those Arabs who
had violated their treaties with the Prophet (PBUH) when they felt
the Muslims were about to meet their match with the Byzantines at
Tabuk.

Relations were on a proper footing with those Arabs without
a treaty but who maintained good relations with the Muslims, and
those who had a treaty, which they observed without treachery.
Several reports speak of the general conditions prevailing at the time
when this declaration was made, as well as the method and the person
chosen for its announcement. Perhaps the most accurate, and most
fitting given the prevailing situation of the Muslim community and
the nature of the Islamic approach, is the one by al-Tabari, an early
commentator on the Qur'an. We will list some of his reports that
support our view of the event and how it took place. The following
report he attributes to Mujahid ibn Jabr, one of the early Qur'anic
commentators of the generation who came after the Prophet (PBUH)
and his companions.

Verse 9:1 states, "A (declaration) of Immunity by God and His
Messenger (is hereby given) to those of the idolaters with whom you
have made a treaty."[130] According to al Tabari this is a reference to the
tribe of Mudalij and to the Arabs who were bound by a treaty with
the Muslims and all other peoples with similar treaties. It is reported
that when the Prophet (PBUH) returned from Tabuk, he wanted to
go on pilgrimage. He then thought that since the Ka'ba was visited
by idolaters who do the *tawaf* (the ritual walk or circumambulation
around the Ka'ba) naked, he would rather delay his pilgrimage until
such a practice was stopped. He sent Abu Bakr and Ali to see people

at the Dhu al-Majaz and other markets as well as at their camps on pilgrimage. They gave notice to all peoples who had treaties with the Prophet (PBUH) that they would have four months. When those four consecutive months were over, beginning with the twenty days remaining of the month of Dhul-Hijjah to the tenth day of Rabi' II, the treaties would end.

As for the notice given by God permitting idolaters with a treaty to "Go freely in the land for four months," al-Tabari says the more accurate view is that this notice was given by God to those idolaters who, despite having peace treaties, collaborated with others against the Prophet (PBUH) and the Muslim community, thus violating their treaties before they ran out. As for those who fulfilled their obligations under such treaties and refrained from collaborating with others, God ordered His Messenger to honor his treaty with them until their term had been completed.[131] This is made clear in the Qur'anic statement "Except for those idolaters with whom you have made a treaty and who have honored their obligations [under each treaty] in every detail, nor aided anyone against you. So fulfil your engagements with them to the end of their term: for Allah loves the righteous" (9:4).[132]

Some may interpret the order to mean that once the truce was over, the Muslims were meant to kill all unbelievers. In support of this view, they may quote the next verse which states, "But, when the sacred months (months of grace) are past, slay the idolaters wherever you find them" (9:5).[133] But this interpretation is wrong. Verse 9:7 confirms and demonstrates the opposite: "How can there be a league [treaty], before Allah and His Messenger, with the Pagans [idolaters], except those with whom you made a treaty near the Sacred Mosque? As long as these stand true to you, stand you true to them: for Allah loves the righteous." People to whom this verse refers to are idolaters, and God commanded the Prophet (PBUH) and the believers to remain faithful to their treaties with them as long as they kept their part and fulfilled their obligations.

Numerous reports confirm that when the Prophet (PBUH) sent Ali to declare the disavowal of treaties to people, he also commanded him to make it clear that whoever had a treaty with the Prophet

(PBUH), that treaty continued until its specified expiration date. This provides clear support of our view. God did not order the Prophet (PBUH) to terminate a treaty with any group of people who remained faithful to it. He only added a four-month notice with those who had violated their treaties and those whose treaties had no specified term limit, or those without a treaty. Treaties with a specific time frame and observed properly by the other side were to remain in force until their term was over. The Prophet (PBUH) sent his companions to announce this policy during the pilgrimage to ensure it was well publicized.

In another comment on the various reports concerning treaties, al-Tabari also says the four-month notice was given to those whom we mentioned. As for those whose treaties specified a term of expiration, God did not allow the Prophet (PBUH) and the believers to terminate such treaties. Hence, the Prophet (PBUH) fulfilled God's order by honoring his commitment to these treaties. This is clearly stated in the Qur'an and confirmed by many reports attributed to the Prophet (PBUH).

The Prophet (PBUH) sent Abu Bakr to lead the pilgrimage that year. The reason was the Prophet (PBUH) did not like to perform the pilgrimage when the idolaters continued their abominable practice of doing the tawaf (the ritual walk around the Ka'ba) in the nude. After Abu Bakr left for pilgrimage, the opening passage of chapter 9 on repentance was revealed. The Prophet (PBUH) dispatched Ali to join Abu Bakr to make the declaration. He outlined the final provisions at the gathering to ensure that all of Arabia would be aware of them. Among them was one that clarified no idolater would be allowed into Mecca to do the tawaf or the pilgrimage.[134]

Al-Tirmidhi related in a report that quotes Ali as saying that God's Messenger (PBUH) had sent him, after the revelation of this chapter, to announce the following four points: no one may do the tawaf naked; no idolater may come near the Sacred Mosque after that year (the Ka'ba had been cleaned of all idols); treaties with God's Messenger (PBUH) would be observed until they expired; and no one may enter heaven except one who submits totally to God. This report is considered the most authentic within the chain of narrations.

"A (declaration) of Immunity by God and His Messenger (is hereby given) to those of the idolaters with whom you have made a treaty" (9:1). This is a general declaration, carrying a sharp rhythm, which outlines the basic principles that governed relations between the Muslims and the idolaters at the time throughout the Arabian Peninsula.

"Go you, then, for four months, backwards and forwards, (as you will), throughout the land, but know you that you cannot frustrate Allah [render Allah incapable], (by your falsehood) but that Allah will cover with shame [disgrace] those who reject Him" (9:2). This statement clarifies the terms now given to the unbelievers: they are given a period of four months during which they can move about freely to carry out their business transactions, fulfill their commitments, and modify their situations in peace. During this period, they must scrupulously honor their treaties. This included idolaters with no treaties or even those idolaters who were quick to violate their treaties when they felt that the Prophet (PBUH) and his followers would never return from their expedition to Tabuk but would instead be taken captive by the Byzantines. That was also the eventuality expected by the hypocrites in Medina. It is pertinent to ask here: when was this notice given outlining this period of truce and security? It followed a long period of treaty violations by the unbelievers and showed that the idolaters would continue to fight the Muslims until they had turned them away from their faith, if they could. These terms were issued at a time when humanity was governed by the laws of the jungle. What dictated relations between communities was merely the ability to invade others without notice, as no commitment was considered binding. Opportunities were taken mercilessly.

This was followed by specifying when this disavowal would be announced to the unbelievers so that they would be fully aware of the time limits imposed, as verse 9:3 specifies: "And an announcement from Allah and His Messenger, to the people (assembled) on the day of the Great Pilgrimage." Reports vary on which was the day of the greater pilgrimage: the day of Arafat (an important place in Islam where, during the Hajj, pilgrims spend the afternoon of the ninth day of pilgrimage) or the day of sacrifice? It is perhaps more accurate to say it was the day of sacrifice. The Arabic term used in this passage for "announcement" or proclamation signifies an assurance to those to whom the proclamation was made and received. This probably took place during the pilgrimage, when the disavowal or immunity by God and His Messenger (PBUH) of all treaties with idolaters were made. An exception was then added in the next verse which allowed certain treaties to run their term.

This warning and encouragement to the unbelievers to mend their ways during a period of treaty violations was indicative of the Islamic approach. It was first and foremost an approach that sought to give guidance to people. The idolaters were given a grace period not only because Islam does not advocate taking anyone by surprise, but also because it did not want to inflict unnecessary humiliation. These have often been the essence of power relations, except under Islam. The truce also gave the idolaters a chance to reflect and reconsider their options. At the same time, it provided reassurance to the Muslims by removing any lingering worries or fears about what may happen.

The exception was then made in the case of treaties that specified a term of validity. These were allowed to remain in force: "Except for those idolaters with whom you have made a treaty and who have honored their obligations [under each treaty] in every detail, nor aided anyone against you. So fulfil your engagements with them to the end of their term: for Allah loves the righteous" (9:4). Perhaps the most accurate report concerning those who benefited from this exception was about the Bakr clan, named the Khuzayma, and the Ibn Amir clan of the Bakr ibn Kinana tribes from Mecca. They were both party to the Treaty of Hudaybiyyah which the Prophet (PBUH) had concluded with the Quraysh and their allies.

This clan did not take part in the Bakr clan's attack against the Banu Khuza'a tribe. That aggression, in which the Bakr were aided by the Quraysh, violated the Hudaybiyyah peace treaty. Thus, that treaty, which was to last for ten years, was treacherously breached after only two years. The Khuzayma clan continued to observe the terms of their agreement while other unbelievers did not. The Prophet (PBUH) was instructed to honor his obligations under the treaty to those people for the remainder of the term.

Our view is confirmed by the statement that followed: "How can there be a league [treaty], before Allah and His Messenger, with the Pagans [idolaters], except those with whom you made a treaty near the Sacred Mosque? As long as these stand true to you, stand you true to them: for Allah loves the righteous" (9:7). These two clans from Kinana were among those who were party to the peace treaty at Hudaybiyyah. They did not violate their treaties and were true to their obligations, aiding no party against the Muslims. It is to them that the exception applies, as confirmed by early scholars and commentators on the Qur'an. Islam honors its obligations to those who are true to theirs and did not give them notice of termination, as it did to all others. Prophet (PBUH) allowed their treaties to run their full term in recognition of their faithful observance of their obligations. This was the Islamic attitude.

It is important to reflect on the comment that concludes the verse requiring Muslims to remain true to their obligations: "So fulfil your engagements with them to the end of their term: for Allah loves the righteous" (9:4). This passage says God considers the fulfillment of obligations an act of worship addressed to Him, and an aspect of the righteousness He loves. This is the basis of Islamic ethics. Islam does not act on the basis of acquiring profits and self-interest, nor on the basis of continually changing traditions. All Islamic ethics are based on worshiping God and fearing Him, which is the essence of righteousness. Muslim bring their behavior in line with that which they know pleases God.

The Qur'anic instruction is very clear. A state of war was then to be declared: "So, when the Sacred Months (months of grace) have passed, slay the idolaters wherever you find them, and take them (captive), and besiege them, and prepare for them each ambush. But if they repent and establish worship and pay the poor-due, then open the way for them. Lo! Allah is Forgiving, Merciful" (9:5).[135]

The word used here to describe those four months in the Qur'anic text is *hurum*, which describes the four months when fighting is not allowed except to repel aggression. These form two periods every year when people can go freely, secure from any danger of war, because of the use of this word.

The correct interpretation, in some commentators' view, is that the four months meant here are different from the four sacred months observed annually. The same description is given to both because fighting during both times is forbidden. This new period of grace applied to all, except in the case of those who had treaties lasting for a specified length of time, in which case such treaties were to be fully honored. Since God has said to them "You may go freely in the land for four months," then the four months must start from the day of the announcement. This interpretation fits with the nature of this announcement.

Moreover, this was not meant as a campaign of vengeance or extermination, but rather as a warning, which motivated them to take a position. "But if they repent and establish worship and pay the poor-due, then open the way for them. Lo! Allah is Forgiving, Merciful" (9:5). For over twenty years they had been listening to the message of Islam put to them in the clearest possible way. However, they kept trying to suppress the message of Islam through persecution, open warfare, and forging alliances to destroy the Islamic state. This long history contrasted with the never-failing tolerance of Islam, as demonstrated by God's Messenger (PBUH) and his companions. Nonetheless, Islam was now opening its arms to them. Instructions were issued to the Prophet (PBUH) and to the Muslims, the very victims of persecution who were driven out of their homeland and suffered a war of aggression, to extend a hand of welcome to those idolaters should they turn to God in repentance. Such repentance should be genuine, confirmed by their observance of the main duties of Islam. This is because God never rejects anyone who turns to Him in sincere repentance, no matter how great his sins: "Lo! Allah is forgiving, Merciful" (9:5). As pointed out earlier:

1. Not all directives mentioned, such as slay, take, besiege, or prepare to ambush, are mandated. The situation, time, and

place relative to idolaters must be considered before choosing one or two of the actions. If, for example, their aggression is stopped by besieging and capturing, then those are the appropriate steps; otherwise, Muslims are permitted to slay.

2. *"Wherever you find them"* is mentioned because idolaters used to attack, kill, and pillage anytime and anywhere they could, and then return to their place of safety, and if they were given any chance, they aimed to wipe out the Muslims everywhere.

3. However, the rest of verse 9:5 says even if these idolaters who murdered, pillaged, and broke treaties repented and embraced Islam, showing sincerity through acts of worship, such as prayer and paying zakat (poor-due), then Muslims must let them go, and God's mercy would be upon them. Yet, despite the declaration of war against all the idolaters after the four-month period ended, Islam continues to demonstrate its grace, as well as a serious and realistic approach. It did not seek to exterminate all idolaters. On the contrary, it also declared a campaign of guidance whenever possible. Individual idolaters who were not part of a hostile and belligerent community were guaranteed safety in the land of Islam. God instructed His Messenger (PBUH) to give them asylum so that they may listen to God's word and become aware of the nature of the Islamic message before they are given safe conduct to their own domiciles. All this, even though they were still idolaters: "If one amongst the Pagans [idolaters] ask you for asylum, grant it to him, so that he may hear the word of Allah; and then escort him to where he can be secure. That is because they are men without knowledge" (9:6). This verse illustrates how Islam was keen to reach out to every heart with its guidance. No single case was to be taken lightly. Whoever appealed for protection shall be granted it. Anyone who sought asylum could not, at the same time, join a hostile force that sought to undermine the Muslim community. Hence, granting protection to such a person provided him or her an opportunity to listen to the Qur'an and to understand

the true nature of the Islamic faith. When God's word is
heard in such an atmosphere, hearts respond positively. Even
if they do not, Muslims are still required to ensure the safety
of anyone who appeals for help until that person is returned
to a place of safety.

Hence, idolaters, or any enemies, who might have persecuted
Muslims are protected. Muslims are required to give safe conduct
until that idolater or enemy has reached a place of safety. Islam seeks
to provide knowledge to those who lack such knowledge, and to give
protection to whomever appeals for protection, even though that person may belong to the enemy camp and might have fought to suppress
the Islamic message.

This termination of the state of peace, based on treaties and agreements, is followed by a rhetorical question stating that it is just not possible for idolaters to have such covenants with God and His Messenger
(PBUH). The very principle of having such agreements is rejected
outright: "How can there be a league [treaty], before Allah and His
Messenger, with the Pagans [idolaters], except those with whom you
made a treaty near the Sacred Mosque?" (9:7).

In order to dispel any misunderstandings, the ruling is restated
once more: "As long as these stand true to you, stand true to them: for
Allah loves the righteous" (9:7). This restatement adds a new provision. The first instruction required Muslims to honor their obligations
to those who had shown true commitment to their peace agreements
and fulfilled their obligations. Now, the second instruction was to
keep faith with them by making it clear Muslims were to honor their
obligations to them for as long as they themselves continued to observe their treaties in full, as they had done in the past.

These verses underscore the fact that the reason to engage in war
was not due to the idolaters' polytheistic beliefs, but rather their aggression and the breaking of treaties.

Last, but not least, regarding ISIS (Islamic State of Iraq and Syria)
using this verse to advance their goals, as mentioned earlier, there
are people who will use and misuse Qur'anic verses to serve their

own purposes. This is standard practice by extremists as well as by critics of Islam. In most cases, it is deliberate and intended to support their agendas. We do not recognize ISIS, or any similar group, as a legitimate authority or a legitimate anything representing Islam. Their views are not echoed by any Muslim outside their camp and are challenged by many scholars and individual Muslims. Therefore, their citing of any verse from the Qur'an, tradition, or any document has no validity or recognition. Many Muslim scholars from around the world have challenged, questioned, and corrected their statements and claims (note a small portion of the open letter signed by 126 Muslim scholars to ISIS leader Abu Bakr al-Baghdadi, was presented in chapter 3). As such, it suffices to repeat: any extremist group can claim anything on any basis to serve their purpose; however, we hope those who are questioning Islam from a scholarly or intellectual point of view would not cite ISIS or any similar group's claims, as almost everyone in the world is now aware of their motives and tendencies.

6.6 "The law of equality (Retribution) is prescribed to you" (2:178–179)

O you who believe! The law of equality [Retribution] is prescribed
for you in the matter of murder: the free for the free, the slave
for the slave, the woman for the woman. But if any remission
is made by the brother of the slain, then grant any reasonable
demand, and compensate him with handsome gratitude, this is
a concession and a Mercy from your Lord. After this whoever
exceeds the limits shall be in grave penalty. And, In the Law of
Equality [retribution] there is (saving of) life to you, o you men
of understanding; that you may restrain yourselves. (2:178–179)

As discussed earlier in this chapter, excess in accepting injustice and forbearance is not always liberating because generalizing it in absolute terms would mean encouraging criminals and oppressors. It also leaves their hands free to commit aggressions against the innocent and the oppressed, which becomes self-defeating and takes away the rights of the oppressed and the innocent, which eventually promotes violence. These verses are about establishing justice in a society, without which life has no sanctity. They refer to punitive measures against criminal acts (which are also prosecuted in any secular court), not an act of violence as a result of a war; however, critics of Islam have included these verses to demonstrate violence in Islam.

In these verses, the believers are informed that retribution in cases of murder is permitted. They are also called upon to reflect on the purpose and wisdom of this legislation, outlined in the second verse. Believers are reminded of the need to enhance their sense of God-fearing, which acts as a safety valve against any excess or injustice in punishing those accused of murder. The statement clearly indicates how retribution ought to be carried out: a free man for a free man, a slave for a slave, a woman for a woman. Verse 178, which states "But if any remission is made by the brother of the slain, then grant any reasonable demand, and compensate him with handsome gratitude," refers to a situation that would arise when a victim's relatives decide to accept financial compensation instead of insisting on punishment of the murderer in retaliation. Once this is agreed upon, the victim's relatives are also under an obligation to seek a fair and amicable settlement, while the murderer's guardian or representative must, on his part, settle readily and honorably. In pre-Islamic days, if a member of a tribe was killed, both tribes would engage in bitter fighting and take revenge against any member of the other tribe. Islam brought justice to individuals by addressing their rights. The verse brings the accuracy of retribution to light by giving an example of a free man retributed by a free man and a slave by a slave. This means any person murdered, regardless of who the murderer is, would be subject to retribution. For example, a slave will not be subjected to pay for another person's crime. Lives and bloods of all Muslims are equal and the individual committing the murder is solely responsible regardless of the gender or the position in the society.

This serves to clear the air and to remove any ill feelings or grudges that would have inevitably arisen between the two parties. It would also be conducive to fostering a friendlier relationship between the living members of both parties. This provision has been laid down by God's grace as a special favor and an act of mercy toward believers: "this is a concession and a Mercy from your Lord" (verse 178). The concession of allowing financial compensation to a victim's family, particularly in cases of murder, was not given to the Jews in the Torah. In Islam, it has been set up as an alternative, aiming to spare lives, when an agreement and amicable settlement can be reached. Of course, another option in Islam is for the victim's family to forgive. This is also reflected in other Qur'anic verses:

The recompense for an injury is an injury equal thereto (in degree): but if a person forgives and makes reconciliation, his reward is due from Allah: for (Allah) loves not those who do wrong. (42:40)

Obviously, these verses are not about war, but about permitting punishment for premeditated murder. In Islam, society's rights are just as recognized as that of the individual's. The verse puts retribution next to reaching a settlement through compensation or forgiveness (with remorse). The aim is to prevent society from trending toward violence on the pretext of establishing justice. Yet it also keeps the option of full retribution on the table so society does not resort to violence on its own without due process in case a settlement is not reached. On the other hand, the end of verse 178 says, "After this whoever exceeds the limits shall be in grave penalty," which is a warning to those who, after a settlement is reached, attempt to harm or kill the murderer. The term "o men of understanding" in the next verse 179 relates to individuals in the community especially officials involved with execution of law who are expected to utilize law of retribution to protect individual's as well as the society's rights, and prevent loss of innocent lives as it says: "And, In the Law of Equality [retribution] there is (saving of) life to you, o you men of understanding; that you may restrain yourselves"(2:179)

6.7   "Then fight in the cause of Allah" (2:244)

> Then fight in the cause of Allah, and know that
> Allah Hears and knows all things. (2:244)

The context here refers to ancient times when thousands of people fled at the same time, whether from a hostile attack or from the outbreak of disease, causing widespread panic. Nevertheless, running away could not save those people from meeting their death, for "God said to them; 'Die' then restored them back to life" (2:243). Then verse 244 says, "Then fight in the cause of Allah and know that Allah Hears and knows all things," which tells Muslims that neither their love of life nor their fear of death should stop them from fighting for God's cause. As the Qur'an stipulates, God determines both death and life, and those who believe should fight for His cause and under His banner alone. They should be mindful that God is aware of what they do and is there to respond to their needs and appreciate and reward their actions. These verses are about advancing human value through struggle and sacrifice. They were revealed during the Battle of Badr, as they point out encountering oppression and injustice and defending human rights and dignity, while raising Muslims' spirit by mentioning this story. It is said after a group of such people died, one of the Prophets (PBUH) from Israelites (Ezekiel) passed by and supplicated that God bring them back to life. God answered his prayer and brought them back to life, as reflected in the Book of Ezekiel 37:1–11.

To fight (qital) for the cause of God in fact means to fight for what is right, and it requires devotion and sacrifice. In the Qur'an, jihad is frequently associated with financial contributions, especially in the early days of Islam when fighters were required to finance their own participation in a war. There were eager and capable fighters who were prevented from riding with the Muslim army due to their lack of means. The emphasis on financial sacrifice was, therefore, essential, as the chapter strongly states in the next verse: "Who is he that will loan to Allah a beautiful loan, which Allah will double unto his credit and multiply many times? It is Allah that giveth (you)

Want or plenty [decreases and increases], and to Him shall be your return" (2:245).

God bestows life and takes it away, and one may go to battle and survive, if it is God's will. Wealth is not lost when spent on a good cause. It is considered a loan to God, whose generous repayment is guaranteed, both in this world and in the life to come. Poverty and wealth are also due to God's will rather than just the outcome of one's financial acumen or frugality or philanthropy. "It is Allah that gives (you) Want or plenty [reduces or increases], and to Him shall be your return" (2:245). Although individuals have a profound role in what they receive, in the end their success is subject to how events develop, which are all in God's hand.

6.8 "Fighting is prescribed for you, and you dislike it" (2:216)

Fighting is prescribed for you, and you dislike it. But
it is possible that you dislike a thing which is good for
you, and that you love a thing which is bad for you.
But Allah knoweth, and you know not. (2:216)

A critic misrepresents this verse by insisting it establishes violence as a virtuous act, but it also contradicts the notion that fighting is intended only in self-defense, since the Muslims were obviously not under attack at the time. From the Hadith, we know that this verse was narrated at a time when Muslims were preparing to raid merchant caravans for goods.[136]

Nowhere in this verse, or any other, does the Qur'an say unjustified violence is virtuous. In Islam, fighting is defined only for a just cause and only when it is unavoidable. This critic completely misses the historical context by which this verse was revealed. He also misses the fact that the war of aggression was started by Meccans (in Mecca) long before the Battle of Badr, and Muslims tolerated these persecutions for thirteen years up until they were forced to migrate to Medina, where they had to defend their existence. The implications of this Qur'anic principle are not limited to fighting, which is only one example of a necessary evil that may ultimately result in something good but extend to all aspects of a believer's life (as preceding verses 214 and 215 speak about struggling and spending in the cause of God). As to what qualifies as justified war (in the cause of God and the truth), it was explained in earlier sections and through verse 2:190 in the context of this chapter.

The Muslims who left Medina on the eve of the Battle of Badr in 624 CE to intercept the Quraysh and their leader Abu Sufiyan (see section 6.3.3 for a more detailed explanation), were hoping to protect their community against a small group; however, they were confronted by a large army from Mecca led by Abu Jahl, as God willed it that the caravan with Abu Sufiyan's men reroute their way back to Mecca. The Muslims found themselves facing the large Quraysh army instead, which was intent on subduing them. How is encountering an army of one thousand well-equipped men who are en route to raid and decimate your town not considered self-defense?

The Muslim army never attacked or looted any caravans. Some critics of Islam refer to the Hadith yet without citing any references.

The outcome of the confrontation was a resounding victory for Islam and the Muslims, which was infinitely better than confronting the small numbers with Abu Sufiyan, who followed the caravan. What the Muslims aimed for was much inferior to what God had in store for them. This verse refers to the fact that God knows best and people do not.

Most of us can recall experiences in which we dreaded certain situations that turned out to be beneficial, as well as other situations that looked appealing and lucrative on the surface but ended in disaster. Often, people bitterly regret missing out on certain things, but as time goes by, they realize that God had spared them certain adverse consequences. While some undergo intense suffering that could drive them to the edge of despair, eventually circumstances bring opportunities for greater happiness and prosperity.

Another critic says that fighting may be defensive but does not seem optional, as the verse uses the term *prescribe*, which means "ordained, intended, destined" by God. The answer is in the critic's own statement and the use of the word *defensive*. If an enemy is determined, mobilized, and on the attack to destroy your very existence, would you not consider it an ordained duty of every able member of your community to defend yourselves?

6.9 "As for those who reject faith (disbelieve), I will punish them" (3:56)

As for those who reject faith [disbelieve], I will punish them with terrible agony in this world and in the Hereafter, nor will they have anyone to help. (3:56)

This verse is a general statement about the concept of punishments and rewards, and many critics conveniently omit the second part—the reward. The full context is about those who believed in Jesus (PBUH) and his message and the disbelievers, as explained fully in verses 3:54–57:

And (the unbelievers) plotted and planned, and Allah too planned, and the best of planners is Allah. Behold! Allah said: O Jesus! I will take you and raise you to Myself and clear you [your name] (of the falsehoods) of those who blaspheme; I will make those who follow you superior to those who reject faith, to the Day of Resurrection: Then shall you all return unto me, and I will judge between you of the matters wherein you dispute. As for those who reject faith [disbelieve], I will punish them with terrible agony in this world and in the Hereafter, nor will they have anyone to help. As to those who believe and work righteousness, Allah will pay them (in full) their reward; but Allah loves not those who do wrong.

This statement proves the seriousness of rewards and punishments and of divine justice, which is absolute and cannot be influenced by people's wishes or fabrications. The return to God is inevitable. His judgment on all matters of dispute is irrevocable. The punishment He inflicts on the unbelievers in this world and in the life to come will overwhelm them, and they will have no one to help them against it. The threat is against those who see and know the truth, yet their arrogance prevents them from acknowledging it. The term *kafir* (disbeliever) literally means the one who covers, and in most cases in the Qur'an refers to the one who covers or rejects the truth due to his or her stubbornness and arrogance.

Not mentioned by critics, in verse 57, are the believers who do good works: "Allah will pay them (in full) their reward" without favoritism, but with great generosity. "Allah loves not those who do wrong." Far be it from Him then, to do anyone any wrong when He Himself does not love the wrongdoers.

6.10   "Soon shall We cast terror into the hearts of the Unbelievers" (3:151)

Soon shall We cast terror into the hearts of the Unbelievers,
for that they joined companions [associated partners] with
Allah, for which He had sent no authority. (3:151)

We note that some critics of Islam claim this verse, which speaks of polytheists, also includes Christians because they believe in the Trinity. If these critics had read the Qur'an, as they claim, they would see that the Qur'an addresses polytheists and Christians separately. The Qur'an calls Christians and Jews People of the Book. An example is "Those who reject (Truth), among the People of the Book and among the Polytheists, were not going to depart (from their ways) until there should come to them Clear Evidence" (98:1), where People of the Book and the polytheist are clearly and separately mentioned.

Furthermore, the context of verse 3:151 does not even concern Christians, which would have been clear had these critics studied the context, which is the Qur'an's review of the Battle of Uhud (with idolaters) and other related events. The Qur'anic comments aim at correcting the concepts of the believers, enhancing their awareness of their situation, warning them of the pitfalls that lie ahead, and warning how the enemy may scheme against them. The passage and this verse reassure the believers and give them positive news of God's plan to cast terror into the hearts of their enemies. Even though the idolaters were apparently victorious, due to their irrational beliefs, rejection of the truth, and with no support from God, they will soon become fearful of you (the believers). According to reports, after defeating Muslims in Uhud, Abu Sufiyan and his army left for Mecca, however, on their way they considered turning back in order to finish off Muslims. However due to news of Muslims regrouping and preparedness, they feared encountering the remaining Muslims, hence returned to Mecca.

6.11 "Let those fight in the cause of Allah . . . whether he is slain or gets victory" (4:74 & 76)

> Let those fight in the cause of Allah who sell the life of
> this world for the hereafter. To him who fights in the
> cause of Allah,- whether he is slain or gets victory - Soon
> shall We give him a reward of great (value). (4:74)

Some critics claim that extremists today are using this verse as a religious or legal basis to justify suicide bombings and acts of terror.

Our response is that extremists will do anything on any basis. We already mentioned in earlier sections that the Qur'an states no Muslim may harm a civilian enemy (Muslim or non-Muslim) under any circumstance. There have been many war crimes against humanity committed by overzealous Christians (throughout Christian history) who have cited biblical verses as well. Another point critics missed, contained in the next verse, explains why Muslims are called upon to defend God's truth and to fight in His path. The passage portrays the integrity, magnificence, and nobility of the aims and objectives of the cause Muslims are urged to fight for: "And why should you not fight in the cause of Allah and of those who, being weak, are ill-treated (and oppressed)? Men, women, and children, whose cry is: Our Lord! Rescue us from this town, whose people are oppressors; and raise for us from thee one who will protect; and raise for us from thee one who will help!" (4:75). But then our dear critics skip verse 4:75 and instead mention verse 4:76, where it repeats fighting for the cause of God: "Those who believe fight in the cause of Allah, and those who reject Faith Fight in the cause of Evil: So fight ye against the friends of Satan: feeble indeed is the cunning of Satan" (4:76).

Verse 74 says that while life has value and pleasure, the life in the Hereafter by comparison is a better, more prosperous place, so those who strive in this life or even fight in the path of God, whether they are victorious or defeated, are ultimately winners in the eyes of God and great rewards await them. The next verse (75) gives examples of what it means to fight in the path of God, defending not just themselves, but helpless men, women, and children who cry for help (referring to their brethren who were still in Mecca under persecution). Due to politics and power plays, extremists have no regard for human life, even the Muslims who represent most of their victims. Although they claim knowledge of the Qur'an, they completely miss verses such as 4:93 which states "If a man kills a believer intentionally, his recompense is Hell, to abide therein (Forever): And the wrath and the curse of Allah are upon him, and a dreadful penalty is prepared for him."

In verse 4:76, the fight is between the advocates of truth and falsehood. Anyone who believes in God would attest to the fact that good and evil exist—there is the truth and then there are falsehoods. This tussle between the forces of good and evil has existed throughout history, starting with Cain and Abel. These verses and similar ones emphasize morality and ideals that believers are fighting for as well as the fallacy and weakness of the unbelievers' cause.

6.12   "But if they turn renegades, seize them and slay them wherever . . ." (4:89)

They but wish that you should reject Faith, as they do, and
thus be on the same footing (as they): But take not friends
from their ranks until they flee [migrate] in the way of Allah
(From what is forbidden). But if they turn renegades, seize
them and slay them wherever you find them; and (in any
case) take no friends or helpers from their ranks. (4:89)

To read this verse without understanding the context, one can deduce this verse was applicable to certain people in a particular situation. But to whom? The hypocrites. Verses 88–91 discuss their division.

First, some important background to consider: the previous verses criticized the Muslim community's hesitation to adopt a firm position toward the hypocrites. The Muslim community was divided by two opinions, leading to some controversy regarding their relationship with a group of hypocrites from outside of Medina. The criticism makes clear that Islam only accepts a firm stance in such matters. It does not allow for hesitation in the Muslim community's approach to such a problem. Such hesitation means accepting the pretense they offer.

The correct approach can only be taken if it is based on a clearly defined plan of action. "Why should you be divided into two parties about the Hypocrites? Allah hath upset them for their (evil) deeds. Would you [wish you] guide those whom Allah hath thrown out of the Way? For those whom Allah hath thrown out of the Way, never shall you find the Way" (4:88).

The report quotes Ibn Abbas as saying this Qur'anic verse speaks of certain people who indicated they were Muslims (as they came to Medina) while, at the same time, they supported the unbelievers when they moved back to Mecca, thinking they were safe, should they encounter the Prophet's (PBUH) companions. When the companions were told of their departure from Mecca, some of them suggested they should mount an expedition to meet those cowards and kill them because they supported the Muslims' enemies. Another group of believers asked how the Muslims could kill people who had made the same declaration of faith they had made. Was it because they had not migrated to Medina that their killing and the confiscation of their property could be sanctioned? This suggests two facts:

1. Muslims were reluctant to fight even those who verbally and deceitfully had accepted Islam.
2. Before receiving any revelation or directive from God, Muslims had the freedom to express their opinions on any

matter. The consultation in all matters was common and the Prophet (PBUH) did not act on his own in various matters.

Both groups maintained their attitudes, and the Prophet (PBUH) expressed no disapproval of either. Hence, Qur'anic verse 89 was revealed: "They but wish that you should reject Faith [disbelieve], as they do, and thus be on the same footing (as they): But take not friends from their ranks." This refers to the situation in which wrongdoers (hypocrites) always feel insecure when alone or with a few, hence they always want others to join them. As such, the verse gives instructions to Muslims not to take them as friends, so the hypocrites do perhaps understand wrongdoing does not deserve company and will mend their ways, as the verse teaches: "until they flee[migrate] in the way of Allah (From what is forbidden)," meaning leave the idolaters and join the Muslims once again. "But if they turn renegades, seize them and slay them wherever you find them; and (in any case) take no friends or helpers from their ranks" (4:89). This means if they decide to stay with combatant idolaters, it is then clear they are adopting the same attitude toward Muslims. The verse then instructs the Muslims to fight the hypocrites like the combatant idolaters. This verse moves closer to exposing the attitude and intentions of the hypocrites. It is not only that they have chosen error in preference to divine guidance and that their deeds and bad intentions have merited that God lets them go further astray, but they have deliberately tried to divert the believers away from their righteous course: "They but wish that you should reject Faith [disbelieve], as they do, and thus be on the same footing (as they)."

The directive to seize them, or to kill them, is conditional on their migration to Medina, which is provided for in verse 89. It is then a warning issued to them to desist from their practices. They might have heeded this warning, and the Prophet (PBUH) would have had no reason to carry out this order. The condition, however, that this threat applies "until they flee[migrate] in the way of Allah" makes it absolutely clear that they were not of the people of Medina. Their migration to Medina was, in fact, required because this whole episode took place before the conquest of Mecca, during the period when migration was meant to move Muslims out of the land of unfaith and into the land of faith (that is, Medina, to join the Muslim community). Otherwise, the identity of those who did not migrate while claiming to be Muslims was questionable. Later in this chapter is a strong denunciation of the attitude of those few Muslims who remained in Mecca despite their ability to migrate to Medina, even though they were citizens of Mecca.

This verse describes those hypocrites as a group in Mecca, or its surrounding area, who claimed to be Muslims while at the same time supporting the Muslims' enemies. This strong denunciation of the believers' hesitant attitude toward those people is then expressed in a rhetorical question: "Why should you be divided into two parties about the Hypocrites? Allah hath upset them for their (evil) deeds. Would you [wish you] guide those whom Allah hath thrown out of the Way?" (4:88). This question emphasizes that it is dangerous for the Muslim community to hesitate when faced with hypocrisy.

Regarding the hypocrites in Medina, discussed in separate verses, we know for certain the Muslims were not given a directive to fight against them. The Prophet (PBUH) never fought against them and never ordered their killing. Instead, there was a different plan for dealing with them, one which tolerated them until they were, over time, naturally cast away due to their attitude and deceit. Their support was weakened by the expulsion of the Jews, who used to encourage them. The believers were very aware of their hypocrisy. The difference in the two cases is that in the one referred to in this verse, some Muslims advocated tolerance toward people living away from Medina because they claimed verbally to be Muslims while at the same time they practically supported the enemies of Islam. Hence, God's view of those people is stated clearly in verse 88: "For those whom Allah hath thrown out of the Way, never shalt they find the Way." When God adopts a certain attitude there is no way a Muslim can adopt a different one. God has cast them off because of their wickedness and bad intentions. This is followed by another reproach in verse 88: "Would you [wish you] guide those whom Allah hath thrown out of the Way?"

The next verse shows they were to be fought not due to their beliefs, but because they had joined the combatant enemy: "Except those who join a group between whom and you there is a treaty (of peace), or those who approach you with hearts restraining them from fighting you as well as fighting their own people" (4:90). This verse suggests it is possible they may not become Muslims nor join the combatant idolaters, or they may join the unbelievers whom Muslims already have a peace treaty with. In either case, Muslims cannot fight those who join a peaceful group. The criteria for fighting in Islam is defined by aggression toward Muslims. Islam is against those who initiate violence due to their acts of aggression, not due to their beliefs. This is further evident where the verse continues: "Or those who approach you with hearts restraining them from fighting you as well as fighting their own people" (4:90), which means when they declare peace, they are inclined to make peace with Muslims and their own people (but keep their own faith). In such cases, there is no reason for Muslims to fight them. Islam is tolerant with the followers of other faiths and ideologies. It does not force itself on anyone.

Non-Muslims who live in a Muslim state, under an Islamic regime, may openly state their beliefs, even if they conflict with the Islamic faith; however, the only caveat is that they not insult Islam. The Qur'an denounces hurling abuse on Islam, as followers of earlier religions had done. Islam does not allow those who live under its regime to criticize its principles in abusive terms, nor distort its facts. It protects the lives and properties of those of other faiths and who live in an Islamic society. Islam further affords them the same benefits, without discrimination, and allows them to implement the rules of their faith in all matters which have no bearing on the general system as it applies to all citizens. Any abuse or disrespect from any Muslim or Muslim nation toward followers of other faiths is not Islamic.

Islam extends tolerance to those who adopt a different faith, but it does not extend it to those who claim to be Muslims and who are aligned with the enemy that Muslims are engaged in a war with.

6.13 "Not equal are those believers who sit (at home) and receive no harm" (4:95)

> Not equal are those believers who sit (at home) not having any
> injury, and those who strive and fight in the cause of Allah
> with their goods and their lives. Allah has granted a grade
> higher to those who strive and fight with their goods and lives
> than to those who sit (at home). To each God has promised the
> ultimate good, yet God has preferred those who strive hard
> over those who sit (at home) with a special reward. (4:95)[137]

Critics claim this passage criticizes peaceful Muslims who do not wish
to join the violence; hence, they are considered less worthy in God's
eyes. The passage also rejects the claim that jihad does not mean holy
war in the Qur'an, but rather a spiritual struggle.

Jihad is a general, overarching term that means to struggle or strive
in different ways, including, but not limited to, financial or physical struggle (fight), none of which refers to holy war. As explained
in chapter 3, the term *holy war* was coined during the Crusades.
However, based on the use of *jihad* in the Qur'an and tradition, the
most important aspect of the term involves self-purification and striving to do better on the path of God. In this verse, the struggle starts
with the decision to strive on the path of God, first with possessions
and then life as it becomes necessary, so it is not purely a physical fight;
hence, the word qital for "combat" is not used. The context provides
further clarification.

The verse addresses a special case within the Muslim community
wherein some followers had demonstrated their reluctance to participate in striving for God's cause, which requires sacrifice of both
possessions and lives. This may be a reference to those who preferred
to stay at home and not migrate to Medina, so they could hold on to
their property and possessions. The unbelievers did not allow anyone
who migrated to Medina to take their wealth. They had to abandon
all of their possessions. Some may have preferred to stay at home to
spare themselves the hardships and the risks of migration. Rarely did

the unbelievers allow Muslims to migrate. In the majority of cases, they imprisoned and treated Muslims poorly, or, more accurately, they intensified their ill-treatment of them if they suspected their intentions were to leave. This is what is meant by the reference to those believers who "*sit (at home).*" It may also refer to those within the Muslim community who did not readily show their willingness to sacrifice their possessions and their lives for God's cause. This obviously excludes the hypocrites who were mentioned in the preceding passage and who tried to dissuade the Muslims from striving for God's cause. This also excludes Muslims with good intentions however with injury preventing them from participation. The description could mean both groups of people in both lands who were not ready to make the necessary sacrifices.

Although this verse addresses a special case, it is phrased to impart a general principle not restricted to a particular time or a particular community. What we have in this verse is a principle describing how God views the believers at any time or place. A distinction is made between true believers and those who remain passive, reluctant to sacrifice themselves or their possessions for God's cause despite having no obstacles, such as a disability, that would prevent them from joining the jihad and making the necessary sacrifices. They are unlike those who come forward and strive hard. In this case their reward is commensurate with their intentions and their efforts.

The principle is stated in the most general terms: "Not equal are those believers who sit (at home) not having any injury, and those who strive and fight in the cause of Allah with their goods and their lives" (verse 95). This is followed by a clarification that leaves no room whatsoever for ambiguity: "Allah has granted a grade higher to those who strive and fight with their goods and lives than to those who sit (at home or remain passive)" (4:95).

Having made a distinction between the believers who remain passive and those who strive for God's cause, this Qur'anic verse says that God has promised a great reward for both: "To each God has promised the ultimate good" (4:95). The very fact of believing in God has its value, which must not be underestimated. Nevertheless, the believers have their ranks according to their willingness to fulfil the duties of faith, especially with respect to self-sacrifice and property. This last statement tells us that those who remain passive are not the hypocrites. They are a group of good believers who have taken their positions alongside other Muslims but have been complacent with regard to this particular duty. Since they are genuine believers, they are urged to overcome their complacency and become active volunteers.

This is followed by a restatement of the original principle, which is reaffirmed here and expanded by way of encouragement to seek the great reward promised to those who strive hard: "Allah has granted a grade higher to those who strive and fight with their goods and lives than to those who sit (at home)... Ranks specially bestowed by Him, and Forgiveness and Mercy. For Allah is Oft-forgiving, Most Merciful" (4:95–96).

6.14 "If you are suffering hardships, they are suffering similar hardships" (4:104)

> And slacken not in following up the enemy: If you are
> suffering hardships, they are suffering similar hardships;
> but you have Hope from Allah, while they have none.
> And Allah is full of knowledge and wisdom. (4:104)

Some critics ask how pursuing an injured, retreating enemy could be considered a fair fight or even an act of self-defense.

Firstly, there is no mention of a retreating enemy in this verse. *"Following up"* or *"seeking out"* means setting out to meet the enemy (not slacking). Secondly, the verse talks about both sides suffering pain as a result of combat, which is obvious. Wars inflict casualties and suffering for both sides. There was violence on both sides. Even individual fighters made mistakes. Here the verse appears to be a consolation from God, but with a distinction in that the believers are promised a reward. This verse concludes with an encouraging note to the believers to continue their struggle, despite the sacrifices they are called upon to make. These simple words draw a distinctive line and reveal the great gulf that separates the two parties. A tired or weakhearted person may become complacent or careless, hence the verse reminds the strivers who endure pain on the battlefield that they are not alone in their suffering. Their enemies also suffer pain and hardship, but their state is different. The believers seek to please God and to await His reward and support. The unbelievers suffer complete loss. If the unbelievers remain steadfast in battle, the believers have all the more reason to do so. They can endure the pain more willingly and with a determined perseverance.

In every campaign of struggle, faith plays a great role. There are moments when the hardship and the pain are overpowering. It is then that an individual needs to tap into an additional source of strength. It is from faith that he or she can more easily draw such strength. This directive is given to the believers when they are engaged in an open battle, when the two sides are at parity, both have their weapons drawn, and both face the prospect of physical pain. It may happen that the believers have to engage in a battle in which their enemies enjoy superiority. This rule, however, holds true in all situations. The only way open to believers is to remain steadfast and not allow themselves to weaken. Moreover, "but you have Hope from Allah, while they have none" is to remember real consolation is found in God.

6.15 "The punishment of those who wage war against Allah and His Messenger," (5:33)

The punishment of those who wage war against Allah and
His Messenger, and strive with might and main for mischief
[corruption] through the land is: execution, or crucifixion,
or the cutting off of hands and feet from opposite sides, or
exile from the land: that is their disgrace in this world, and
a heavy punishment is theirs in the Hereafter. (5:33)

This verse and the following lay down the punishment for a particular crime that wicked adversaries commit. This is known in the Islamic punitive legal code as the punishment for waging war (with arms) against Islam, Muslims, their lives, possessions, and society as a whole. In the Qur'an, corruption or mischief on earth means destroying lives and property. The crime to which this legislative statement refers to involves rebellion against a true Muslim ruler from within the nation or society, not a war waged by an outside enemy. Of course, we are referring to a true Muslim nation, not the Muslim lands of today with so-called Muslim leaders and governments. In other words, a despotic ruler who claims to be Muslim cannot use this verse to suppress people's voices and those defending the rights of people in the land protesting unjust and corrupt rule. In a situation where rebels gather to renounce the authority of a true Muslim ruler, they cause fear within the Muslim community and commit aggressions against the people and their property. Such rebels do not merely fight the ruler or the community, but they make war on God and His Messenger (PBUH), since they fight God's given law, wage an assault against the community, and threaten the land. In doing so, they also spread corruption.

It is hard to imagine how there could be such rebels in a true Islamic society or nation where liberty and justice exist, and citizens enjoy God-given freedoms under a government ruled by God-fearing people for the people of all races, ethnicities, and faiths within that nation. History has shown it can happen. According to reports, a group from the A'rina tribe came to the Prophet (PBUH) and accepted Islam. They later fell sick, so the Prophet (PBUH) sent them to a place with comfortable accommodations where they could relax and be taken care of by the local camel herders until their recovery. Once they recovered, they renounced Islam, killed the camel herders in a horrible way, and stole their camels. They continued their mischief by ambushing visitors on the roads, killing their men, raping their women, and stealing their possessions. It was due to such corruption that the above injunction was issued by God[138]. In the case of rebels, the Qur'anic statement also signifies that the ruler entitled to enforce these punishments against those who rebel against him is the ruler who is actually God-conscious himself and implements God's directives in the Muslim land.

Let us consider a situation in which an armed group rebels against the authority of a Muslim ruler who has implemented these Islamic directives. The rebels threaten the lives and properties of Muslims living in a Muslim land. The punishment for those who join such a group is commensurate with their crimes and can range from exile to execution. Furthermore, these laws are designed to deter any future unjustifiable acts of rebellion; however, scholars have widely different views on whether a Muslim ruler has the right to choose any of these punishments or whether each punishment is implemented in a particular case. Implementation of these punishments or alternative forms (based on the situation and circumstance) gives a Muslim ruler the right to take preventive and deterrent measures to allay any future rebellion. Those who threaten the security of a Muslim community thus face a stern punishment because the Muslim community deserves to live in peace and security.

Scholars also differ in their understanding of what is meant by banishing the rebels, and whether they should be removed from the land where they committed their crimes or from the land where they have their freedom. In the latter sense, they are imprisoned.

Verse 33, which states "that is their disgrace in this world, and a heavy punishment is theirs in the Hereafter," means that their punishment in this life does not waive the punishment in the hereafter, as is the case with certain other crimes. This emphasizes the gravity of the crime and doubles its punishment, the reason being that the Muslim community should be able to live in peace and security in the land of Islam and that a true Muslim ruler should be obeyed. Such a social setup and such a just and perfect system deserves to be protected against any attempts to undermine it. If the rebels realize their mistake and turn to God in repentance when they still have their strength, then their punishment is waived and the Muslim ruler has no way of punishing them. God will forgive them eventually: "Except for those who repent before they fall into your power: in that case, know that Allah is Oft-forgiving, Most Merciful" (5:34).

The wisdom behind discounting the crime and waiving punishment in this case is clear. For one thing, it is an appreciation of their repentance when they still have their power. It is taken as evidence of their good intentions. For another, they are encouraged to repent so that the Muslim nation is spared the need to fight them.

6.16 "I will instill (cast) terror into the hearts of the Unbelievers" (8:12)

> Remember your Lord inspired the angels (with the message): "I am with you: give firmness to the Believers: I will instill[cast] terror into the hearts of the Unbelievers: smite you above their necks and smite all their finger-tips off them". (8:12)

Some critics say that the verse is not referring to spiritual struggle. As defined in the next verse, the targets of violence are unbelievers, further defined as those who contend against Allah.

First of all, the critics conveniently removed the beginning of the verse that says "Remember your Lord inspired the angels (with the message): I am with you: give firmness to the Believers." Again, this relates to the Battle of Badr (see section 6.3.3), and there is neither mention of the word *jihad*, nor the order for soldiers (believers) "to strike, and cast terror"—both of which refer to the presence of angels. There are numerous detailed reports that mention angels who came to support the Muslims on the day of the Battle of Badr; the number of angels, their part in the battle, their words of reassurance to the believers, and what they said to dishearten the unbelievers. Earlier verses 9–10 say, "Remember you implored the assistance of your Lord, and He answered you: 'I will assist you with a thousand of the angels, ranks on ranks,'" which reveals the number of angels who came to assist. And, "Allah made it as good news and an assurance to your hearts: (in any case) there is no help except from Allah." God inspired the angels to encourage the believers and promised to strike fear in the hearts of the unbelievers. He also commanded the angels to take an active part in the battle: "Remember your Lord inspired the angels (with the message): 'I am with you: give firmness to the Believers. I will cast terror into the hearts of the Unbelievers. Smite you their necks and smite all their finger-tips off them'" (verse 12).

Such was the task assigned to angels, not to the Muslim fighters. The term *wahy* (inspiration) means quick and secret announcement (to angels in this case). The message was "I am with you: give firmness to the Believers" which means with My support aid the believers and strengthen their resolve against their enemy.

We should keep in mind that God did not abandon the Muslim community to their own devices on that day, when they were much inferior in number to their enemies. Muslims believe that among God's creation is a type called the angels. We know of their nature only by what God, their Creator, has told us. We cannot fathom exactly how they participated in the Muslim victory at Badr, except in as far as the Qur'an tells us. Their Lord inspired them by saying that He was with them and commanded them to encourage the believers. The angels complied because they always do what they are commanded. We, however, do not know how they fulfilled this task. We learn that angels are tasked not only to bring revelations to the prophets (PBUT), but to inspire and encourage others to stand firm, as they did here in preparation to face the enemy. Knowledge of all this is merely a detail of knowing the nature of angels, which we know only by what God has chosen to tell us. Furthermore, God promised to strike terror in the hearts of the unbelievers, and this was certainly the case because God always fulfills His promises.

At the end of verse 13, we have a statement clarifying the reality beyond the battle and the rule that shapes events to bring about victory or defeat: "This is because they have contended against Allah and His Messenger. If any contend against Allah and His Messenger, Allah is strict in punishment." It is not by mere coincidence that God has granted support to the Muslim army and has stricken terror into the hearts of its enemies and commanded the angels to fight them in support of Muslims. This verse follows verse 12 regarding the aggressors who faced the Muslims. In general, it refers to those who defy God and all His messengers and who will eventually receive God's retribution for their evil deeds.

This is in the context of war, and yes, the instruction was given to defend against those who disbelieve. Critics, however, twist the words to make it sound as if the disbelievers defy and disobey God, thus permitting believers the right to pull them out of their homes and strike their necks. But the order is to the angels and not to the Muslim fighters. Furthermore, the context is a battle, not during a period of peace. (The rights of unbelievers are discussed in chapter 3.)

6.17 "When you meet the Unbelievers in hostile array, never turn your backs" (8:15–16)

> O you who believe! when you meet the Unbelievers in hostile array [marching for battle], never turn your backs to them If any do turn his back to them on such a day - unless it be in a stratagem [maneuvering] of war, or to retreat to a troop (of his own)- he draws on himself the wrath of Allah, and his abode is Hell,- an evil refuge (indeed). (8:15–16)

Although few, if any, critics have commented on this verse, we want to comment further. This verse relates to the same context as mentioned in the previous section. The decisive victory in the Battle of Badr has been attributed to the following factors: God's planning and support, and the believers' reliance on Him alone and their acceptance of whatever eventuality He determines. The believers are given an order to remain firm whenever they meet unbelievers in battle. They must never run away, since victory or defeat are determined by God's will and the various factors contributing to either scenario is different from human perception.

These verses begin with a strong warning. Should the believers face their enemies who may in essence present themselves in a great show of power, they must not, under any circumstances, turn away, except for tactical reasons. These might include choosing a better position, carrying out a more effective plan, joining another group of believers, or moving to another Muslim stronghold in order to resume the fight. Deserters and those who turn away in flight deserve the worst punishment for incurring God's wrath. Some scholars have expressed the view that this ruling applies only to those involved in the Battle of Badr or to a battle in which the Prophet (PBUH) himself took part. But the overwhelming majority of scholars have emphasized its general application. They consider fleeing from battle as one of the gravest sins, because when a Muslim enters a battle based on his faith and then turns away, leaving his fellow soldiers, he has in fact rejected his faith. This implies a limited worldly life is more important to him than the truth—the hereafter and God's glad tidings, and the lives of his brothers in faith. This is why God reaffirms in the next verse "If any do turn his back to them on such a day - unless it be in a stratagem [maneuvering] of war, or in an endeavor to join another troop - he shall incur the wrath of Allah, and his abode is Hell, an evil refuge (indeed)" (8:16). In other words, for the one who claims God and His pleasure is above everything else in life, when faced with a situation where he must choose between this life and the hereafter, and he chooses this life, it then becomes clear how his belief ranks. However, the verse mentions a few exceptions in which turning away is part of strategic maneuvering and is allowed.

6.18 "And fight them on until there is no more tumult or oppression" (8:39)

And fight them on until there is no more tumult or oppression, and there prevail justice and faith in Allah altogether and everywhere; but if they cease, verily Allah doth see all that they do. (8:39)

While this verse is self-explanatory, a critic of Islam insists there is an aspect of violence and force in all of these verses and claims that some translations interpret *fitna* as persecution or oppression; however, the traditional understanding of this word is not supported by the historical context. The critic adds that Meccans were refusing Muhammad (PBUH) access to their city during Hajj, while other Muslims were allowed to visit—just not as an armed group, because Muhammad had declared war on Mecca prior to his eviction. He then says that Meccans acted in defense of their religion because it was Muhammad's intention to destroy their idols and establish Islam by force, which he did later. Hence, the critical part of this verse is to fight until *"religion is only for Allah"* (as translated by some), meaning that Muslims' justification for violence was the unbelief (or disbelief) by the opposition.[139]

Firstly, verse 8:39 follows what was said in verse 8:38 (and "them" refers specifically to disbelievers mentioned), which is the following: "Say to disbelievers that if they cease (from persecution of believers) that which is past will be forgiven; but if they persist the punishment of those before them is already (a matter of warning for them),"[140] which means the path to reform and the return to God from past crimes is open. However, if they persist in wrongdoing, a fate similar to that of their predecessors will draw near to them, which is affirmed in the next verse addressing Muslim fighters with combative idolaters: "And fight them on until there is no more tumult or oppression, and there prevail justice and faith in Allah altogether and everywhere; but if they cease, verily Allah doth see all that they do" (8:39). Fight them (referring to idolaters mentioned in verse 38) until their persecution is ended. Here, persecution means by force using the sword to turn Muslims away from their faith. "And there prevail justice and faith in Allah altogether and everywhere" means creation of an environment where there is freedom of faith to practice one's faith, the obstacles to truth are removed, and a monotheistic faith prevails. Obviously, if provocation of the enemy were removed, meaning coercion to idolatry was eliminated, monotheism *would* prevail. However, as we see, some either misunderstand or purposely misrepresent this verse to mean forcing others to accept Islam. Of course, under such a situation hypocrisy would prevail, not the religion of God. Furthermore, as indicated earlier, such a directive would be in contradiction with the higher goals and aim of Islam and verses such as 4:90, 2:256, 60:8. From an Islamic perspective, Muslims fight only those who are armed, who commit aggressions against them, or who have prevented them from believing in one God and practicing their faith (see sections 6.4 and 6.5).

Secondly, we already responded to one critic's confusion over verse 2:193. Regarding this critic's comment, "the Meccans were refusing

Muhammad access to their city during Hajj (pilgrimage) and other Muslims were allowed to travel there—just not as an armed group", when Muhammad (PBUH), for the first time (after his forced migration), arrived and camped outside Mecca for his pilgrimage, neither he nor his companions were armed for war (aside from a few swords required to protect the caravan). They even declared their intention to the Meccan idolaters. Since they still were not allowed to visit the house of God, they returned to Medina. This is when the Treaty of Hudaybiyyah was signed, and according to this treaty, Muslims and the Prophet (PBUH) would be allowed to return for Hajj in four years, but within two years Meccans broke the treaty. Furthermore, during this time, Muslims in Mecca were still boycotted and persecuted. How could they then allow Muslims (not the Prophet (PBUH)) for Hajj? Why did they not allow Muslims who accompanied the Prophet (PBUH) to complete their pilgrimage if they did not have any issues with unarmed Muslims? Due to persecution, Muslims were forced to secretly escape from Mecca up until the conquest of Mecca. How could they then be allowed to travel to Mecca? The critic seems to be making statements that are in denial and that contradict historical facts. If the Meccans were forced to accept Islam, why didn't they later revert to "their religion" when he and his successors were no longer present? Was there any violence when the Prophet (PBUH) and Muslims conquered Mecca? Has this critic read about general amnesty given by the Prophet (PBUH) to all people of Mecca (including the idolaters who persecuted Muslims for many years)? For a quick review of the Treaty of Hudaybiyyah, see chapter 3.

6.19   "Against them make ready whatever force and war mounts you can muster" (8:59–60)

Let not the unbelievers think that they can get the better (of the godly). They will never escape (be beyond) (God's) grasp. Against them make ready whatever force and war mounts you can muster, strike terror into (the hearts) of the enemies of Allah and your own enemies. (8:59–60)[141]

Some critics assert this verse commands and encourages Muslims to be ready to fight as much as possible and can be afforded.

Again, the historical context and to whom this verse applies cannot be ignored, not to mention the verses that follow. Verses 8:55–63, at the beginning of the passage, deal primarily with a real situation that the Muslim community had to come to grips with when the first Muslim state was established in Medina. These verses provided the Islamic leadership with guidance and rules to apply in dealing with that particular situation. They represent a basic element in the international relations between the Muslim community and other groups.

These verses illustrate that it is perfectly appropriate to conclude agreements of peaceful coexistence with other communities and groups, as long as such agreements are to be taken seriously, respected, and honored. If the other camp manipulates these agreements and uses them as a shield to cover up treacherous intentions, taking steps to launch an assault against the Muslims, then the Muslim leadership is fully entitled to terminate these agreements and make the other side fully aware of that termination. On the other hand, those who are interested in genuine peace with the Muslims and who have no intention of opposing their message or stopping its advocacy and who demonstrate an inclination toward peace, may enjoy a peaceful relationship.

All of this was clearly meant to deal with real situations that affected relationships between the Muslim state and neighboring camps. When the Muslim state enjoys security and has no physical impediments to its task of peacefully conveying God's message to people everywhere, it then has no reason to refuse peaceful coexistence. At the same time, it does not allow for peace agreements to be used as a cover-up for intended treachery.

At that point in history, the unbelievers were divided into three categories with regard to their relationship with the Prophet (PBUH) and the Muslims. In the first category were those with whom he concluded a peace treaty. The second category included those who were at war with the Prophet (PBUH), while the third were those who had submitted to his authority and were under his protection.

The Prophet (PBUH) was ordered to fulfill his obligations under any peace treaty as long as the other party fulfilled their obligations. Should he fear that they may resort to treachery, he should give them notice of the termination of their treaty. He must not fight them until he had informed them of such termination.

We should remember that these regulations were revealed at a time when the whole of humanity could not have aspired to such a high ideal. The law of the jungle prevailed, which meant the powerful could use their power without restraint. The same law of the jungle continued to dominate in all ignorant communities until the eighteenth century. Europe had no concept of international codes and laws except for what it learned through its dealings with the Muslim world.

The verse before says "If you fear treachery from any group, throw back (their covenant) to them, (so as to be) on equal terms: for Allah loves not the treacherous" (8:58). The term *fear* comes with an emphasis that if you have reason to believe their treachery, then you can announce the dissolution of the treaty. Being true to the treaty has been emphasized in the Qur'an (5:1), given the other side is also true to the agreement. This verse emphasizes that first it should be announced before dissolution takes place.

In return for such clear honesty, God promises victory to the Muslims and He tells them that the unbelievers have no real power: "Let not the unbelievers think that they can get the better (of the godly). They will never be beyond (God's) grasp" (8:59). Their treachery will not enable them to take the lead and outstrip the Muslims, because God will not abandon the Muslims or allow the traitors to triumph. The unbelievers are too weak to escape from God when He moves against them. Nor can they escape from the Muslims when God is supporting them. Elsewhere the Qur'an says, "Do those who practice evil think that they will get the better of Us? Evil is their judgment!" (29:4) and "know that you cannot frustrate (escape) Allah and that Allah will bring disgrace to the disbelievers" (9:2).[142]

Believers' efforts aim to liberate humanity from the worship of creatures so that only the Creator is worshiped. Islam, however, sets out to make real preparations that are within the capability of the Muslims so that victory becomes achievable. It does not raise the sights of the Muslim community toward that sublime horizon without making sure it has firm ground upon which to stand. Islam also makes sure the Muslim community is well prepared for its practical tasks: "Against them make ready whatever force and war mounts you can muster, strike fear into (the hearts) of Allah's enemies and your enemies and others besides, whom you may not know, but whom Allah does know. Whatever you shall spend in the cause of Allah, shall be repaid unto you, and you shall not be treated unjustly" (8:60).[143]

The terms *"force"* and *"war mounts"* imply that Muslims must always be well prepared and ready to face aggressors. Regarding the context and the time of the revelation of this verse, it refers to Muslims who were outnumbered and ill equipped during the Battle of Badr; however, the directive here is for them to be better prepared for the next encounter. The second part of the verse points out that being well prepared does not necessarily mean to engage in a fight, but rather to be a deterrent to those who might commit aggression against them.

The first objective is to get all the forces ready to establish peace and security for those who have chosen to accept the Islamic faith so that they do not suffer any persecution as a result of their choice. Secondly, it deters the enemies of Islam from contemplating aggression against the Muslim land. In other words, the Muslim state must always surrender to truth and justice, but at the same time be strong and prepared to defend itself. In the third part of the verse, the Qur'an says, "and others besides, whom you may not know, but whom Allah does know," meaning Muslims must be prepared to face any enemy, not just those whom they have identified due to present or past confrontations; there may be others they are unaware of, but God knows. In the case of early Muslims, they were to be prepared not just for the combatant idolaters and some Jewish tribes (as known enemies), but for any other foe that may come along. This applies to Muslims at any point in time or place.

Acquiring such forces and having them ready can only be done if the resources are available. Since the Islamic system stresses collective responsibility and mutual support, the duty of jihad goes hand in hand with the duty of spending money for God's cause: "Whatever you may spend in God's cause shall be repaid to you in full, and you shall not be wronged" (60).

Whatever investment members of Muslim nations make to defend their God-given rights will not go to waste, and it will protect them against any aggression. Thus, right at the outset, Islam rules out any war undertaken for the glory of individuals and states. It rejects all campaigns that seek to exploit resources and open markets or to subjugate and humiliate other communities. Islam has nothing to do with any war that tries to establish the superiority of one class, race, nation, or state over another. The only type of campaign that Islam approves of is one undertaken for God's cause. The recognition of His sovereignty and submission to Him alone brings honor, freedom, goodness, and blessings to all mankind.

The third ruling in this passage, which cannot be missed, concerns those who wish to live in peace with the Muslim community. The ruling specifies that they be genuine in their desire—in word and action—and have a friendly and peaceful relationship with Muslims. The Prophet (PBUH) is instructed "But if the enemy incline towards peace, do you (also) incline towards peace, and trust in Allah: for He is One that hears and knows (all things)" (8:61). Islam is in peace with the peaceful.

In verse 61, the use of the word *"incline"* is very apt, as it gives connotations of a gentle attitude, one who prefers peace and friendly relations. The instruction to be inclined toward peace is coupled with placing trust in God—He who hears and knows everything and is aware of all that is harbored behind words and appearances. That is, even if someone tends toward deceit, Muslims are still instructed to be inclined toward peace, because placing their trust in God is sufficient for ensuring protection and security, as the next verse indicates: "Should they intend to deceive you, then indeed Allah is Sufficient for you. It is He who has strengthened you with His aid and with (the company of) the Believers" (8:62).[144]

6.20 "O Prophet! rouse [urge] the believers to fight" (8:64-65)

> O Prophet! sufficient unto you is Allah,- (unto you) and unto
> those who follow you among the Believers. O' Prophet! rouse
> [urge] the believers to fight If there are twenty amongst you,
> patient and persevering, they will vanquish two hundred: if
> a hundred, they will vanquish a thousand of the Unbelievers:
> for these are a people without understanding. (8:64-65)

These verses continue the discussion from the previous section and include the context of verses 59–60. The passage reassures the Prophet (PBUH) and the Muslim community yet again that God is on their side. The Prophet (PBUH) is also instructed to encourage the believers to fight for God's cause, for they are equal to a force that outnumbers them by ten to one. It is a reminder that believers are always ready to face oppressors. Even at their weakest, the believers are more than a match for twice their number.

We can contemplate the difference between God's invincible, overwhelming power and the small force that tries to suppress the truth and the divine message. The difference is too large to allow any meaningful comparison. Hence, the outcome of the battle is a foregone conclusion, as the following verse implies: "O Prophet! sufficient unto you is Allah,- (unto you) and unto those who follow you among the Believers" (64). Following earlier verses that directed Muslims to be well prepared and well equipped, an order is given to the Prophet (PBUH) to urge the believers to fight for God's cause, now that every soul is ready for the engagement: "O' Prophet! rouse [urge] the believers to fight" (65). It is an opportunity to serve God and the truth. Rouse them to arms, for they are a match for their enemies, even though they may be inferior in number: "If there are twenty amongst you, patient and persevering, they will vanquish two hundred: if a hundred, they will vanquish a thousand of the Unbelievers" (65). Armed with faith, each fighter equipped with the power of belief is equivalent to ten unbelieving fighters who have narrow worldly views and desires. The reason for such a great difference in real power comes as a surprise, but it is true and incisive: "For these are the people without understanding" (65).

So what is the link between understanding and victory? There may seem to be very little on the surface, but the link is real and strong. The believers are distinguished by the fact that they know their way, which they have chosen, after deep thought. They understand the course they follow in this life, and they are well aware of the purpose of their existence. Their mission is to struggle for God's cause, build a humane civilization, and establish the rule of justice among all people. All of this understanding pours enlightenment, confidence, strength, and reassurance into the believers' hearts. They are then motivated to go into their campaigns of struggle with certainty of the outcome. Their enemies, on the other hand, are devoid of understanding. Their hearts are sealed, and their eyes are blinded by worldly desires. Their forces are without power, although they may appear to be superior. That is because their link to the source of real power has been severed.

It is important to note the Prophet (PBUH) is ordered to "rouse" or urge the believers to go to the battle, but not to institute a draft. The reason for urging them to fight is explained in earlier verses. Muslim fighters volunteer to engage in battle in order to seek God's pleasure and to strive in the path of God. As such, in early days, they provided their own arms, mounts, and provisions. Often those who wished to join but could not afford the expense were left behind, regretting the lost opportunity.

6.21   "Fight them, Allah will punish them by your hands" (9:14)

> Fight them, Allah will punish them by your hands, and will
> bring them disgrace; and will help you (to victory) over
> them and will heal the hearts of the believers. (9:14)[145]

Some critics claim this verse advocates humiliating and killing disbelievers, which has the approval and blessings of Allah, and by "punish them by your hands" it means killing them, which also heals the hearts of Muslims.

This is another example of critics who cherry-pick a verse and take it out of context. The earlier verses in the passage explain the context, which is about the very principle of a treaty or a covenant being granted to the idolaters by God and His Messenger (PBUH):

> And if they violate their oaths after their covenant, and revile your religion, then fight the chiefs of disbelief – for their oaths are nothing to them – in order that they may desist. Will you not fight against people who have broken their solemn pledges and plotted to expel the Messenger, and who were the first to attack you? Do you fear them? Nay, it is Allah whom you should justly fear, if you are true believers. Fight them, Allah will punish them by your hands, and will bring them disgrace; and will help you (to victory) over them and will heal the hearts of the believers, removing all angry feelings from their hearts. God will turn in His mercy to whom He wills. Allah is All-knowing, All-Wise.[146] (9:12–15)

Verses 12–13 set up the context: The fighting idolaters were given the choice to either accept Islam based on submission to God alone or to fight, *except* for the person who seeks refuge with the Muslims but keeps his own faith. Such a person was given shelter and invited to listen to God's revelations before he was escorted to his place of security. The reason for questioning the principle itself was that the idolaters would never respect any agreement or obligation of honor with regard to any believer once they prevailed over the Muslims.

They reneged on their treaty, as their leaders encouraged and provoked them to do so. The Prophet (PBUH) was instructed to face them first in order to stop their aggression. On the other hand, the idolaters taunted and reviled the Islamic faith as they breached their agreement.

These verses were revealed at a time when most likely the Muslim population increased. The Qur'an addresses all the feelings and fears of some Muslims by reminding them of their experiences with the idolaters' attitudes and their treaties with the believers. It reminds them of when the idolaters tried to expel God's Messenger (PBUH) from Mecca before he left to settle in Medina. It also reminds them that it was the idolaters who were the aggressors when they first attacked the Muslims in Medina. It then arouses their sense of shame should they fear confronting the idolaters on the battlefield. If true believers, they should fear God alone.

"Will you not fight against people who have broken their solemn pledges and plotted to expel the Messenger, and who were the first to attack you? Do you fear them? Nay, it is Allah whom you should justly fear, if you are true believers" (9:13). The entire history between the idolaters and the believers was characterized by the violation of solemn pledges and agreements. The most recent historical example was the violation of the peace treaty concluded at Hudaybiyyah. Acting on instructions from his Lord, the Prophet (PBUH) accepted their conditions, which were felt by some of his best companions to be unfair to the Muslims. He fulfilled his obligations under that agreement as meticulously as possible. For their part, the idolaters did not respect their agreement, nor did they fulfill their obligations. Within two years, and at the first opportunity, they committed a flagrant breach of their obligations by extending active support to their allies who launched a treacherous attack against the Prophet's (PBUH) allies. Muslims from Banu Khuza'a were slaughtered by supporters of the Bani Bakr and the Quraysh.

Moreover, the idolaters had tried to expel the Prophet (PBUH) from Mecca and were determined to kill him. This was before he migrated to Medina. It was in the Sacred Mosque, the inviolable house of worship, where even a murderer was sure to be unharmed. In the case of Muhammad (PBUH), they did not respect even that obligation of honor.

It was also the idolaters who tried to fight the Muslims in Medina. Under Abu Jahl's leadership, they insisted on fighting the Muslims even though the Prophet (PBUH) made every attempt to dissuade them. They went on the offensive in the Battles of Uhud and the Trench, and they mobilized other tribes against the believers in the Battle of Hunayn. All these encounters and events were still fresh in the memories of the believers. They all confirm the persistent attitude of the idolaters, which is described by God in the Qur'an: "They shall not cease to fight you until they force you to renounce your faith, if they can" (2: 217). This is clear in the nature of the relationship between the camp that worships all sorts of deities and the one that worships God alone.

With their feelings so heightened, they are encouraged to fight the idolaters and are promised victory over them: "Fight them, God will punish them by your hands, and will bring disgrace upon them; and will help you (to victory) over them and will heal the hearts of the believers, removing all angry feelings from their hearts" (9:14–15).

In essence, this verse told the believers the following: When you fight them, God will bring about their punishment by your hands, causing them to be defeated after they have arrogantly demonstrated their power. With the victory He will grant you, God will make the believers who had been at the receiving end of the idolaters' repression and persecution happy. This happiness will come about as a result of the complete victory of the truth and the defeat of falsehood (and injustice) and its advocates. Some commentators have said the verse applied to group of Muslims from Banu Khuza'a who were murdered by Quraysh and Bani Bakr clans after the treaty of Hudaybiyyah.

But that was not all. There would be more good news and rewards: "God will turn in His mercy to whom He wills" (15). When the Muslims achieved their victory, some of the idolaters opened their hearts to the truth. They were able to recognize that this victory was achieved through the help of a power superior to all that human beings can muster. What was the outcome in the end? The Muslims were victorious and forgave the Meccans as they entered Mecca. They entered peacefully without any harm to anyone. All past infractions were forgiven, and their exemplary conduct won the hearts of the Meccans and the surrounding tribes, as they all eventually embraced Islam. Forgiveness from a position of power has a greater impact than from a position of defeat.

6.22 "And suffer exile and strive with might and main, in Allah's cause" (9:20)

> Those who believe, and suffer exile and strive with might
> and main, in Allah's cause, with their goods and their
> persons [lives], have the highest rank in the sight of Allah:
> they are the people who will achieve (salvation). (9:20)

Some critics comment that in this verse the term *strive* is from the same root as jihad, hence another example of holy war.

Since the meaning of jihad ("to strive") was discussed in chapter 3, suffice it to say that it is a general term, especially if one reads this verse even by itself. Jihad can be applied to many things. For example, one can offer his property or life (in a noncombative or combative situation), as the verse says to strive hard with their property and life. Critics, however, want to force and limit the meaning to a strictly physical fight and label it "holy war," a term that neither exists in the Qur'an, nor in Arabic language texts, as discussed in chapter 3.

This verse simply refers to true believers (like the Emigrants and Helpers), who proved their loyalty and commitment through sacrificing and striving for their beliefs, not the glitter of this world. In other words, the good deeds are the result of true belief.

6.23 "Fight against those who . . . believe not in Allah nor the Last Day" (9:29)

> Fight against those who — despite having been given
> earlier Scriptures —believe not in Allah nor the Last
> Day, and do not consider as forbidden that which Allah
> and His Messenger have forbidden, and do not follow
> the religion of truth, till they pay the Jizya (tribute) with
> willing hand, after they have been humbled. (9:29)[147]

Some critics have said that according to this verse, People of the Book or people of earlier scripture (Christians and Jews) are to be subjugated, for the sole reason of being non-Muslims. Some have said this is an open-ended command to fight them.

This second passage of chapter 9 provides the final rulings concerning relations between the Muslim community and the people of earlier revelations, just as the first passage defined the final rulings on relations between the Muslim community and the idolaters in Arabia. However, the first passage addressed the situation that prevailed at the time in Arabia regarding the Arab idolaters and their attitudes and events related specifically to them. The second passage is more general and applicable to all people of earlier revelations at the time.

By the time this passage was revealed, most encounters with internal enemies and military conflicts with the Jews had already taken place, but no such conflict took place with any Christian communities. According to some reports, by this time most people of earlier revelations within Arabia had accepted the Muslims' central rule, hence there were no internal conflicts. As such, the revelation may refer to enemies along the Muslim community's borders. The verse was directed to People of the Book who did not truly believe in God and the hereafter and never consciously practiced what was permitted or forbidden. They neither joined the Muslim community nor followed their own faith's directives, and only understood wealth, power, and conquests. They often attacked the Muslim community.

No peace agreement could be made with them except on this basis of submission, which would be evident by the payment of a special tax which gives them the right to live in peace with the Muslims (see chapter 3 for details on jizya). On the other hand, if they become convinced of the truth of Islam and accept it, they are considered part of the Muslim community, which then requires them to pay zakat (dues for the poor) as part of their worship. Never will they be forced to accept the Islamic faith. A basic Islamic tenet states: "Let there be no compulsion in religion" (2:256). But they are not given a peaceful status unless they are bound by a covenant with the Muslim community.

The attitude of the people of earlier revelations (People of the Book) toward the Muslims is stated several times in the Qur'an. On certain occasions, God speaks of them alone, while on others, He groups them with the unbelievers, where the two groups are united in their attitudes toward Islam and the Muslim community. At times, the Qur'an speaks of certain positions taken that exposed their bias against Muslims. Of course, the context refers to those with hostile attitudes toward Muslims, not those who believed in peaceful coexistence (hence the words like "among," "group of," and "party of," are used to separate them); therefore, there is no open-ended command toward any or all People of the Book.

The following Qur'anic statements themselves are too clear and decisive to require further comment:

It is never the wish of those without Faith among the People of the Book, nor of the Pagans [idolaters], that anything good should come down to you from your Lord (2:105).

Many among the People of the Book wish they could Turn you (Muslims) back to unbelief after you have believed from selfish envy, after the Truth has become Manifest unto them (2:109).[148]

It is the wish of a section of the People of the Book to lead you astray. But they shall lead astray (Not you), but themselves, and they do not perceive! (3:69).

A section of the People of the Book say: "Believe in the morning what is revealed to the believers, but reject it at the end of the day; perchance they may (themselves) Turn back; (3:72).

Have you not turned your sight to those who were given a portion of the Book? they barter it away for error, and wish that you should lose the right path? But Allah has full knowledge of your enemies (4:44–45).[149]

These examples illustrate the attitude of some of the people of earlier revelations toward Muslims and defines their attitude by insisting they become Jewish or Christian. They would not enter into true peace with them unless the believers abandoned their faith altogether. As a result, they conspired multiple times with the idolaters and others during the Prophet's (PBUH) time and later. They went as far as testifying to the idolaters that their idolatry was better guided than Islam (see "Were All Battles Defensive?" in chapter 6). "Never will the Jews or the Christians be satisfied with thee unless thou follow their form of religion" (2:120).

6.24 A Deeper Look at History

In early Muslim history, some of the Jews repeatedly violated their treaties with the Muslim state in Medina and schemed against the Muslims. These violations led to conflicts with the Jewish tribes of Banu Qaynuqa, Banu Nadir, and Banu Qurayza, and included the Battle of Khaybar. Their efforts to bring together all the forces hostile to Muslims in an unholy alliance, with the aim of exterminating Islam altogether, are well known.

Other people of earlier revelations, the Christians, have been no less hostile. Enmity between the Byzantines (Christians) and the Persians goes back centuries. Nevertheless, as soon as the church felt that Islam, the new faith, represented a threat to its version of Christianity, the Byzantines and Persians buried their age-old hatred to confront the new faith together.

The Byzantines and their allied Arab regime of Ghassanid started to gather forces to fight Islam and its followers. They killed the Prophet's emissary, at a time when emissaries were traditionally given full protection. As a result, when the Prophet (PBUH) sent a small force of three thousand to stop the provocation, an army that included, according to historical reports, a hundred thousand Byzantines and Christian Arabs under their rule, confronted them. This was the Battle of Mu'tah, which took place in the year 629 CE, in which three Muslim commanders—Zayd ibn Haritha, Ja'far ibn Abi Talib, and Abdullah ibn Rawahah—fell, leaving the Muslims defeated. The Muslim army's expedition to Tabuk followed, which is the major subject of this chapter section. The news of Byzantine forces mobilizing in Syria reached the Muslims as both armies prepared to meet in Tabuk; however, when the Muslims reached Tabuk, they did not encounter any army, so the Prophet (PBUH) instead signed a peace treaty with Banu Ghassan. When the Byzantine emperor Heraclius heard this news, he grew furious and ordered the deaths of some of the Ghassan tribe's leaders. This event was followed in the year 636 CE by the march of the Muslim army, led by Usamah ibn Zayd, who faced the Byzantine forces in Yarmuk, along what today are the borders of Syria–Jordan and Syria–Israel. This became known as the Battle of Yarmuk, where Muslims achieved a great victory and ended Byzantine rule in Syria.

The religious campaigns of the Crusades have been well documented, but the battles mentioned above were much earlier campaigns. They started when the Byzantines and Persians mended their longtime hostilities and joined forces to fight the Muslims in present-day northern Arabia and Jordan. This animosity was at its most brutal when European forces, motivated by the Crusaders' zeal, swept through the Islamic base in Spain and committed some of the worst atrocities in history. The same sort of hatred and violence carried out during the Crusades was also on display in these earlier campaigns against Muslims.

Gustav Le Bon, a French Christian author who wrote *The World of Islamic Civilization*, refers to the compassionate treatment Muslims extended to their enemies. He states that during the Crusades, the first thing King Richard I of England (also known as Richard the Lionhearted) did was kill three thousand Muslim prisoners after he had pledged to spare them. His soldiers then continued to kill and loot. This angered Salahuddin Yusuf ibn Ayyub (the first Sultan of Egypt and Syria), who had exercised noble and compassionate treatment of the Christians in Jerusalem and even sent provisions to King Philip II of France and King Richard when they were ill.[150]

Another Christian writer, quoted in Arabic sources, says the Crusaders made a brutal start during their march into Jerusalem. A group of Christian pilgrims killed those whom they found in the palaces that fell to them. They demonstrated their brutality by opening their victims' stomachs to look for any gold that they might have swallowed. In contrast, when Salahuddin conquered Jerusalem, he granted security to the Crusaders and fulfilled all his pledges to them. The Muslims showed their defeated enemies unparalleled magnanimity. King al-Adil, Salahuddin's brother, freed one thousand prisoners and ensured the safety of all the Armenians. He allowed the patriarch to carry the cross and any other church ornaments. The queen and the princesses were also allowed to visit their husbands.

A proper examination of the long history of Christian hostilities toward Muslims around the world is beyond the scope of this text. We will only say, however, that the hostilities continued. To describe the Christians' antagonistic view of Islam, European author George Brown wrote the following in 1944:

> We used to be warned against dangers posed by different nations, but experience has shown that there is no cause for worry. We were warned against the Jewish threat and the threat of the yellow races and the Bolshevik threat. But none of these warnings has come true. We have found the Jews to be very good friends, which means that anyone who persecutes them is our enemy. We have also found out that the Bolsheviks are our allies. The yellow races are being taken care of by powerful democracies. The only real threat is that of Islam because of its dynamism and ability to spread and attract new followers. It is the only real obstacle that stands up to Western imperialism.[151]

There have been hostilities and genocides against Muslims in recent years in Bosnia and Myanmar. Brown's remarks should be sufficient and further details on these hostilities may be sought elsewhere.

Today, opponents of Islam continue spreading their venom, as Edward Said, a professor at Columbia University explains: "What matters to 'experts' like Judith Miller, Samuel Huntington, Martin

Kramer, Bernard Lewis, Daniel Pipes, Steven Emerson, and Barry Rubin, plus a whole battery of Israeli academics, is to make sure that that the 'threat' [of Islam] is kept before our eyes, the better to excoriate Islam for terror, despotism and violence, while assuring themselves profitable consultancies, frequent TV appearances, and book contracts. The Islamic threat is made to seem disproportionately fearsome, lending support to the thesis that there is a worldwide conspiracy behind every explosion."[152]

Despite this violent history, the general Qur'anic attitude toward the People of the Book is that of an invitation:

Say: O' people of the Book! come to common terms as between us and you: That we worship none but Allah; that we associate no partners with him; that we erect not, from among ourselves, Lords and patrons other than Allah. (3:64)

And dispute not with the People of the Book, except with means better (than mere disputation) [in good manner], unless it be with those of them who inflict wrong (and injury): but say, 'We believe in the revelation which has come down to us and in that which came down to you; Our Allah and your Allah is one; and it is to Him we bow (in Islam).' (29:46)

6.25 More Insights into Verse 9:29

Fight against those who—despite having been given Scriptures— believe not in Allah nor the Last Day, and do not treat as forbidden that which God and His Messenger have forbidden, and do not follow the religion of truth, till they pay the Jizya with willing hand, after they have been humbled. (9:29)[153]

As explained earlier, this verse and the verses to follow were meant to prepare Muslims for their expedition to Tabuk and their confrontation with the Byzantines and the Christian Arab regime known as the Ghassanid.

The conditions for battle, which the Qur'anic verses (9:29–34) make clear, does not require non-Muslims to accept Islam. There is no compulsion in matters of faith, and no one is forced to accept Islam at any time. The only condition is that they pay the jizya (tax) and agree to be subdued. By paying jizya, they are agreeing that they will not stand in physical opposition to Islam on Muslim land. They are also helping pay for the defense of the land (including their own property, honor, and family).

Islam guarantees protection for all those who pay the jizya tax. To ensure this, Islam defends those under its protection against all internal and external enemies. They contribute to the treasury of the Muslim state, which guarantees a decent standard of living for all those who are unable to work, including those who pay the tribute, without any distinction between them and the Muslims who pay zakat (dues for the poor). We discussed in detail those who should pay jizya in chapter 3, along with references that may be consulted for further details.

6.26 "Unless you go forth, He will punish you with a grievous penalty" (9:38–39)

O' you who believe! what is the matter with you, that, when you
are asked to go forth in the cause of Allah, you cling heavily to
the earth? Do you prefer the life of this world to the Hereafter?
But little is the comfort of this life, as compared with the
Hereafter. Unless you go forth, He will punish you with a grievous
penalty and replace you by other people. You will not harm
Him in any way, for God has power over all things. (9:38–39)

Some critics claim these two verses signal a warning to anyone who refuses to fight that they will be punished in hell.

Upon closer examination, these verses refer to the mobilization of Muslim forces as they prepare for a confrontation. Although the verses refer to a specific case in a specific point in time, their message can be applied generally to a similar situation should a Muslim community be threatened. But it cannot be applied haphazardly to any situation that arises, as the critics suggest. The explanation of the verse will clarify how its message is to be applied.

Let us first examine the context: most likely these passages were revealed after the order was given to the Muslim army to mobilize for the expedition to Tabuk. According to history books, the Prophet (PBUH) received intelligence that the Byzantines were deploying large forces in southern Syria near the borders of Arabia. He also learned the Byzantine emperor had ordered all soldiers to receive their salaries a year in advance as enticement to fight the Muslims. However, once the Muslims arrived at Tabuk to set up camp, they waited several days, but when there was no army to confront, they returned home.

A number of Arab tribes in the area, such as the Lukham, Judam, Amilah, and Ghassan, had also joined the Byzantine forces. Advance units had already been deployed in al-Balqa' in Palestine. Therefore, the Prophet (PBUH) issued an order to prepare for battle with the Byzantines. Whenever he left Medina to confront an enemy, his standard strategy was to keep his destination unknown in order to maintain an element of surprise. This time, however, the Prophet (PBUH) made his objective known ahead of time due to the long distance and difficult circumstances involved. This expedition coincided with the burning heat of summer, when people would seek the shade and be keen to enjoy the summer fruits. At such a time, all physical activities, let alone military confrontations far from home, were avoided. Hence, some Muslims voiced their hesitations, which the hypocrites took advantage of by trying to dissuade them from joining the Prophet (PBUH). They advised them against marching in the hot summer heat and warned them of the might of the Byzantine army, in addition to the long distance they would have to travel. Hence, some people began to feel uneasy. This passage then deals with their reluctance to go on the journey.[154]

The passage begins with a word of reproach and a warning against their reluctance to join the campaign. The believers are reminded of the help God gave to His Messenger (PBUH) even before any of them had joined him, and of His ability to help the Prophet (PBUH) to victory without them. In such an eventuality, they would have nothing except their disobedience of God, and their failure to support His Messenger. "O' you who believe! what is the matter with you, that, when you are asked to go forth in the cause of Allah, you cling heavily to the earth?" (9:38).

Such reluctance to march in support of God's cause was motivated by worldly considerations and ambitions. People may have feared for their lives and their property. They were keen to protect their interests and preserve their pleasures and would have preferred a settled life of ease and comfort. They thought primarily of their present lives, immediate objectives, close relatives, and physical needs. They also ignored the fact their comfort zone was about to be invaded. In addition, joining a campaign for God's cause represented freedom from the shackles of this earthly life and its physical pleasures: "Do you prefer the life of this world to the Hereafter? But little is the comfort of this life, as compared with the Hereafter" (9:38). Even from the perspective of this world, the verse is given in the context of defending the homeland.

It comes down to whether a person believes in the hereafter and its rewards. No one who believes in God would hesitate to set out to fight for God's cause unless there is some weakness in his or her faith. Of course, we are referring to a true cause, not a made up one with ulterior motives.

Hypocrisy is a character trait of a person who claims to believe in God yet avoids joining the fight for God's cause because he or she fears death or poverty, even when life and death are determined by God, and all provisions and wealth are granted by Him. Besides, all the comforts and pleasures of this life are petty and meaningless when compared with what is in store for the believers in the life to come. A stern consequence then follows: "Unless you go forth, He will punish you with a grievous penalty and replace you by other people. You will not harm Him in any way, for God has power over all things" (39). The address here is made to certain people during a specific time period, but its import applies to all those who believe in God. The punishment with which they are threatened is not limited to the life to come, but it also includes a punishment in this life. They will suffer humiliation that afflicts all those who refrain from fighting for God's cause when their enemies have power over them.

They are also deprived of the enjoyments and comforts of this life, which will be taken up by their enemies. In addition, their loss of life and property is far greater than what they will lose when they fight in support of God's cause. Whenever a community abandons God and refuses to fight for God's cause (which is really defending their own liberty and justice), they are bound to suffer defeat.

Part of verse 39 states "He will replace you by other people," meaning those who will guard their faith and who are prepared to make the necessary sacrifices without yielding to God's enemies. Also from verse 39, "You will not harm Him in any way" and "For God has power over all things" mean we do not determine the outcome, and He can easily cause us to perish and bring about a different community to replace us, as we have seen empires come and go.

God then gives an example from the history which they themselves had witnessed, showing how He supported His Messenger (PBUH) and gave him a great victory without their support at the Battle of Badr. After all, victory is granted by God's hand:

If you help not him [your leader]; (it is no matter) for Allah did indeed help him, when the Unbelievers drove him out: he had no more than one companion; When these two were alone in the cave, and he said to his companion, "grieve not, for Allah is with us" : then Allah sent down His peace upon him, and strengthened him with forces which you saw not, and humbled to the depths the word of the Unbelievers. But the word of Allah is exalted to the heights: for Allah is Exalted in might, Wise. (9:40)

This references a time when the Quraysh had lost all patience with Muhammad (PBUH) and his message. It is the same with all tyrannical authorities when they lose patience with the message of the truth after realizing they cannot stifle or suppress it. The Quraysh held their consultations and decided to murder Muhammad (PBUH). God then informed the Prophet (PBUH) of the plot and instructed him to leave. He departed Mecca alone except for his trusted companion Abu Bakr. He had neither troops nor weapons with which to confront his numerous enemies. The odds were heavily against him. The following passage describes vividly the situation of the Prophet (PBUH) and his friend: "When these two were alone in the cave" with several bands of Quraysh chasing them in all directions. Abu Bakr was sad and worried about the Prophet (PBUH).

The assailants were so close at one point that Abu Bakr said to the Prophet (PBUH), "Should any one of them look down where he is standing, he would surely see us." But the Prophet (PBUH) remained calm and with an inner peace bestowed on him by God. He reassured his companion by saying, "Abu Bakr, what do you think of two men who have God on their side?"

The two were then called upon to mobilize their forces and not to allow any impediment to stand in their way. If they wished to attain what was best for them in this life and in the life to come, then they should not allow any factor to interfere with their response to such a call, as verse 41 makes clear: "Go you forth, (whether equipped) lightly or heavily, and strive in the cause of Allah with your wealth and your lives. This will be best for you if you but knew it." They must withstand their circumstances, strive hard, and be ready to sacrifice their wealth and their lives, seeking no excuses.

The sincere believers set forth on their campaign in support of God's cause. Although they had many impediments and no shortage of excuses if they wished to justify staying behind, they sought none and marched on. Hence, God enabled them to liberate the hearts and minds of other communities and to liberate their lands as well. He allowed His word to triumph at their hands and enhanced their position by being its advocates. He thus enabled them to achieve miraculous victories, unparalleled in history.

6.27 "If there had been immediate gain (in sight)" (9:42)

If there had been immediate gain (in sight), and the journey easy, they would (all) without doubt have followed you; but the distance was long, (and weighed) on them. They would indeed swear by Allah, 'If we only could, we should certainly have come out with you'. They destroy their own soul [bring ruin upon themselves]. Allah knows that they are certainly lying. (9:42)

One critic asserts this verse contradicts the claim that Muslims must fight only in self-defense, because the wording implies a battle will be waged far from home, perhaps in another country and, in this case, on Christian soil, as history books have indicated.[155]

The critic, however, does not cite any historians or history books to support his assertion. To grasp the deeper meaning of this verse one must first understand the historical context, which we will discuss here, based on well-documented historical records by al-Tabari, al-Maghazi, and others. This verse is the continuation of verses 39–41, discussed in the previous section, about the Battle of Tabuk. The critic asserts "in another country and, in this case, on Christian soil". Had he checked a map, he would have realized Tabuk is and always has been part of Arabia and is well within its border where its residents were all Arab tribes, some of whom had aligned themselves with the Byzantine emperor and some of whom were killed by him because they embraced Islam. Tabuk was the place Muslims camped and awaited the encounter with the Byzantine army. One might question this critic as follows:

- Since when is moving within one's territory considered an offensive measure?
- When defending your country or territory, do you wait until the enemy reaches your capital city, or do you deploy to meet them at or near the border, before they invade your land and control your towns (in this case, Muslim and non-Muslim tribes who lived in the area)?

- If, in fact, this was not a defensive measure, but rather an offensive move to invade the Byzantine Empire, why did the Muslims not continue and march toward the border and into Byzantine territory (when no army showed up in Tabuk) but instead return to Medina?

As mentioned in the previous section, the Prophet (PBUH) was informed that the Byzantine emperor had ordered all soldiers to be paid a year in advance to entice them to fight the Muslims. Arab tribes in the area, including the Lukham, Jutham, Amilah, and Ghassan tribes, joined the Byzantine forces, while advance units had already been deployed in al-Balqa' in Palestine.

Muslims showed fringe Arab tribes that they were a force to be reckoned with and that they should not carry out raids on Muslim tribes or Arab tribes under Byzantine control who desired independence. Naturally, the Byzantine rulers had to react, and with the support of the local Ghassanid tribe, organized a revolt against the Muslims. In the meantime, the Muslims were wary of such a coalition and considered the encounter with the Byzantines and its allies difficult.

The Prophet (PBUH) received news from merchants traveling from Sham (Syria) that the emperor, with cooperation from the above Arab tribes, was mobilizing an army in Sham to attack the Muslims. Their army had already reached al-Balqa' in Palestine (under Roman control), on its way down to Mu'tah, about 200 km north of Tabuk. The Prophet (PBUH) started preparing for an encounter during a drought and intense heat. It was a season when most men disliked traveling. With a long and daunting journey ahead of them, the Prophet (PBUH) was concerned about the formidable Byzantine army and its advancing coalition, and that if they did not stop them, the enemy would reach their doorstep and finish them off. Atypically, he made his objective very clear because of the difficult circumstances. According to al-Maghazi, he began to prepare and asked for help from Muslims beyond Medina and Mecca.

During the month of Rajab, in the ninth year after migration they started their journey, some on foot and some on horses and camels.

They estimated the encounter with the Byzantine army would take place in Tabuk. They had a limited amount of water, and, at one point, ran out, but through the will of God they received ample amounts of rain to wash up and refill their water containers.[156] With renewed strength, the Muslims were ready to face the Byzantine army when they reached Tabuk; however, upon their arrival there was no army to confront. Multiple reports indicated there were signs of a Roman army in the area earlier; however, they may have withdrawn once they heard a Muslim army was on the way. The Muslims stayed in Tabuk for twenty days and then the Prophet (PBUH), along with companions, made the decision to leave. Muslims declared the event a victory without bloodshed. This verse is really about those who prefer the ease and comforts of this world and would only accompany the Prophet (PBUH) if there was safety and some worldly benefit to them. However, if it involves a hard task and a faraway journey, they will decline and try to justify their disinclination with excuses, to which God says they are liars.

6.28 "O Prophet! strive hard against the unbelievers and the Hypocrites" (9:73)

O Prophet! strive hard against the unbelievers and the
Hypocrites and be firm against them. Their ultimate
abode is Hell,- an evil refuge indeed. (9:73)

One critic claims this verse is a reminder to Muslims that unbelievers are merely fuel for the fires of hell, thus making it easier to justify their killing. It further explains why today's devout Muslims generally have little regard for people outside their faith. The inclusion of the term hypocrites (nonpracticing Muslims) within the verse also contradicts the notion that the targets of hate and hostility are wartime enemies, since there was never an opposing army made up of nonreligious Muslims in Muhammad's time.[157] Other critics commented this verse is a general and open-ended command.

In the first instance above, the critic somehow defines hypocrites as "nonpracticing" Muslims. We have discussed multiple verses that talk about fighting the idolaters that fight you and not fighting the idolaters with whom you have a treaty. How can these passages be interpreted to mean the Prophet (PBUH) should strive hard and press hard against Muslims who are nonpracticing? Firstly, the term *nonpracticing* is subjective. How would the Prophet (PBUH) and others determine who is practicing and who is not and by how much? Secondly, if a person does not practice, it is an issue between that individual and God. The Messenger of God is merely a bearer of good news, a warner and a guide, as indicated throughout the Qur'an (by terms *mubashir* and *munzer*). Why would he and other Muslims be firm against those who were nonpracticing? Thirdly, the term *munafeqeen* (hypocrites), as mentioned in this verse, has been well defined by their characteristics in the Qur'an in a chapter called al-Munafeqoun (The Hypocrites, chapter 63) as well as other chapters. The following verses from the Qur'an further exemplify these points:

> When the hypocrites come to you they say: 'We bear witness that you are indeed the Messenger of Allah. Allah knows that you are indeed His Messenger, and Allah bears witness that the hypocrites are indeed liars! They have made their oaths a screen (for their misdeeds): thus they obstruct (men) from the Path of Allah: truly evil are their deeds.' (63:1–2)

> They are the ones who say, 'Spend nothing on those who are with Allah's Messenger, to the end that they may disperse (and quit Medina)'. But to Allah belong the treasures of the heavens and the earth; but the Hypocrites do not understand. They say, 'If we return to Medina, surely the more honorable (element) will expel therefrom the meaner'. But honor belongs to Allah and His Messenger, and to the Believers; but the Hypocrites know not. (63:7–8)

> Truly, if the Hypocrites, and those in whose hearts is a disease, and those who stir up sedition in the City, desist not, We shall certainly stir thee up against them. (33:60)

The Hypocrites, men and women, (have an understanding)
with each other: They enjoin evil, and forbid what is
right and just, and are close with their hands. They
have forgotten Allah; so, He has forgotten them. Verily
the Hypocrites are rebellious and perverse. (9:67)

Does one who obstructs and conspires against Muslims sound like a Muslim who is not practicing Islam? Unfortunately, the extremists also use the term *hypocrite* loosely to define a Muslim majority who do not share their murderous views. To them, the Muslim majority has left the faith and hence their killing is justified.

To the explanation of why today's devout Muslims generally have little regard for people outside their faith, the critic uses the word "devout" to implicate Islam as a faith that disregards other faiths. Just like followers of any other faith, there are zealous Muslims who are not aware of the Qur'anic attitude toward non-Muslims (especially the People of the Book), as discussed earlier, whom Muslims can visit, share meals with, and marry. A devout Muslim would be aware of such an Islamic attitude toward others.

Returning to verse 9:73, chapter 9 gives a clear outline of the essential characteristics of true believers and those of the hypocrites who claim to be believers. This is now followed by an order from God to His Messenger (PBUH) to strive against the unbelievers and the hypocrites. The Qur'an makes it clear that the hypocrites certainly disbelieved after they had claimed to be Muslims. They tried something that only their disbelief could have led them to contemplate, but God foiled their attempts.

One wonders about their hostile attitude toward the Prophet (PBUH) when they gained nothing but peace, good will, and justice from his message. It invites them to repent and change their attitude, as the next two verses elaborate:

O Prophet! strive hard against the unbelievers and the
Hypocrites and be firm against them. Their ultimate
abode is Hell,- an evil refuge indeed. (9:73)

> They swear by God that they have said nothing (wrong). Yet
> they certainly uttered the word of unbelief, and disbelieved
> after they had professed to accept Islam, for they aimed
> at something, which they could not attain. They had no
> reason to be spiteful or blasphemous, except that God and
> His Messenger had enriched them out of His bounty. If they
> repent, it will be for their own good; but if they turn away,
> Allah will cause them to endure grievous suffering both in this
> world and in the hereafter. They shall find none on this earth
> to be their companion or to give them support. (9:74)[158]

At the time of this revelation, the unbelievers were the aggressors from the outside because, by this time, most Arabs had accepted Islam and there were no internal conflicts. This was about striving hard against the Byzantines, as the earlier verses 9:27–29 indicate. The critics do not seem to have understood the context and the conflicts instigated by the Byzantines. Striving or being firm against them would have been in the context of war, due to the Byzantines' attempt to invade and seize control over the local tribes. Muslims fought them to defend their territory, not because of their faith but their aggressions. In some cases, Muslims even defended the Christian tribes within their own territory. Unlike the recorded Christian holy wars, none of the Prophet's (PBUH) campaigns were about gaining more territories nor were they politically motivated. Nothing about physical fighting in Islam is ever open-ended. All the conditions and restrictions for physical altercations apply, as discussed in earlier sections.

In practical terms, the Prophet did not kill any hypocrite, and had been very lenient with them, forgiving them and turning a blind eye toward their actions. At this point, however, such leniency was no longer useful. He was commanded by his Lord to take a new approach in his dealings with them. There are times when it is more suitable to take a harder stance, while at other times it is wiser to be lenient. When a period of patience and tolerance is no longer advisable, then it is time to be tough. A practical movement has different requirements at different times, and its method of action may move from one stage to another.

In general terms, verse 74 portrays the consistent attitude of the hypocrites, which was reflected through a range of incidents. For example, they mocked the Prophet (PBUH) and denied doing so (see verses 64–67). It also refers to their various attempts to harm the Prophet (PBUH) and the Muslim community. "They aimed at something which they could not attain" (74) refers to a group of hypocrites who plotted to kill the Prophet (PBUH) on his way back from Tabuk.

This event reveals the degree of their treacherous intentions. The Qur'an wonders at their attitude: "They had no reason to be spiteful, except that God and His Messenger had enriched them out of His bounty" (74). Islam had caused them no harm to justify such hostility.

This is followed by a clear verdict concerning their case: "If they repent, it will be for their own good; but if they turn away, God will cause them to endure grievous suffering both in this world and in hereafter. They shall find none on this earth to be their companion or to give them support" (74).

The door to repentance and mending one's ways remains wide open. Those who are keen to do themselves good, let them enter through that open door. Such remained the Islamic attitude after all the mockery, slander, and treachery. Doors of forgiveness are always open; as such Islam conquered the hearts, something no sword or excommunication can ever accomplish.

But those who wish to continue along their evil path should also know their fate. They will be made to suffer God's severe punishment in this life and in the life to come, while they can rely on no one's support in this world. Since the alternatives have been made clear, they can make their own choice. We ask again, do any of the above characteristics mentioned for hypocrites, and the one who conspires and attempts to harm the Messenger of God sound like a Muslim who does not practice?

6.29 "God has purchased of the believers their lives and their property" (9:111)

God has purchased of the believers their lives and their property, for theirs (in return) is the garden (of Paradise):

they fight in His cause and slay and are slain. This is a true
promise which He has made binding on Himself in the Torah,
the Gospel and the Qur'an. And who is more faithful to his
promise than Allah? Rejoice, then, in the bargain you have
concluded [with him]. That is the supreme triumph. (9:111)

Some critics assert that in this verse God has made a bargain with
believers in return for their struggle and ask how a true believer is
defined in the Qur'an. The Qur'an identifies a believer in the next
verse within the context of this passage, and many other places, but
first let us delve into verse 9:111. Embracing Islam is described as a
deal with God in which believers surrender what they possess to God,
including property and their lives, and in return they will receive admittance to heaven for their sacrifice and struggle in the path of God.
God's word should be supreme, and all submission is made to God
alone. The price a believer receives in this deal is a favor from God.

The people who enter into this deal are a select few with distinctive qualities, some of which apply to them in their direct relationship with God and to their feelings and their worship. Their other
qualities (as believers) are concerned with the duties under this deal,
which require them to work for the establishment of the truth, enjoin
what is right, forbid what is wrong, and make sure God's bounds are
respected: "Those that turn (to Allah) in repentance; that serve Him,
and praise Him; who contemplate (Allah and His creation), who bow
down and prostrate themselves in prayer; who enjoin good and forbid
evil; and observe the limit set by Allah;- (These do rejoice). So, give
the glad tidings to the Believers" (9:112).[159]

"Rejoice, then, in the bargain you have made with Him. That is
the supreme triumph" (9:111). Believers rejoice at having dedicated
their souls and their property for God's cause in return for admittance
into heaven, as God Himself has promised. What do believers miss
out on when they honor this part of the deal? They do not miss out
on anything. They are certain to leave this world, and their wealth
cannot go with them, whether they spend it to serve God's cause or
in any other way. Being in paradise is a great gain, which believers

actually attain for nothing, since the price they offer would be gone anyway, whichever course of action they follow. We need not mention the position of honor they attain when they conduct their lives in line with what God requires. If they attain victory, then it is a victory achieved to make God's word supreme, to establish the faith God has revealed, and to liberate God's servants from subjugation by human beings.

God's promise in the Torah and the Gospel to those who strive for His cause needs clarification. The Torah and the Gospel in circulation today cannot be described as (exactly) the ones that God— limitless is He in His glory—revealed to His noble messengers Moses and Jesus (PBUT). Even the Jews and the Christians do not make that claim. They agree the original versions of these scriptures are not in existence. What they have today was written long after the revelations in these books, when all that was left was committed to memory after more than one generation. Much was added to small, memorized portions.

Nevertheless, jihad is referenced in the Old Testament, and the Jews are encouraged to fight their pagan enemies in order to ensure the triumph of their faith. Furthermore, in the Talmud we read that the spirit of those who are just and who do good will benefit from the great bounty in the abode of the seven heavens, the first of which is filled with martyrs who gave their lives protecting their faith. On the other hand, the Gospels circulating among Christians today do not include explicit references to jihad beyond some verses on fighting and sacrifice in Matthew 10:33–42 and 16:24–28, which also implies struggling. However, we must recall the Gospels, as written today, have been modified over time and through translations, a fact conceded by Christian scholars. What we can confirm is what God said in the Qur'an (His final testament) in which He refers to His true promise in the Torah, the Gospel, and the Qur'an (verse 9:111). As such, those who struggled for the truth and to keep their faith in the path of God should "rejoice in the bargain they have made with Him. That is the supreme triumph" (9:111).

What this statement means is that jihad, or striving for God's cause, is a binding deal for anyone who believes in God, ever since God sent messengers to mankind to preach His faith. But to strive for God's cause does not mean rushing to fight the enemy. It is the practical translation of a principle of faith designed to influence a believer's feelings, attitudes, behavior, and worship. The faith and characteristics of those with whom God has made this deal are outlined in the next verse. Hence the answer to the critic's question is found in the next verse:

> Those that turn (to Allah) in repentance; that serve Him, and
> praise Him; who contemplate (Allah and His creation), who
> bow down and prostrate themselves in prayer; who enjoin good
> and forbid evil; and observe the limit set by Allah;- (These do
> rejoice). So, give the glad tidings to the Believers. (9:112)

As the verse indicates, the first of these qualities is to turn to God in repentance. Believers must appeal to Him for forgiveness, regret any mistakes they may make, resolve to turn to Him, and follow His guidance in their future days. They must also not revert to sin. They must endeavor to do only good actions in order to make their repentance a reality. They then must purge themselves of temptation and resolve to mend their ways, so they can earn God's acceptance.

"Serve Him, and praise Him" means believers must submit and dedicate their worship to Him alone, acknowledging that He is God, the only Lord. This is a basic quality manifested through their worship and also by dedicating all their deeds and statements to the pursuit of God's pleasure. Their worship is a practical confirmation of their belief in God's oneness. They praise Him continuously, for true praise is expressed not only during times of ease and happiness but during times of adversity as well, thus recognizing that God does not put believers through trials unless it is for their own good. A believer may not know the reasons for a hardship, but God knows.

"Who contemplate (Allah and His creation)". The meaning of the Arabic term for contemplation and its translation here is not readily apparent. There are several interpretations of what contemplation means. The qualities of contemplation and reflection are better understood in the following Qur'anic passage:

> Behold! in the creation of the heavens and the earth, and
> the alternation of night and day,- there are indeed Signs for
> men of understanding, who remember God when they stand,
> sit and lie down, and reflect on the creation of the heavens
> and the earth: "Our Lord, You have not created all this in
> vain. Limitless are You in Your glory. Glory to you! Give
> us salvation from the penalty of the Fire." (3:190–191)

Through repentance, worship, and praise of God one develops the quality of reflecting on God and His dominion, which will inevitably lead to turning to Him and acknowledging His wisdom manifested throughout all creation.

"Who bow down and prostrate themselves." This phrase speaks of the believers who attend to their prayers, which becomes an essential part of life. Praying becomes one of their distinctive characteristics.

"Who enjoin good and forbid evil." When a Muslim community is established to conducts itself in accordance with divine laws, making clear that it submits to God alone, the quality of enjoining to do what is right and to forbid what is wrong is seen to be fully operative within this community.

"And observe the limit set by Allah." Believers should make sure to implement God's directives in their own lives and in the community and to resist temptations and anyone who tries to forestall this progress. By definition, such a community acknowledges God's sovereignty as the only God. To summarize, following are the distinctive qualities of believers:

- They repent, which brings a human being back to God's ways, stops a person from committing sin, and motivates them to do what is right.
- They worship, which maintains a believer's close relationship with God and makes seeking His pleasure their aim.

- They praise God equally in times of happiness and in adversity, as a manifestation of total submission to Him alone, suggesting complete trust in His justice and wisdom.
- They reflect on God's attributes and the signs that indicate His wisdom and perfection of creation;
- They enjoin what is right and forbid what is wrong in order to ensure that the whole community is set on the right course;
- They keep within the limits set out by God to ensure their implementation and to prevent any violation.

6.30 "When We decide to destroy a population, We (first) send . . ." (17:16)

When We decide to destroy a population, We (first)
send a definite order [our commend] to those [affluent]
among them who are given the good things of this life
and yet transgress; so that the word is proved true against
them: then (it is) We destroy them utterly. (17:16)

In this verse, one critic infers the crime is a "moral" transgression, but the punishment will be "utter destruction."[160]

Firstly, the critic added the word "moral" before the term *transgression*, even though *moral* is not used in this Qur'anic passage; if it were, more applicable terms would be used. Secondly, moral decay does not only apply to the affluent; it includes the nonaffluent as well. However, the verse mentions the affluent, who not only enjoy wealth, servants, luxuries, comfort, and power, but are prone to carelessness and decadence. These vices can lead to a life of corruption, transgress all limits, trample values, desecrate sanctities, and defile other people's honor. This influence extends to the community, which is impacted as well. Unless the affluent are taken to task for their misdeeds, they will spread corruption and indecency throughout their community. They will debase the sound values and principles which every community needs to observe in order to survive. The laws of cause and effect take over. Thus, their corruption will lead to the loss of strength, vigor, and means of survival by the whole community. It then becomes lifeless and is soon overtaken by destruction. The verse here restates this law, which God has set in motion. When God determines a certain community should be destroyed, this is the natural outcome of its destructive ways and practices.

When the affluent become too numerous and no one takes any action to curb their transgressions, corruption spreads little by little until the entire community becomes corrupt. Consequently, it is liable to the effects of God's natural law, thus condemning such communities to destruction. Indeed, the community in question is responsible for the destruction it suffers, because it did not take the necessary action to stop its foul practices. Had it done so, it would have been spared destruction.

God has willed that human life should run according to set laws that never fail or change. A cause has its effect, and the effect takes place as a result of God's will. The mention of God's will in the verse—"When We decide to destroy a population, We (first) send a definite order [our commend] to those [affluent] among them who are given the good things of this life"—does not mean a commanding will that initiates the cause. It is will that brings the effect when the cause takes place. It is known as formative or determinative will. Thus, the effect becomes inevitable as a result of God's laws of nature: "So that the word is proved true against them (judgment is irrevocably passed)." Similarly, in the same statement, "commend" does not refer to a directive requiring them to indulge in transgression. It simply refers to the natural consequences for those who led such a life. Hence, the verse states they "and yet transgress; so that the word is proved true against them: then (it is) We destroy them utterly" (17:16). If they continue to transgress, judgment is irrevocably passed, and they are utterly destroyed. This statement highlights the responsibilities of every community, as it makes clear that this law has remained in operation since Noah's time, as the next verse states: "How many generations have We destroyed after Noah? Suffice it that your Lord is well aware of His servants' sins and observes them all" (17).

6:31   "(Moses) said: 'That was (the place) we were seeking after!'" (18:64–81)

> [Moses] said: 'That was [the place] we were seeking
> after!' So, they went back. . . (18:64–81)

A critic claims this is a parable for laying the legal and theological groundwork for honor killings in which a family member is murdered because he or she brought shame to the family, either through apostasy or perceived moral indiscretion. This verse talks about Moses encountering a man with "special knowledge" who carries out tasks that do not make sense on the surface but are later justified. In the story, one task was to murder a youth for no apparent reason (18:74). Later, the sage explains that it was feared the boy would "grieve" his parents through his "disobedience and ingratitude" (18:80). He was killed so Allah could provide them with a "better" son. The critic then adds that this story, along with verse 58:22, "Thou will not find any people who believe in Allah and the Last Day, loving those who resist Allah and His Messenger, even though they were their fathers or their sons, or their brothers, or their kindred," is the major reason honor killings are sanctioned by Shari'a. As further confirmation, he cites the *Reliance of the Traveller* (the translation of *Umdat al-Salik*) where it says that punishment for murder is not applicable when a parent or grandparent kills their offspring.[161]

We will explain the verses, but first a response to this critic's claims:

1.   A clarification: In verse 80, it is not "disobedience and ingratitude," as some have translated, but rather rebellion or wickedness and disbelief or rejection. Hence, the more accurate translation would be "and as for the youth, his parents were people of Faith (believers), and we feared that he would grieve them by obstinate rebellion (wickedness) and unbelief" (18:80).[162]

2.   This is a parable about a series of events that explains divine destiny. The story also serves as a gateway to the unseen and

to divine wisdom, which no human being has access to, even the Messenger of God (PBUH). It involves putting faith and trust in divine wisdom concerning situations that may seem negative at first but end up positive in eventuality. In this case, it is a reminder to a parent who has tragically lost a child that a divine plan exists and that there are many things we cannot know but must trust in God's plan. It operates beyond human and religious laws, including Shari'a. It does not, by any means, sanction crime, including honor killings (which do not exist in Islam). The Qur'an states: "And so for all things prohibited,- there is the law of equality. If then any one transgresses the prohibition against you, Transgress you likewise against him. Fear Allah and know that Allah is with those who restrain themselves" (2:194); and "And We ordained therein for them: 'Life for life, eye for eye, nose for nose, ear for ear, tooth for tooth, and wounds equal for equal.' But if any one remits the retaliation by way of charity, it is an act of atonement for himself. And if any fail to judge by (the light of) what Allah has revealed, they are (No better than) wrong-doers" (5:45); and "We ordained for the Children of Israel that if any one slew a person - unless it be for murder or for spreading mischief in the land - it would be as if he slew the whole people: and if any one saved a life, it would be as if he saved the life of the whole people" (5:32). How then could a religion that has *qisas* (retribution laws) saying an eye for an eye, or ransom, or forgiveness (as a response) is to sanction murder (of an innocent child, in this case)? This is why Moses (PBUH), driven by human laws and his own Shari'a, protested such action. The sage who accompanied Moses (PBUH) had deeper knowledge and power beyond that of a human being; perhaps he was an angel, as some commentators have speculated. He was given permission by God to execute the action, much like an angel of death who operates under God's command. His action, however, is separated from that of a mortal being.

3. Although verse 58:22 (Thou wilt not find any people who believe in Allah and the Last Day, loving those who resist Allah and His Messenger, even though they were their fathers or their sons, or their brothers, or their kindred) has no relevance to the verses above nor sanctions murder (or honor killings, as the critic puts it), its passage refers to those who oppose God and His Messenger and says they will be among the lowest. The verse refers to those who believe in God and the last day and who will not *love* those who oppose God and His Messenger (PBUH), even though they may be their fathers, sons, brethren, or clan. As such, God has written faith upon their hearts and has strengthened them in his spirit. This verse speaks of not loving them, yet being their friends. Therefore, how could this verse sanction honor killings? It does not.

4. Honor killings do not exist in Islam and Shari'a for any member of the family, much less a child. Many Muslim commentators and organizations condemn honor killings as an un-Islamic cultural practice. Tahira Shaid Khan, a professor of women's studies at Aga Khan University, says "There is nothing in the Qur'an that permits or sanctions honor killings." Khan instead blames them on attitudes across different classes, ethnicities, and religious groups that view women as property, with no rights of their own, as a motivation for honor killings.[163] Ali Gomaa, Egypt's former Grand Mufti, has also spoken out forcefully against honor killings.[164]

In a more generic statement reflecting a broader Islamic scholarly view, American scholar Jonathan A.C. Brown says:

> Questions about honor killings have regularly found their way into the inboxes of muftis. No Muslim scholar of any note, either medieval or modern, has sanctioned a man killing his wife or sister for tarnishing her or the family's honor. If a woman or man found together were to deserve the death penalty for

fornication, this would have to be established by the evidence required by the Qur'an: either a confession or the testimony of four male witnesses, all upstanding in the eyes of the court, who actually saw the act.[165]

We acknowledge that honor killings exist in many communities around the world, especially in some Muslim communities, probably because the concept of family honor is extremely important in many Muslim and Eastern communities. The family is viewed as the primary source of honor, and the community highly values the relationship between honor and the family. Family members who commit inappropriate acts bring shame to their families in the eyes of the community. Unfortunately, this is a cultural practice that is often confused as a religious sanction. Widney Brown, the advocacy director of Human Rights Watch, said the practice goes across cultures and across religions.[166]

It is noteworthy to mention a few examples regarding the sources of such practices. During the Roman Empire, the Roman law *Lex Julia de adulteriis coercendis*, implemented by Augustus Caesar, permitted fathers to murder their daughters and lovers who committed fornication, and also permitted husbands to murder an adulterous wife's lover.[167] The Napoleonic Code, however, did not allow women to murder unfaithful husbands, while it permitted husbands to murder their unfaithful wives.[168] Article 324 of the Napoleonic Code, which was passed in 1810, permitted the murders of an unfaithful wife and her lover at the hand of her husband.[169] It was abolished only in 1975. Middle Eastern Arab countries actually copied the 1810 penal code of Article 324. It inspired Jordan's Article 340, which permits the murder of a wife and her lover if caught in the act at the hands of her husband, and still applies to this day. France's Article 324 also inspired the 1858 Ottoman Penal Code Article 188, which was retained even after a 1944 revision of Jordan's law.[170]

The French Mandate over Lebanon resulted in France's penal code imposed there in 1943–1944. The French-inspired Lebanese law for adultery allowed for the mere accusation of adultery against a woman to result in a maximum punishment of two years in prison. Men, on the other hand, must be caught in the act, not merely accused. They are punished with only one year in prison.

5. Regarding the critic's reference to the *Reliance of the Traveller*, as we discussed in chapter 3, the sources for Islamic law and the evidence must come from the Qur'an or an authentic narration. When there are explicit verses in the Qur'an and authentic narration of the Prophet (PBUH) regarding any legal issue, these are the first sources one must turn to before going to any book or report based on any scholar's opinion. In Islam, retribution only applies after the crime has been committed, not before. Our dear critic claims to have read all Jewish and Christian sources yet did not take his time to read the Qur'an. Regarding children and what was customary among pagan Arabs who killed their children for fear of poverty, the Qur'an says: "Kill not your children for fear of want[poverty]: We shall provide sustenance for them as well as for you. Verily the killing of them is a great sin" (7:31). And regarding those who buried their infant girls alive due to shame and fear for possible dishonor, the Qur'an describes the father's expression as "When news is brought to one of them, of (the birth of) a female (child), his face darkens, and he is filled with inward grief" (16:58). The Qur'an draws a vivid picture of the day of accountability for fathers when these girls will be spoken to: "When the female (infant), buried alive, is questioned; For what crime she was killed" (81:8–9). This is followed by "(Then) each soul shall know what it has put forward" (81:14). There is also a general rule given in this verse: "And if a man kills a believer intentionally, his recompense is Hell, to abide therein (Forever): And the wrath and the curse of Allah are upon him, and a dreadful penalty is prepared for him" (4:93).

When there are explicit verses like these that condemn and hold responsible parents who kill their child for reasons of poverty or shame, and when there is no verse about killing an offspring (due to dishonor or otherwise), why would one go to another source for an injunction? How could a faith with the above condemnations say that punishment for murder is not applicable when a parent or grandparent kills their offspring? Does this not seem contradictory to the Qur'an? And for what crime should a child be killed? Who decides what is a fair punishment? What about an adult son or daughter who commits a crime: does the father arbitrarily decide whether his offspring should be killed and then carry out the punishment? In Islam, parents are strictly forbidden to kill a child born out of wedlock or by rape. Any civil or criminal punishment is decided and carried out by an Islamic court, not by the parents or any other members of the society, including the police or community officials.

The following briefly explains the verses that refer to murder.

Verses 18:64–81 refer to a conversation between Moses (PBUH) and a sage—one sent from God who had knowledge of the future. The conversation was based on the sage's actions, which Moses (PBUH) questioned. The actions were taken preemptively, and, of course, seemed unjustified from the perspective of human laws; however, from a divine perspective, the realm beyond human perception, it is possible or plausible they were taken for a greater purpose, unknown to the human mind at the time they occurred. For example, a prophet is not allowed to cause a calamity, like a flood or disease, in order to test or punish a community, but God can. No human is allowed to kill another human even with the absolute knowledge that he or she in the future would be inflicted with an incurable disease, but God can terminate a life out of His mercy. Verses 18:64–81 refer to a divine system in which God's will takes place through the hands of a sage. On the surface, however, these actions appeared to have no logical justification whatsoever. They could not be understood without accessing the divine wisdom dictating them, which most people would struggle to comprehend. Verse 74 states, "Then they proceeded until, when they met a young man. [The sage] slew him." The first action exposed the boat and its passengers to certain risks. Now, a young man is murdered without provocation or justification. This was too much for Moses (PBUH) to tolerate patiently (despite all the promises he had given not to question anything he saw). Hence, in the same passage, "Moses said: 'Have you slain an innocent person who had slain none? Truly a foul thing have thou done!'" This suggests that Moses (PBUH) was not unmindful of his promise. He probably remembered it but was unable to keep quiet when he witnessed the murder. To him, the young man was innocent (according to human laws and his Shari'a); he had not perpetrated anything to justify his death.

Verse 18:80–81 continues: "As for the youth, his parents were people of Faith (believers), and we feared that he would grieve them by obstinate rebellion (wickedness) and unbelief. And so we desired that their Lord would give them in exchange (a son) better in purity (of conduct) and closer in affection." Although this young man appeared at the time to be deserving of no punishment, God revealed the boy's true nature to the sage. We realize now that he harbored all the seeds of wickedness and unbelief, which were bound to increase as he grew up. Had he lived, he would have caused his parents, believers as they were, much trouble and grief. He might have influenced them (out of love for him) to follow him in his wickedness. Hence, God directed His goodly servant to kill the boy in order to replace him with one who would be better and more dutiful.

If the issue were based on human knowledge alone, the sage would have had no justification for killing the boy, particularly since he appeared to be underage, having done nothing to deserve capital punishment. It is not up to anyone to take another's life, other than God Himself or one to whom God imparts knowledge to do so. Nor is it permissible to make such knowledge the basis of any action other than that in which appearances allow. But God may command what He wills, as He does in this case. By no means does this verse sanction murder or command anyone to kill one's child. The implication of the parable in these verses is a series of events that help illustrate divine destiny as a gateway to divine wisdom and the unseen. It is beyond human perception and capacity hence unseen. It entails lessons to be learned about divine wisdom; what might appear bad may end up being good in eventuality. It operates beyond human and religious laws, such as Shari'a.

6:32 "Therefore listen not to the Unbelievers, but strive against them with" (25:52)

> Therefore listen not to the Unbelievers, but strive against them with the utmost strenuousness with (the Qur'an) (25:52)

In this verse, some critics claim the root word for jihad is used twice here, although it may not have been referring to *holy war* when revealed, since it was prior to the migration to Medina. The "with" at the end of the verse is thought to mean the Qur'an. Hence, the verse may have originally been meant as nonviolent resistance. This changed with the migration. After the Meccan period, jihad is almost exclusively meant within the context of violence and the enemy is always defined as the people, rather than ideas.

We discussed jihad in detail in chapter 3 and noted the term *holy war* does not exist within the Qur'anic vocabulary. So if the verse is referring to the period in Mecca (which is true) and a nonviolent struggle, then physical fighting in this context would be meaningless. To "strive" or "struggle" from within would be appropriate, which is consistent throughout the Qur'an, during Mecca or thereafter. It is true this verse was revealed during the early period in Mecca, hence *jihad* means to struggle to educate (with the Qur'an). Hence, if the root term for *jihad* or struggle is used in a nonviolent context before migration as well as the violent period after migration, as the critic acknowledges, then the critic should also acknowledge that the term *jihad* has a broader meaning and application than just physical fighting (which some critics insist on)—a point we have been trying to drive home throughout this text.

We also explained the Muslims' situation after migration. Had the Meccans not instigated, provoked, and schemed against Muslims, no physical encounter or fight (qital, not jihad) would have occurred. Had the Meccans stopped persecuting Muslim families who were still in Mecca, Muslims, who at the time did not have an army, would have continued with their lives in Medina and would have honored the peace treaty between them. Had the Meccans not broken their treaty with the Muslims and had allowed Muslims to travel to Mecca for pilgrimage and to visit their families, conflict would have been avoided. The critic says, "The enemy is always defined as people, rather than ideas."[171] If by "idea" the critic means their ideology, Muslims never fought anyone based on their ideology, as Islam dictates. Hence, the enemy *was* defined as a people, those who fought Muslims regardless of their faith. On the other hand, Muslims did not fight people, regardless of their faith, with whom they had signed peace treaties.

As the critics correctly indicated, the reason scholars have not been able to associate this verse with physical fighting is due to the word *behee* (or "with it"), a preposition and pronoun used in the Qur'an to mean to begin striving with the Qur'an to educate and invite. Indeed, from this verse, we realize that to strive to educate takes priority over to strive in combat, as we confirmed by studying the Prophet's (PBUH) biography by Ibn Ishaq's *Seerat Rasool Allah* and books of history by al-Tabari's *Tarikh* and Ibn al-Athir's *Al Kamel Fe Tarikh*. Only when the Messenger of God invited people to Islam for several years and the enemy persecuted the Muslims and became determined to kill the Prophet (PBUH) was he forced to migrate and to defend Muslims, which is explicitly mentioned in the Qur'an, as it speaks about the reason to engage in battle: "To those against whom war is made, permission is given (to fight), because they were wronged;- and verily, Allah is most powerful for their aid. (They are) those who have been expelled from their homes unjustly only because they said: Our Lord is Allah" (22:39–40). Note, for an explicit physical fight, the term *qital* is generally used in the Qur'an.

The Meccan people were the enemy, not due to their belief system, but because of their combative attitude toward Muslims. "To those against whom war is made, permission is given (to fight), because they were wronged" says nothing about who they are and their beliefs. However, Muslims did strive to educate them about Islam, and while they were amazed by the Qur'anic verses, their arrogance and stubbornness did not allow them to acknowledge Qur'an's uniqueness and excellence; hence, they resorted to violence.

The Qur'an has great power and influence. When God's Messenger (PBUH) used the Qur'an to address the Arabs, it pierced their hearts and consciences. They tried hard to counter its effects, employing every means at their disposal, but all their efforts were useless. The Quraysh elders did not want their people to listen to it carefully: "The Unbelievers say: 'Listen not to this Qur'an, but talk at random in the midst of its (reading), that you may gain the upper hand'" (41:26). This illustrates their profound fear that the Qur'an would touch their own hearts and the hearts of their followers who might embrace Islam. They were also aware of how deeply affected people were by Muhammad's readings of the Qur'an, and they worried that these listeners might accept his message. Indeed, their statement is indicative of how worried they were about the impact of the Qur'an. Hence, the struggle started with the education of others, and conflict was unavoidable once the enemy (as defined) instigated violence.

6.33 "If the hypocrites, and those in whose hearts is a disease" (33:60–62)

If the hypocrites, and those in whose hearts is a disease and those who stir up sedition in the city do not desist, We will stir (rouse) you up against them, and then they will be your neighbors for only a little while. They shall have a curse on them: whenever they are found, they shall be seized and slain. Such has been Allah's way with those who lived before. No change will you find in Allah's way. (33:60–62)

A critic argues that the verses in this passage sanction slaughter (rendered as "merciless" and "horrible murder" in some translations) against three groups: the hypocrites, those Muslims who refuse to fight in the cause of Allah and hence do not act as Muslims should (3:167); those with "diseased hearts," which includes Jews and Christians (5:51–52); and agitators, those who speak out against Islam. The critic adds that victims are to be sought out, which is what terrorists do today.[172]

It is amazing how critics of Islam simplify and pontificate in order to justify their position, as they mix and match verses without thorough analysis, conveniently selecting verses that suit their purpose. Given what we have already said about the hypocrites and the Prophet's (PBUH) leniency toward them, the passage concludes with a stern warning to the hypocrites and those who had diseased hearts. It includes those who circulated false rumors, requiring them to stop their wicked actions and to refrain from affronting the believers and the Muslim community as a whole. Unless they stopped, God would empower His Messenger (PBUH) to drive them out of Medina; subsequently, if they continued their ways, they could be killed. The term *quttelou taqtila* does not mean to slaughter mercilessly; it means to seize and kill without hesitation (or to be done away with). We do acknowledge that there are wrong or exaggerated translations of the Qur'an out there. This powerful warning gives us a clear impression of the Muslims' strong position in Medina after the Banu Qurayza affair. Indeed, the Muslim state was now in full power. The hypocrites could only scheme in secret.

Verse 60 warns hypocrites, deviants, and rumormongers, who had caused insecurity and mayhem within the community, that if they did not desist, the Prophet (PBUH) would be directed to take action and exile them. Verse 61 says even if exiled by the Muslims, these people who are cursed with wickedness will be seized and killed by any ruler of any land.

Verse 61 ties this message to God's way, tradition, or practice that, in any land and at any time, those who cause turmoil and threaten the citizens' security and laws will be dealt with as has happened in the past. Some reports indicate that those who continued their ways, while even in exile, were killed. We will now address the specific comments made by the critic.

We start with his definition of hypocrites as *"Muslims who refuse to fight in the way of Allah (3:167), and who don't act as Muslims should."* However, the Qur'an characterizes hypocrites in the following way:

1. They do not say what is in their hearts, as the Qur'an states: "And the Hypocrites also were told: 'Come, fight in the way of Allah, or (at least) drive (The foe from your city).' They said: 'Had we known how to fight, we should certainly have followed you.' They were that day nearer to Unbelief than to Faith, saying with their lips what was not in their hearts but Allah hath full knowledge of all they conceal" (3:167). Does this sound like *"Muslims who do not act as they should"* or those who align themselves with the enemy (directly or indirectly) or who lack courage to defend their own city?

2. They cause mischief, as the Qur'an says: "The Hypocrites, men and women, (have an understanding) with each other: They enjoin evil, and forbid what is just, and are close with their hands. They have forgotten Allah; so, He has forgotten them. Verily the Hypocrites are rebellious and perverse" (9:67). True Muslims enjoin what is good and just and forbid evil.

3. They do not tell the truth: "When the Hypocrites come to you they say: 'We bear witness that you are the Messenger of Allah.' Allah knows that you (Prophet Muhammad) are indeed His Messenger, and Allah bears witness that the hypocrites are truly liars" (63:1).

4. They scheme in secret: "Certain of the desert Arabs round about you are hypocrites, as well as (desert Arabs) among the Medina folk: they are obstinate (and well versed) in hypocrisy: you know them not: We know them." (9:101).

5. They fear their intentions will be revealed: "The Hypocrites are afraid lest a Sura [chapter] should be sent down about them, showing them what is (really passing) in their hearts. Say: "Mock you! But verily Allah will bring to light all that you fear (should be revealed)" (9:64).

6. They have no sense of honor. "It is they that say: 'Spend nothing on those who follow the Messenger of Allah until they disperse (and quit Medina).' Yet to Allah belong the treasuries of heavens and the earth, but the hypocrites do not understand. They say, 'If we return to Medina, surely the more honorable (element) will expel therefrom the meaner [most contemptible].' But honor belongs to Allah and His Messenger, and to the Believers; but the Hypocrites know not" (63:8–9).

The critic then asserts that verses 33:60–62 apply to *those with 'diseased hearts', which includes Jews and Christians* (5:51–52). Firstly, according to verses 5:51–52, those with disease in their hearts do not include Jews and Christians, but rather those who joined Jews and Christians and took them as allies (sometimes translated as "friends and protectors"). The term *alliance* or its Arabic equivalent *wala'* (or *awlia'* as allies) is well known and has a precise meaning in Islamic terminology. It occurs in the context of the relationship, one that the Muslims in Medina were to have with the Muslims who did not migrate to the land of Islam (from Mecca to Medina). God says in the Qur'an "You have no alliance with them until they have emigrated" (8:72). What is meant here is not the support in faith, because every Muslim is a supporter in faith to every other Muslim in all situations. The reference here is to the sort of alliance and patronage that required cooperation and military assistance for protection. This latter relationship did not exist between Muslims in the Muslim land.

Secondly, Islam commands that its followers maintain a peaceful attitude toward the people of earlier revelations (Christians and Jews). At the individual level, Muslims may develop a friendly or spousal relationship, and nations may develop peaceful, cooperative, and commercial relationships. To take them as allies, however, is a different matter altogether.

One should not confuse the emphasis Islam places on extending a tolerant attitude toward the people of earlier revelations, plus the need to treat them with kindness within the Muslim community with the alliance that is owed by every Muslim to God, His Messenger, and the Muslim community. One might forget the Qur'an asserts that the people of earlier revelations were allied with one another to fight the Muslim community. They had been hostile toward Muslims because of their faith. They would not be happy with Muslims unless Muslims abandoned their religion and followed theirs. Hostility may be obvious in their words, but their hearts conceal much worse. Of course, on an individual level there were many Muslims who established personal relationships with people of earlier revelations and even married them, as allowed by Islam. The reference here is to communities and nations who are hostile toward Islam and Muslims; as a result, Muslims cannot have a strategic alliance with them.

Those very people of earlier revelations used to tell the pagan Arabs that they were "better guided in the way than the believers" (4:51). It is they who stirred the unbelievers and mobilized them to launch a determined attack against the Muslim community in Medina. Those people of earlier revelations were the ones who launched the Crusades against the land of Islam, which extended over a period of two hundred years. It is they who organized the Spanish Inquisition. In recent history, they turned the Muslim Arabs of Palestine out of their land in order to give it to the Jews. Here, as Muslims engaged in a fight to establish their new system as a living reality, the Qur'an provides them with the necessary concept to create, in their subconscious, a sense of distinction between them and all those who oppose their community. This distinction does not preclude tolerance and kind treatment, for these come naturally to a Muslim (as they should). It only precludes a relationship of alliance, of the sort a Muslim owes only to God, His Messenger, and the community of believers.

Thirdly, the Qur'an, in many cases, mentions together hypocrites and those with disease in the hearts as they conspired and aligned themselves with the enemy. The Qur'an says:

Lo! the hypocrites say, and those in whose hearts is a disease:
'These people, – their religion has misled them.' But if any trust
in Allah, behold! Allah is Exalted in might, Wise. (8:49)

> Is it that there is a disease in their hearts? or do they doubt, or
> are they in fear, that Allah and His Messenger will deal unjustly
> with them? Nay, it is they themselves who do wrong. (24:50)

> Or do those in whose hearts is a disease, that Allah will
> not bring to light all their (secret) hate? (47:29)

Does all this mean Muslim individuals or communities should be hostile toward people of other faiths, including those of earlier revelations? Does it mean Muslims should arm themselves and randomly attack people of other faiths, including innocent civilians, because of their faith or association with certain countries or communities? Does it mean Muslim communities should sever ties with any non–Muslim nations and disregard implicit or explicit international laws for peaceful relations, coexistence, and trade? The emphatic answer is absolutely not from over a billion Muslims throughout the world, with the exception of a few extremists whose lone violent acts have occurred only in more recent years. Unfortunately, the attitude of extremists (like ISIS and others) toward others feeds the critics of Islam with a pretext to attack Islam, which in turn becomes a pretext for the extremists to promote their cause, their hate, and their attack on anyone with opposing views (including Muslims). In general, the Qur'an says:

> And do not dispute (discuss) with the People of the Book,
> except with means better (than mere disputation, in good
> manners), unless it be with those of them who inflict wrong
> (and injury): but say, "We believe in the revelation which has
> come down to us and in that which came down to you; Our
> Allah and your Allah is one; and it is to Him we bow." (29:46)

On an individual basis, Christian hospitality toward Muslims is neither new nor unusual. It is a fourteen hundred-year-old tradition that began in 615 AD when Muhammed (PBUH) started preaching his message of one God in Mecca. He gathered a few followers around him, who for years were tortured and persecuted by the pagan majority in Mecca. Five years into his ministry, Muhammed (PBUH) asked some of his followers who suffered the most to migrate to Abyssinia, which was ruled by a Christian king. King Negus was a pious man who gave refuge to the immigrants and the protection to live safely and practice their faith. Muslims to this day remember and cherish King Negus.

Within five years of the birth of Islam, Muslims were migrating to Christian lands in search of religious freedom. While fourteen hundred years ago only a few sought the safe haven of Christian Abyssinia; today, over three million Muslims enjoy the same in the US as the original immigrants (and more so in Europe), followed by second- and third-generation Muslims. Many prominent Muslim Americans have gone on record saying that they feel freer to practice Islam in America (and in the West) than in their country of origin. It is a fact that Islam thrives where there is democracy as much as it did fourteen hundred years ago in Arabia.

6.34 "Therefore, when you meet the Unbelievers (in fight), smite at their necks" (47:3–4)

This because those who reject Allah follow vanities, while those who believe follow the Truth from their Lord: Thus, does Allah set forth for men their lessons by similitude. Therefore, when you meet the Unbelievers (in fight), smite at their necks, when you have thoroughly subdued them, bind a bond firmly (on them): thereafter (is the time for) either generosity or ransom [set them free either by an act of grace or against ransom]: Until the war lays down its burdens. Thus (are you commanded): but if it had been God's Will, He could certainly have exacted retribution from them (Himself); but it is his will to test you all, by means of one another. But those who are slain in the Way of God- He will never let their deeds be lost. (47:3–4)

Some critics add the term *jihad* in parentheses to verses wherever they can. They assert this verse advocates holy war against those who reject

Allah, and that unbelievers are to be killed or wounded. One critic in particular adds that survivors are to be held captive for ransom, and the only reason Allah does not do the work Himself is to test the faithfulness of Muslims; those who kill will pass the test.

The fact remains that critics of Islam do not intend to conduct impartial and scholarly work to understand why such verses are revealed. Their goal is not to rely on the facts, but rather to criticize and blame God's revelations and the faith itself by relying on snapshots, something that can be done with other books. Their goal is to portray Islam, a faith followed by a quarter of the world's population, as a villainous religion, one that preaches violence. They blame this violence, in parts of the world, on the faith, rather than on the particular people and their circumstances. We have already discussed and acknowledged that verses of violence exist in all holy books for multiple reasons (often due to injustice and persecution), and Islam is no exception. All major religions have had such encounters in their history, and by all means Christianity has had the most (and unjustified, we might add). Thus, we will not repeat that discussion; however, the Qur'an and its verses have existed for fourteen hundred years, yet most of the violence we are witnessing, and to which critics refer to, belongs to recent years. Any violence by any extremist from any faith can be justified by many verses in holy books. Is there no other underlying reason for the recent so-called Muslim violence?

As to the above verse, the principle stated in the first verse of chapter 47 is to the believers to fight the unbelievers. The believers are the ones who follow the truth. The unbelievers, on the other hand, follow falsehoods. The following verse refers specifically to meeting the unbelievers in battle:

Therefore, when you meet the Unbelievers (in fight), smite at
their necks, when you have thoroughly subdued them, bind
a bond firmly (on them): thereafter (is the time for) either
generosity or ransom [set them free either by an act of grace or
against ransom]: Until the war lays down its burdens." (47:4)

Before the revelation of this chapter, idolaters lived in the Arabian Peninsula, some of whom were at war with Muslims and some who were bound by peace treaties. Thereafter, *combatant* idolaters were to be killed if they were found anywhere in the Arabian Peninsula (as in a state of war). In addition the first verse of this chapter describes the unbelievers as: "Those who reject Allah and hinder (men) from the Path of Allah,- their deeds will Allah render [in vain] astray (from their mark)." (47:1) They are hostile to the believers and will do anything to turn them to bar them from their belief as we have seen throughout history many have done so not just with sword, but through speeches, books, articles and broadcasts, with no success and left this world with no meaningful results. On the other hand it describes the believers as: "But those who believe and work deeds of righteousness, and believe in the (Revelation) sent down to Muhammad- for it is the Truth from their Lord,- He will remove from them their ills and improve their condition" (47:2). Verse 4 then says believers can defend themselves against the combatant unbelievers (as described), if unbelievers arm themselves and come to fight (in a battle as "until the war lays down its burden", and the commend on what to do with the captives refer to). Once they are overcome, they are to be kept as captive, so they do not run away and return to fight. After the battle is ended, they can be freed or ransomed or exchanged. This rule did not apply to idolaters outside the Arabian Peninsula; they could continue to live in the Muslim state but only in accordance with the rules of the Islamic community (for example, not causing rebellion and paying the jizya for the reasons discussed).

Eliminating the aggression of those who are hostile to Islam must be the first objective of warfare. When the Muslim community increased in numbers and became more powerful, God established this ruling concerning those who are taken captive during war. This is the only Qur'anic text stating a ruling on such captives: "Thereafter, set them free either by an act of grace or against ransom" (47:4). This means that captives of war are to be set free (the critic above conveniently removed this option from his statement) with or without ransom. The Qur'anic verse does not mention a third option, such as putting captives who are idolaters to death. It is all a test for mankind, which determines everyone's position: "Thus, had God so willed, He could have punished them Himself, but it is His will that He tests you all by means of one another. And as for those who are slain in God's cause, never will He let their deeds go to waste" (47:4).

He can indeed punish the aggressors without using any forces. God, however, wants to put forth a scene where truth encounters the falsehood, so members of each group earn positions and results they deserve. God wants the best for the believers. He tests them and cultivates what is good in them, making it easier for them to do good works and bringing out the best potential in people. The highest-level human beings attain is when the truth they believe in becomes so dear to them that they will fight for it, even exposing themselves to death ("But those who are slain in the Way of Allah,- He will never let their deeds be lost"). They simply will not compromise on the truth they believe in and cannot live or love life unless it be under such truth. God wants to cultivate the believers so that every desire and aspiration pertaining to this transitory life on earth, dear as they may be to most people, are progressively valued less. They do not make their choices on impulse, but on the basis of careful consideration. God also wants to elevate the believers.

Moreover, such a test provides the means to put the affairs of a community on sound footing, placing its leadership in the hands of those who strive strenuously for God's cause and who are ready to sacrifice themselves for it. Such people care little for worldly riches and luxuries. When they are the leaders of a society, the whole world can potentially be set on the right footing. Furthermore, it facilitates ways for people to earn God's pleasure and His rewards, without having to face a reckoning. By contrast, those in the opposing camp find it easier to do what incurs God's displeasure and what exposes them to His punishment. Indeed, this was the thinking of early Muslims that caused many to embrace Islam. We strongly encourage and invite the critics to consider the preceding facts from a historical, contextual basis and with a deeper look at the concepts behind them.

6.35 "You should be uppermost (have the upper hand): for Allah is with you" (47:35)

Be not weary and faint-hearted, crying for peace, when you should be uppermost [have the upper hand]: for Allah is with you, and will never put you in loss for your (good) deeds. (47:35)

To fully understand this verse, we must first consider the preceding verse. Abdullah ibn Umar (one of the Prophet's companions and a prominent authority in Hadith) said that they, the Prophet's companions, used to think that every good deed would inevitably be accepted by God, until this verse was revealed. They wondered what could render their deeds worthless. They thought that it must be cardinal sins. However, God revealed the following verse: "Allah forgives not (the sin of) associating other gods with Him, but He forgives whom He pleases for other (lesser) sins" (4:116).

Such reports show how the sincere Muslims were receptive to the Qur'anic verses. They were profoundly affected by them, feared every warning, careful lest they applied to them and keen to do what the Qur'an required of them. Verse 34 explains what fate awaits those who are hostile to the Prophet (PBUH): "Those who reject Allah, and hinder (men) from the Path of Allah, then die rejecting Allah [as disbelievers],- Allah will not forgive them" (47:34). The chance to ensure forgiveness of sins is available only in this present life. The gates of repentance, which ensure forgiveness, are open to both unbelievers and sinners up to the moment of death.

Verses such as this one address both the believers and unbelievers. They warn the latter to take the right action before it is too late, to repent and turn back to God before the chance is lost and the doors are closed. This is understood by the fact that what the believers are cautioned against in the next verse is what can lead to the same fate of the unbelievers, as mentioned in the preceding verse: "Be not weary and faint-hearted, crying for peace, when you should be uppermost [have the upper hand]: for Allah is with you, and will never put you in loss for your (good) deeds" (47:35). Such are the actions believers

are cautioned against. They are presented with the fate of the unbelievers who are hostile to the Prophet (PBUH), so that Muslims take
care not to do anything that brings them nearer to such an outcome.
This warning suggests that there may have been Muslims who feared
or felt burdened by the stress of fighting. They might have weakened and advocated for a peace agreement in order to avoid fighting.
Some might have looked to their relatives who were unbelievers or
been involved financially with them. All of these possibilities could
influence a person's preference for a peaceful arrangement. Verse 35
addresses the believers, telling them not to be forced to make peace
based on fear of weakness and intimidation; God is with them and
their strength comes from Him and their true faith. Their good deeds
will never be lost, as verse 34:37 confirms: "It is not your wealth nor
your sons [children], that will bring you nearer to Us in degree: but
only those who believe and work righteousness."

6.36 "No blame is there on the blind, nor is there blame on the lame" (48:17)

> No blame is there on the blind, nor is there blame on the
> lame, nor on one ill (if he joins not the war): But he that
> obeys Allah and his Messenger,- (Allah) will admit him to
> Gardens beneath which rivers flow; and he who turns back,
> (Allah) will punish him with a grievous Penalty. (48:17)

Some critics say that Muslims often claim that jihad means spiritual
struggle, and if that is so, then why are the blind, lame, and sick exempted? Some add the verse also stipulates that those who do not fight
will be punished in hell.

To clarify, jihad is a general form of struggle or striving, starting
with self-struggle and self-improvement, which is the larger part of
the meaning. Striving can be at the individual or community level
and can be carried out in many ways, one of which is via a physical
fight, as explained in detail in chapter 3.

The term *jihad* is neither mentioned in verse 48:17 nor in the preceding verse. In 48:16, the verb *tuqatalounahum* ("fight them"), from the root word *qital*, is used here, not *jihad*. Therefore, since the context and the terminology are about fighting a war, it then makes sense why the blind, lame, and sick would be exempt. It seems some critics are trying hard to interject the term *jihad* into the Qur'anic verse. We have already explained that the term has a broad connotation, one of which can imply physical struggle, although in many verses related to war (such as 48:16), the term *qital* is used, which explicitly means a physical fight, as in a battle. Unfortunately, one who is not familiar with the Qur'anic verses and their meanings might actually take these critics' comments as true statements, which they are not.

The verse refers to a person who is blind or has a disability and who is therefore exempt from military engagement. A person who is sick is also temporarily exempt. Ultimately, it is all a question of obedience and disobedience. It is a mental attitude, not a technical situation. Those who obey God and His Messenger (PBUH) are rewarded. And those who run away from their duty ultimately suffer. Anyone can balance the hardship of fighting for God's cause against the safety and comfort of staying behind. Individuals must make their own choices.

6.37 "Muhammad is the Messenger of God; and those who are with him are . . ." (48:29)

> Muhammad is the Messenger of God; and those who
> are with him are strong [firm] against the unbelievers,
> but compassionate toward one another. (48:29)

Critics sometimes use this verse to assert that Islam does not treat everyone equally. They claim two distinct standards exist and are applied based on one's religious status. They then add that the terms used for "hard" or "ruthless" in this verse share the same root as the word translated as "painful" or "severe" that is used to describe hell in other verses, including 65:10, 40:46, and 50:26.

Firstly, *ashaddu* means "stern, firm, strong" and comes from the root word *shadd* or "strength." Nowhere in this verse do we see the term "ruthless," nor is it used in any translation of this verse or other verses, including 65:10, 40:46, and 50:26, as well as others.

Secondly, these critics are using this verse to make a blanket statement about Islam. How could the Qur'an make such a generalization when it also says the following: "O you who believe! Stand out firmly for Allah, as witnesses to fair dealing, and let not the hatred of others to you make you swerve to wrong and depart from justice. Be just: that is next to piety: and fear Allah. For Allah is well-acquainted with all that you do" (5:8)? What about the rights of the unbelievers in Islam, as mentioned in chapter 3?

Thirdly, here is what the verse is specifically referring to: It includes several snapshots or images depicting the believers' main conditions, both subtle and apparent. One portrays their attitude toward the unbelievers and to one another. They stand firm in their beliefs, despite the fact that those unbelievers include their family and friends. Thus, they are "strong [firm] against the unbelievers, compassionate toward one another." Another image shows them as they are in worship: "You will see them bow and prostrate themselves (in prayer)." Yet a third image reveals what preoccupies their minds and characterizes their feelings: "Seeking Grace from Allah and (His) goodly Pleasure." A fourth focuses on how worship is reflected in their faces when they dedicate all to God: "On their faces are their marks, (being) the traces of their prostration, this is their similitude in the Torah." Other images tell us how they are described in the Gospels: "And their similitude in the Gospel is: like a seed which sends forth its blade, then makes it strong; it then becomes thick, and it stands on its own stem, (filling) the sowers with wonder and delight; As a result, it fills the Unbelievers with rage at them" (48:29).

The verse begins by confirming the Prophet's (PBUH) status, denied by the Quraysh negotiator, Suhail ibn Amr, and the unbelievers he represented at the time: "Muhammad is the Messenger of God." Needless to say, the believers experience different conditions and situations during their lifetimes. However, the images in the verse highlight their beatific features. The selection of these particular images shows that God wants to bestow honor on this pleasing community. This is reflected right from the very first image that describes them as: "Strong [firm] against the unbelievers, but compassionate toward one another." They are instructed to take a firm and unyielding attitude toward the unbelievers, not yield to their ways, and to stand firm in their beliefs.

This means that in both conditions of unyielding firmness and flowing mercy, the determining factor is faith. There is absolutely no personal consideration. They are to discard selfish thoughts and make their bond with God the only one to which they attach any value. Again, God's wish to honor this community is apparent by emphasizing their condition during worship: "You will see them bow and prostrate themselves (in prayer)." This portrayal is their permanent condition, one that we see whenever we look at them. In fact, bowing and prostration represent worship, core aspects of who they are. Therefore, it is expressed in a way that makes it permanent during their lifetime, as if they spent their entire lives bowing and prostrating.

The same applies to the third image, which concentrates on their inner thoughts and feelings: "Seeking Grace from Allah and (His) Pleasure." Such are their permanent feelings and what preoccupies them. All they aspire for is God's favor and earning His pleasure. The fourth image focuses on how worship and inner feelings are reflected in their appearance: "On their faces are their marks, (being) the traces of their prostration." Their faces shine with transparent clarity and the warmth that worship imparts. The mark of this submission is seen on their faces; in other words, there are no traces of pride, arrogance, or selfishness. Instead, their faces reflect noble characteristics of humility, purity, and a serenity that adds to the shine on a believer's face. The symbol "their similitude in the Gospel is: like a seed which sends forth its blade, then makes it strong; it then becomes thick, and it stands on its own stem," at the end of verse 48:29 refers to a similar symbol in Matthew 13:31.

6.38 "Truly Allah loves those who fight in His Cause in battle array" (61:4)

> Truly Allah loves those who fight in His Cause in battle array, as if they were a solid cemented structure. (61:4)

A critic contends this verse explicitly refers to "rows" or "battle array," meaning it speaks of physical battle. A few verses later (61:9) the cause is defined as "He it is who has sent His Messenger (Mohammed) with guidance and the religion of truth (Islam) to make it victorious over all religions even though the infidels may resist." (See the response to 61:10–12 in the following section.) That is to say, infidels who resist Islamic rule are to be fought.[173]

Again, the term *infidel* does not exist in the Qur'an. It was initially coined by Christians to refer to those who did not believe in Christianity, and, unfortunately, found its way into a few Islamic books and translations of the Qur'an. None of the most common translations use this term. The Qur'an uses either the term *kuffar,* meaning unbelievers (those who hear the message properly and reject it) or the term *mushrekeen* (idolaters), which is used in verse 61:9.

To begin with, the verse indeed refers to battle because the term *yuqateloun* is used, which means "those who physically fight." Hence, the critic works hard to prove the obvious by saying the verse refers to "rows" or "battle array," meaning physical conflict, which the verse already explicitly states.

Since the verse refers to a physical fight, what is to be concluded here? We have repeatedly said that Islam does not allow any physical fights without a just reason, and many related verses were explained as to why Muslims engaged in those battles, all within Islamic bounds and with valid reasons. It seems the statement "fighting in cause of God" triggers an alert mechanism in some critics who fail to consider the verses before and after in order to properly understand the context. Instead, they rush to the conclusion that anyone who disagrees with Islam or Muslims is to be fought.

In fact, this critic says, "Infidels who resist Islamic rule are to be fought." If by "resist" he means they only rejected Islam (or disagreed with it) but remained peaceful toward Muslims (some of whom did so and signed treaties), then Muslims had no reason to fight them (as explicated in multiple earlier verses). However, if he means they were hostile, picked up arms, and physically fought Muslims, it would be naïve to think Muslims would not have responded accordingly.

To understand the full context, we must first consider the preceding verses. A group of believers are strongly reproached for something they did that was particularly hateful to God. This was inappropriate behavior for these believers:

> O you who believe! Why say you that which you do
> not [do]? Grievously odious [Most loathsome] is it in the
> sight of Allah that you say what you do not do! Truly
> Allah loves those who fight in His Cause in battle array,
> as if they were a solid cemented structure. (61:2–4)

Ibn Abbas reports that some believers used to say: "We wish that God would tell us what action is most loved by Him so that we could do it." God instructed His Messenger (PBUH) to say that what God loves most is a belief in Him that allows no room for doubt and striving against deviant people who reject the faith. However, when the order came, a few believers found it difficult, and disliked it. Hence the revelation of the verse "O you who believe! Why say you that which you do not [do]? Grievously odious [Most loathsome] is it in the sight of Allah that you say what you do not do!" (61:2–3). Al-Tabari also confirmed this in his commentary. Al-Qatadah says that this verse reproaches those who used to boast about their exploits, claiming that they had fought and killed the enemy when they had not done so.

The passage starts then with a reproach for behavior concerning one or more actual events: "Why say you that which you do not [do]?" (61:2). It then denounces this action and its lack of morality in a doubly powerful way: "Grievously odious [Most loathsome] is it in the sight of Allah that you say what you do not do!" (61:3). What

God views as most loathsome must certainly be hateful and repugnant. This statement is sufficient to make believers view this in the vilest of terms, particularly as God addresses them as people who have accepted His religion and believe in Him.

The next verse refers to that particular matter when they did something different than what they used to profess, namely the struggle. It defines what God likes in this question and what earns His pleasure: "Truly Allah loves those who fight in His Cause in battle array, as if they were a solid cemented structure" (61:4). This is not mere fighting but fighting for God's cause in collaboration with the Muslim community, within its ranks, and with resolve and steadfastness, so that believers remain "in solid ranks, as though they were a solid cemented structure." A well cemented and reinforced structure stands integrally and uniformly strong. A strike on one corner will not shake the entire structure.

A Muslim is not a Muslim unless he or she functions within a community. It is inconceivable for Islam to be practiced unless it functions in a community and within well-defined relationships, a system, and goals. Its ultimate goal applies to the community as a whole and to each individual.

When we examine these three verses we find that the morality of the individual is intertwined with the needs of the community, under the authority of the faith. The first two verses under discussion refer to God's punishment and a strong censure if believers say something that is belied by their deeds. Thus, these two verses delineate the hugely important qualities of truthfulness and consistency in a Muslim's conduct.

Muslims' inner life must be reflected and consistent with their outer life or appearance. Their actions must be consistent with their words. This applies to all situations and goes far beyond the call to fight to which the third verse refers. The Qur'an places great emphasis on this Islamic characteristic, which is also repeatedly emphasized in the tradition.

Let us now consider the issue of fighting, which these verses addressed at the time of their revelation. There are several points here that should be considered: These verses refer to a group of Muslims who, according to some reports, belonged to the Muhajereen, the early Muslims who migrated with the Prophet (PBUH) from Mecca to Medina. While in Mecca, they wished, with enthusiasm, that God would allow them to fight, but they were told to hold back and attend to their worship duties instead. However, later in Medina, they were told to fight, which was considered appropriate then, so they adopted a different attitude:

Had you turned your vision toward those who were told, to hold back their hands from fighting, but establish regular prayers and spend in regular charity (i.e. the purifying dues)? When the order for fighting was issued to them, behold! a section of them feared men as – or even more than – they should have feared Allah said, "Our Lord! Why have you ordered us to fight? If only You had granted us a delay for a little while." (4: 77)[174]

Other reports suggest this passage refers to a group of Muslims who asked about the action God loves most so they could perform it. However, when they were ordered to fight for God's cause, they disliked it.

As we reflect on this passage, we realize that regular and repeated encouragement, directives, and strengthening are all necessary for the human soul when faced with difficult tasks and responsibilities. Moreover, we realize that we must not ask for great goals when we face neither pressure nor difficulty, because we may not be able to fulfill what we ask God to assign to us. Here, we see a few early Muslims weakening to the extent that they say one thing and do another. Hence, they faced this strong reproach from God.

Furthermore, we need to reflect on the phrasing of the verse that speaks of God's love for those who fight for His cause in closed ranks, as though they were a firm and solid structure. This represents profound encouragement to fight for God's cause. Islam neither likes nor encourages fighting, but it makes it a duty of Muslims because life necessitates it, and the purpose behind it is very important.

Regarding the critic's last statement that "this is followed by (61:9)," which defines the cause: "He it is who has sent His Messenger (Mohammed) with guidance and the religion of truth (Islam) to make it victorious over all religions even though the infidels may resist." We will first explain verse 61:9 and then address 61:10–12 in the following section.

The correct translation of the verse says: "It is He who has sent His Messenger with guidance and the religion of truth, so that He may proclaim it over all other religions, even though the idolaters may detest (it)" (61:9).

God testifies that Islam is *"guidance and the religion of truth"* as the final word. God's will has been fulfilled. It has prevailed by its very nature as a religion. No other religion compares to it by its nature. Pagan and idolatrous religions cannot stand up to its monotheistic message for a moment. Divine religions, on the other hand, find it as their final and complete version. We discussed in chapter 2 what constitutes "one religion." In essence, Islam is the perfect and complete version of these divine faiths, and it will preserve its pure form until the end of time.

Earlier divine religions were eventually distorted by omissions, additions, extractions, and misquotations. Even if they had remained intact, they are no more than earlier versions of the divine faith that did not cater to ever-increasing life requirements, because they were intended by God to serve for a limited time only.

6.39 "That you strive (your utmost) in the cause of Allah" (61:10–12)

O you who believe, shall I lead you to a bargain that will save you from a grievous Penalty [painful doom]? That you believe in Allah and His Messenger, and that you strive (your utmost) in the cause of Allah with your property and persons [lives]. That will be best for you, if you but knew. He will forgive you your sins, and admit you to Gardens beneath which Rivers flow, and to beautiful mansions in Gardens of Eternity. That is indeed the supreme achievement. (61:10–12)

Some critics believe these verses sanction physical conflict in order to give Islam victory over other religions and that the verses use the Arabic root word for jihad.

Jihad and the Qur'anic phrase "your property and persons [lives]" means a struggle with possessions first and not just life, in the path of God (all-inclusive as we discussed in section 3.4), which is all about sacrificing in His cause with anything that you may have in your possession, whether your own or supplied by others, and implies using one's abilities to confront an opponent. This could be done through writing, speaking, and educating based on the circumstance. For this reason, the term *qital* (physical fight) is not used in the verse. Of course, the verse includes both personal and communal struggles. However, the struggle is still bound by the Qur'anic rules of law and engagement, as discussed earlier.

An important prerequisite for the verses relating to God's promise of a reward in this life and the hereafter is a belief in God. There will be a Day of Judgment when everyone will be held accountable for his or her actions. But without a firm belief in God, these verses cannot be fully understood.

With the final version of the divine faith, the Qur'an addresses the believers—those living at the time of revelation and those of later generations—offering them the bargain of their lives. This is a transaction in which the merchandise is faith and the means to achieve it is jihad.

The verse begins by addressing the reader in the name of faith: "O you who believe!" It is followed by an inspiring question by God, Who holds their expectation of an answer: "Shall I lead you to a bargain that will save you from a grievous Penalty [painful doom]?" (61:10). A bargain that yields a prosperous life here in this world and hereafter. The reference is to individual as well as the community.

Who would not wish to know what this bargain is and its terms? The answer is given in the next verse: "That you believe in Allah and His Messenger." Since they are truly believers in God and His Messenger (PBUH), they are happy they have already fulfilled this request. "And that you strive (your utmost) in the cause of Allah with your property and persons [lives]." This is the main theme of the chapter, and it is given here to reiterate a message that has already been clarified. God knows that human beings need such repetition and variety of modes and styles in order to rise to the occasion. Realizing this, they will exert their maximum efforts to establish and preserve the divine system.

Then the Qur'an presents the bargain in an even more attractive way: "That will be best for you, if you but knew" (61:11). Who would need any further reward when he or she is assured of God's forgiveness? Who would begrudge anything if he or she is certain to obtain God's forgiveness? But God's grace is limitless, for the reward also includes something for the life to come. God "will forgive you your sins, and admit you to Gardens beneath which Rivers flow, and to beautiful mansions in Gardens of Eternity" (61:12). The term "best" in "That will be best for you, if you but knew", relates to the fact that opposite of "best" will result if the Muslims abandon higher goals and cling to material world.

In addition, the believers are promised a victory in this life in the next verse: "And another (favor will He bestow,) which you do love, - help from Allah and a speedy victory. So give the Glad Tidings to the Believers" (61:13).

Such a believer cannot sit idle and live in a world devoid of faith, not striving to establish a just community governed by the faithful. In the next verse, the Qur'an gives an example within the same context:

O you who believe, Be helpers (in the cause) of Allah; as said Jesus, the son of Mary to the disciples: "Who will be my helpers to (the work of) Allah?" The disciples said: "We are Allah's helpers," then a portion of the Children of Israel believed, and a portion disbelieved. But We gave strength to those who believed against their enemies, and they became the ones that prevailed. (61:14)

As this verse points out, helping God's cause means helping His Messenger (PBUH) and his faith. The twelve apostles of Jesus Christ (PBUH) were close and dedicated pupils. They continued to spread his message and the commandments after his life. Although this verse does not give us a detailed story, it gives us a sense of how a follower of faith should cultivate the proper attitude. Hence, we view it in the context given and for the purpose it serves. "O you who believe, Be helpers (in the cause) of Allah" (61:14). Rise up to the noble position to which He elevates you. Is there any higher and nobler position than being a supporter of God and struggling for His cause?

6.40 "Strive hard against the Unbelievers and the Hypocrites, and be firm" (66:9)

> O Prophet! Strive hard against the Unbelievers and
> the Hypocrites, and be firm against them. Their
> abode is Hell,- an evil refuge (indeed). (66:9)

A critic argues that the root word for jihad is used in this verse and that the context implies holy war with the difference being that the scope of fighting is extended. The scope of violence is broadened to include hypocrites—those who call themselves Muslims but do not act as such.[175]

We discussed similar verses that deal with hypocrites in section 6.31. Hypocrites did not have a peaceful and honest attitude toward Muslims. They had conspired against Muslims and allied themselves with the idolaters. Again, despite the critic's insistence, there is no mention of holy war in verse 66:9, as it refers to struggle or jihad, which we have discussed in earlier sections.

The verse was revealed in the context of protecting the first Muslim community when the Prophet (PBUH) issued a command to strive against those who take a hostile stand toward Islam. Thus, oppressive and wicked groups are not allowed to attack the Muslims whether from outside the community, as the unbelievers used to do, or from within the community as the hypocrites did.

In its order to strive against the enemies, this Qur'anic statement groups together the unbelievers and the hypocrites because they shared the same mission: to destroy the Muslim community or at least hasten its disintegration. The command to Prophet is to be alert, firm and to neutralize their schemes against Muslims. The relation between the Muslims and the unbelievers or hypocrites who mean to harm cannot be that of friendship. To strive and be hard against them protects the believers from their hostilities. As for the life to come, the Qur'an says of the unbelievers and hypocrites, "Their abode is Hell,- an evil refuge (indeed)" (66:9). Therefore, the believers are striving to protect their faith but they are not against those who want to coexist peacefully, regardless of their faith or opinion of Islam. In such cases, Muslims have no reason to declare jihad against them.

6.41 "And say not of those who are slain in the way of Allah: They are dead" (2:154)

And say not of those who are slain in the way of Allah: 'They are dead.' Nay, they are living, though you perceive (it) not. (2:154)

This verse is often cited by critics of Islam who claim leaders of extremist groups use it to rally their followers to commit suicide bombings.

Before addressing the verse, we must note that leaders of any group may generalize any statement from a well-known person or book (especially a holy book) in order to influence people's thoughts and psyches. Extremists are no exception.

The verse prepares Muslims for potential encounter with the combatant enemy and the oppressors mentioned in earlier verse 2:150. It describes those who risk their lives and who fight for God's cause as honorable people with pure hearts. If they are killed in such a struggle, they must not be considered or described as dead. They continue to live, as God Himself clearly states. They live beyond our material world, one beyond our perception. Although they may appear lifeless, life and death are not judged by superficial physical means alone. Life is chiefly characterized by what one stands for—one's activities, growth, and persistence—while death is a state of lifelessness and total loss of function. But the death of those who are killed for God's cause lends greater impetus to the cause. Their influence on those left behind also grows and stands as a lesson in history. Thus, after their death, their memory remains an active force in shaping and giving direction to their community. It is in this sense that such people, having sacrificed their lives for the sake of God, retain an active existence in everyday life.

One notable example whose name stands for justice and is always remembered in Islamic history and hailed as a lesson in fighting for freedom and against injustice is the great martyr Hussain ibn Ali. He was the grandson of the Prophet Muhammad (PBUH), who refused to pledge allegiance (fealty) to Yazid ibn Mu'awiyah, a self-appointed, unjust ruler who demanded Hussain's pledge of allegiance. Many who became the subject of Yazid's persecution and slaughter did not recognize his rule. Thus, Hussain ibn Ali led the resistance against injustice, as he saw Yazid unfit to rule the Muslim nation. There were other martyrs in Islamic history that gave their lives in battles, including some of the Prophet's (PBUH) companions and his Uncle Hamza.

Throughout the centuries, Hussain and all the martyrs in Islamic history remain highly revered by Muslims throughout the world for their sacrifice and stands for justice. Their names will continue to be remembered until the end of time. On the contrary, Muslims will not remember the names of extremists and their leaders who incite violence against innocent people. Their names will not be recorded in Islamic history in the same manner as the martyrs mentioned above.

6.42 "It is not fitting for a Prophet that he should have prisoners of war" (8:67)

It is not fitting for a Prophet that he should have prisoners of war unless he has subdued [battled strenuously in] the land. You look for the temporal goods of this world; but Allah looks to the Hereafter: And Allah is Exalted in might, Wise. (8:67)

Some critics draw on this verse to claim a defensive fight is unlimited in scope and that the Prophet did take prisoners, even though it commends the Prophet (PBUH) not to take prisoners.

Firstly, the correct translation, as above, is "unless he has subdued [battled strenuously in] the land," which means the Prophet (PBUH) has achieved victory after a war. Secondly, in following the analysis of the earlier verses on war, the Qur'an now addresses the issue of taking prisoners. "It is not fitting for a Prophet" makes the message absolute and nonexclusive to Prophet Muhammad (PBUH). The verb *yuthkhen* refers to strenuously overcoming a challenge or a decisive victory by engaging in a full-scale war. The verse then says it is not becoming of any Prophet (PBUH) to take captives *without* achieving a decisive victory through a legitimate, recognized battle (not through a non-battle mean, which was customary during pre-Islamic times). In this context, it refers to encounters before the Battle of Badr, when some Muslims took captives and released them for ransom. The verse specifies that taking prisoners must only be done through a legitimate battle and victory over the enemy, not from an encounter or skirmish. The goal must not be to acquire spoils or other gains. Finally, when the Battle of Badr concluded with their victory, the Muslims took prisoners (as this was their first full battle). The Prophet (PBUH) consulted his companions because verse 47:4 had not yet been revealed regarding how to deal with prisoners of war ("and afterward either free them by grace or ransom till the war lay down its burden"). Some suggested killing the prisoners while others recommended freeing them for ransom as a way for Muslims to improve their reputation with the unbelievers. By freeing them, they would still be following God's guidance. The Prophet (PBUH) took this suggestion and freed the captives for ransom.[176]

Thirdly, following the same passage is verse 8:70, in which the Prophet (PBUH) is told "O Prophet! say to those who are captives in your hands: 'If Allah finds any good in your hearts, He will give you something better than what has been taken from you, and He will forgive you: for Allah is Oft-forgiving, Most Merciful.'" Had these critics read this verse, which follows 8:67, they would have realized the Prophet (PBUH) did take prisoners but did not kill them, as some of his companions suggested doing, but rather freed them.

6.43 "And if you are slain, or die, in the way of Allah, forgiveness and mercy" (3:157–158)

> And if you are slain, or die, in the way of Allah,
> forgiveness and mercy from Allah are far better than all
> they could amass. And if you die, or are slain, Lo! it is
> unto Allah that you shall be gathered. (3:157–158)

Some critics interpret this verse to mean that God implores His people not to fear death, but to be mindful of the rewards that await them in the next life. This is conveyed through Muhammad (PBUH); however, Jesus (PBUH) blessed those who made peace. In Islam, those who wage war (jihad) rank highest among the believers. According to verses 9:19–20, those who suffer exile and strive in God's cause with their possessions and lives have the highest rank in the eyes of God.

But some critics try to conflate extremists' behavior with the ideals of Islam—its goals, intentions, and accomplishments, including early Muslims' achievements and conduct in the eyes of God. Some commentators attribute the violent conduct of a few Muslims today to Islamic teachings and then contrast it with Christianity. They say that Jesus (PBUH) advised, "Blessed are the peace makers." We previously discussed the verses of violence in today's version of the Bible and said that one cannot compare a snapshot of the past to that of the present. When Jesus (PBUH) left this world, he had few disciples and was in no position to form a state or even a small community. At best, one might compare his situation to the first two years of Prophet Muhammad's (PBUH) life in Mecca, in which we see verses urging his first few followers to be patient, tolerant, and steadfast. Furthermore, these critics do not present any evidence to answer this: if the number of early Christians had risen to the number of the Muslims in Medina so that they would have had their own community, what would have been their reactions to the hostilities of the ruling Jews and the Romans, assuming their goal was the same as the Quraysh and the Meccans? In that case, what would have been God's instructions given through Jesus (PBUH)?

We have discussed verse 9:19 in earlier sections. Those who surrender to God their possessions and life, and endure hardships (for example, exile) rank high in the eyes of God. In verses 3:157–158, as viewed by a believer, a natural death or a violent death fighting for God's cause is superior to life and all the riches, position, and authority of the world. This is because it ensures God's forgiveness and grace—two objectives God wants His believers to attain most. Those of faith are not to work for personal glory or material gain, but rather to ensure that He bestows His grace on them. Although dying in the path of God can take many forms, including battle, *jihad fee sabil Allah* (struggle in the path of God), however, does not always mean to take up arms, as was discussed in chapter 3.

According to Islam, true believers will return to God, whether they die in their own beds or defending Muslims on the battlefield. Death is the destiny of all people, and it comes at its appointed time, and all are gathered before God on the Day of Resurrection. They either receive God's grace or suffer His punishment. It tells the believers their physical death is not end of life for them as they will be gathered before God in an everlasting higher life.

6.44 "O you who believe! fight the unbelievers who gird you" (9:123)

> O you who believe! fight the unbelievers who gird you
> about [are near you], and let them find firmness in you: and
> know that Allah is with those who fear Him. (9:123)

Some critics interpret this verse as an open-ended command for Muslims to engage in physical fights with unbelievers, while others assert it is in reference to an offensive fight.

Firstly, the verb *yaluuna* is written in the imperfect tense (referring to both present and future) and means those who are coming near you. The verse refers to fighting against a specific group and is not an open-ended directive to fight any and all unbelievers. At the time this chapter was revealed in the year 9 AH, almost all of Arabia had embraced Islam; hence, the unbelievers were those who lived on the outskirts of Arabia, as expressed in the phrase unbelievers "who are near you."

According to historian al-Tabari and others, this verse refers to Byzantines who had fought their way into Muslim territory and taken control of several local towns and tribes. With the help of their Ghassinid ruler, Shurahbil ibn Amr, Byzantines killed several members and leaders of these allied tribes because they had embraced Islam. The Prophet (PBUH) sent Harith ibn Umayra as an emissary with a letter for Ghassanid, who ruled Bosra, a town on the southern border of modern Syria. Ghassanid killed the Prophet's (PBUH) emissary, even though emissaries at the time were traditionally given full immunity. As a result, when the Prophet (PBUH) sent a small force of three thousand men to stop the provocation, they were confronted by an army of a hundred thousand Byzantines and Christian Arabs. This confrontation became known as the Battle of Mu'tah (a village in southern Jordan), which took place in the year 8 AH (629 CE), and left three Muslim commanders, Zayd ibn Haritha, Ja'far ibn Abi Talib, and Abdullah ibn Rawahah, defeated and killed because they were unprepared and outnumbered. Khalid ibn al-Walid (the Muslim commander after them) and a few others retreated and returned to Medina to report the outcome.[177]

Verse 9:123 was revealed after this conflict, and the Prophet (PBUH) mobilized the Muslim army for an encounter at Tabuk, based on information that Byzantine forces were preparing for a larger offensive. Thus, the verse enjoins Muslims to be firm and to show strength in the face of the Byzantine army in an effort to prevent their imminent attack. None of the battles Muslims fought were offensive fights, including the battle of Tabuk, as was discussed in detail in section 6.24. One might ask how could moving within one's territory be considered an offensive measure. When defending your country or territory, do you wait until the enemy reaches your capital city, or do you deploy to meet them at or near the border before they invade your land and control your towns (in this case Muslim and non-Muslim tribes who lived in the area)? If, in fact, this was not a defensive measure, but an offensive stance to invade the Byzantine Empire, why did the Muslims not march onward into Byzantine territory, especially when no army showed up in Tabuk to fight? The Muslims instead returned to Medina.

Chapter 7
Parting Thoughts

IN CHAPTER 6, WE listed the most commonly misinterpreted verses cited by critics of Islam, their comments on these verses, and our responses. Verses not addressed in chapter 6 would be either a repeat of the same verses or similar ones; hence, mentioning them would be repetitive. In this chapter, we offer a few parting thoughts on the critics' opinions regarding Islamic attitudes on war and violence.

1. The most common mistake critics of Islam make in their interpretation is to overlook the context in which each verse was revealed. This is essential to a deeper textual understanding, especially in verses that reference wars and conflicts. One can explain Qur'an with Qur'an. Since the Qur'an is not ordered by topic (like textbook chapters), it is necessary for one to be thoroughly familiar with other texts in the Qur'an, which deal with the same topic or relate to it. Failure to do so may alter the overall message of the Qur'an concerning that topic. In fact, other texts in the Qur'an may be highly significant in determining the true meaning of a given text. Critics have also relied on narrow definition of key terms, especially jihad (struggle), which has led to further misinterpretations. Offensive jihad, or an offensive physical fight as some critics suggest, does not exist in Islam. However, if by offensive jihad, critics mean introducing, propagating, and preaching

Islam through education, then such is a form of jihad that does exist in Islam, just as it does in Christianity. This is evident by the letters of invitation the Prophet (PBUH) wrote to a Persian king, a Roman emperor, and other rulers inviting them to accept Islam but with no further action required. The choice was up to them to accept or decline the invitation. Muslims would have had no way to pursue this further and certainly not through force or violence.

2. The verses that refer to war or struggle are historic and related to specific situations Muslims encountered at a particular time. Some of these situations may not exist today and if they are, they may take a different form. Verses revealed to deal with certain situations should not be unnecessarily generalized. There are many history books available that describe these events in detail.

3. Since these verses are historically based, does it mean they are irrelevant to our times? Not exactly. The Qur'an mentions Muslims' struggles with their enemies and their mode of behavior. It then instructs them on how to cultivate the proper attitude and character in order to deal with specific and sometimes adverse situations. Each is a reminder to future generations of the lessons learned about Muslim unity, reliance on God, commitment to striving on God's path, and cultivating patience and perseverance. Naturally, Muslims should defend themselves when aggressed upon, defend against injustices, and avoid all transgressions

4. In reading about the early years of Islamic history and related Qur'anic passages, one can see how Islam evolved from a small group of followers to a large number and eventually to statehood—a situation that did not occur with earlier Prophets like Moses and Jesus (PBUT). These changes occurred over a span of twenty-three years in which Islam began with a few individuals who were under persecution in Mecca and who were then forced to migrate to Medina. There, the number of people who embraced Islam grew rapidly and the

community grew until it became a state, governed by the Prophet (PBUH) himself. During this time, Islam flourished throughout Arabia. As a new nation, Muslims experienced commerce, new relations with neighboring lands, treaties, and battles.

5. As a fundamental rule, Islamic principles are based on peace and justice. Islam is at peace with the peaceful. Islam advocates peace and calls on all nations to be peaceful regardless of their faith. Advocating peace means Islam and its followers stand for peace and justice. At the same time, Muslims should be ready to stand up against injustice, corruption and destruction. Any act of war or violence is a consequence of an attack or a desire to keep a Muslim society or nation safe, including non-Muslim citizens. If we look at Islamic history in its early years, we will find that Islam brought peace, justice, and order to any society it adopted. One clear example was Medina, a city in chaos prior to the arrival of the Prophet (PBUH) and his followers. Many tribes were at war with each other and there was infighting among the elites. When the Prophet (PBUH) entered Medina, he was welcomed because the people of Medina had heard of his wisdom, truthfulness, and trustworthiness. As such, they respected his balanced and impartial opinions. He rendered judgment in many disputes and brought peace to the entire community through his wisdom and statesmanship in a predominantly non-Muslim community. All the events during the twenty-three years of his prophethood, including his transparent life, have been extensively and consistently reported in multiple authentic history books and biographies, which we've mentioned in this text.

6. In laws of jurisprudence and any court of law, there is the principle of the absolute (general) and the condition (constraint), which says the absolute cannot be applied when there is a condition or a constraint. Once all relevant scriptural passages have been collected, the "general" has to be distinguished from the "specific" and the "conditional" from the

"unconditional." Also, the "unequivocal" passages have to be distinguished from the allegorical ones. Moreover, the reasons and circumstances for the revelation (*asbab al-nuzul*) must be distinguished for all the passages and verses. When there are clear verses in the Qur'an about physical fighting and its conditions, one cannot apply absolute terms or make generalizations. The Qur'an explicitly divides unbelievers into two groups or types: the first group is hostile, combative, and expels believers from their homes or reneges on their treaties; the second group is peaceful and honors their treaties, as verse 60:8 says: "Allah forbids you not, with regard to those who fight you not for (your) Faith nor drive you out of your homes, from dealing kindly and justly with them: for Allah loveth those who are just"; whereas, verse 60:9, which follows, explicitly forbids surrendering to injustice: "Allah only forbids you, with regard to those who fight you for (your) Faith, and drive you out of your homes, and support (others) in driving you out, from turning to them (for friendship and protection)." In Islam, surrendering to oppression and injustice is considered a form of injustice. When the Qur'an mentions fighting, it always qualifies to do so only when faced with hostility and in no way advocates killing for other reasons. Therefore, how could one claim that Islam advocates killing unbelievers? Unfortunately, there are those who do not wish to conduct a proper contextual analysis of the Qur'an nor consider a historical perspective in order to fully understand the passages. They merely wish to use a cut-and-paste method to convey a biased message of their choice. They do not know or care to know about the principle of absolute and constraint. In addition, language plays a very important role in understanding Qur'anic verses especially when it comes to Islamic law. This means mastering Arabic grammar, syntax, morphology, rhetoric, poetry, etymology, and Qur'anic exegesis. Without mastery of these disciplines, erroneous understanding will be likely, indeed inevitable.

7. There have been many books written about qital (battle).
    Although the Qur'an clearly spells out the rules of engage-
    ment in a physical battle, some critics have preconceived no-
    tions and no book or verses will convince them otherwise.
    Two verses in particular summarize Islam's philosophy of war:
    "By Allah's will they routed them; and David slew Goliath;
    and Allah gave him power and wisdom and taught him what-
    ever (else) He willed. And did not Allah Check [repel] one
    set of people by means of another, the earth would indeed
    be full of mischief" (2:251) and "(They are) those who have
    been expelled from their homes in defiance of right,- (for no
    cause) except that they say, 'our Lord is Allah'. Did not Allah
    check [repel] one set of people by means of another, there
    would surely have been pulled down monasteries, churches,
    synagogues, and mosques, in which the name of Allah is com-
    memorated in abundant measure." (22:40).

8. Another myth perpetuated by critics is that none of the wars
    Muslims fought were defensive, which they try to prove
    through Qur'anic verses such as 2:191, 2:216, 8:67, 9:42, 9:123
    (as addressed in chapter 6). But there are verses proving oth-
    erwise, such as "Will you not fight people who violated their
    oaths, plotted to expel the Messenger, and did attack you
    first?" (9:13). While the critics do acknowledge that Muslims
    were killed, persecuted, and tortured during their thirteen
    years in Mecca, they do not consider that experience as a
    conflict or a war. The multiple attempts made to annihilate
    Muslims and force them to leave Mecca with their lives, aban-
    doning their homes and possessions, is not considered a state
    of war. Hence, Muslims had no right to defend themselves.
    How then do critics define a defensive war? They do not
    consider verses such as 22:40 above, or the preceding verse:
    "To those against whom war is made, permission is given
    (to fight) [and defend], because they were wronged" (22:39).
    In this verse, the verb *yuqatalun* refers to "those who are at-
    tacked," which means they were attacked first and then says

"they were wronged." How is this not considered a defensive war? For the critics who believe in freedom of religion and expression, why do they consider Islam to be an exception? Even after Muslims migrated, the enemy did not stop their intimidations and threats, as was discussed earlier. Muslims were given an ultimatum to either be killed or return to the Prophet (PBUH) in Medina. Even if Muslims returned to Mecca to visit relatives or the house of God, they would be arrested, tortured, and killed. Nonetheless, the Qur'an says, "But if the enemy incline towards peace, you (also) incline towards peace" (8:61). As a result, the Messenger of God initiated and signed numerous peace treaties with those who were inclined toward peace.

9. There are no verses in the Qur'an and no authentic narrations from the Prophet (PBUH) commending or urging Muslims to fight non-Muslims (be they idolaters, unbelievers, Jews, Christians, or followers of any other faith) in an effort to convert them. Nor are there verses requiring their conversion to be a condition for peace. As we discussed earlier, conversion by force is in contradiction to the Qur'an and its fundamental teachings and will only produce hypocrites. Non-Muslims who lived in a Muslim state were only required to pay jizya (a tax) for their protection, which was much less than what Muslims paid in zakat. Furthermore, Islam does not consider People of the Book as enemies who must be killed or subjugated, as some critics suggest. This is false and illogical, as the Qur'an makes it clear: "And dispute you not with the People of the Book, except with means better (than mere disputation) [in good manner]" (29:46) and "The food of the People of the Book is lawful for you, and your food is lawful for them. (Lawful unto you in marriage) are the virtuous women of the believers and the virtuous women of the People of the Book when you give them their due dowers not in fornication, nor secret intrigues" (5:5). If they were truly enemies, how could they visit one another, share food, or

marry? What about the one who converts to Islam? Would his or her parents and siblings suddenly become enemies?

10. Islam is not about expansionism, as some critics suggest. Islam is about winning hearts, not territories. Islam encourages preaching and propagation of the faith through education, righteous acts, and exemplary human behavior, not through force and violence. It promotes peaceful coexistence with non–Muslims within Muslim nations, as well as with the rest of the world. If some Muslims or nations behave differently (or did so in the past), they do not represent Islam. Sometimes their actions conform in various degrees to Islamic teachings. However, there are also times when their actions are either independent of, or even in violation of Islamic teachings. Offending acts are often falsely committed in the name of faith as a result of ignorance, or sincere misunderstandings, misinterpretations, or even deliberate misrepresentations in order to justify such acts. The Qur'an repeatedly said to the Prophet (PBUH): "And we did not send you except to give glad tidings and warning" (25:56)[178] and "We made you not one to watch over their doings, nor are you set over them to dispose of their affair" (6:107). However, Islam also advocates strength and unity among Muslim communities and nations, so they can defend their faith, their lives, and their land should it become necessary. This is apparent in some of the verses we addressed related to the battles early Muslims fought.

11. Although our focus has been on certain Qur'anic verses and a few authentic narrations, we acknowledge there are many opinions (some by well-known Muslim scholars), narratives, and misquotations regarding war, violence, and jihad, some of which have found their way into major books of Hadith (narrations). Extremists who want to promote their version of Islam to uneducated, uninformed Muslims (and non-Muslims) and brand it as Islam, exploit such misrepresentations in order to gain support for their cause. While there are several ways to authenticate narrations, injunctions, and reports, the

first step for any truth seeker is to contrast any claim with the Qur'anic verses (using well-known translations by Yusuf Ali, Marmaduke Pickthall, T.B. Irving, M.A.S. Abdel Haleem or Sahih International). If it contradicts the Qur'an, it is either invalid, misquoted, or someone's opinion. If critics of Islam who put forth such evidence are genuinely concerned and interested in learning about Islam and its attitude toward war and peace, they should pursue it through scholarly methods, such as engaging well-known contemporary Muslim scholars in a debate or pursuing fact-finding inquiries in order to clarify such misunderstandings and misconceptions. There are numerous books written on the topic of Islam, violence, and related history, such as *The Preaching of Islam: A History of the Propagation of the Muslim Faith* by Thomas W. Arnold, *Understanding the Qur'an* by Muhammad Abdel Haleem, and *Silent No More: Confronting America's False Images of Islam* by Paul Findley, and many more on the biography of the Prophet (PBUH), the history, and the Qur'anic perspective, which are all available for those who wish to study further.

Notes

1   *The Qur'an*, translated by Abdullah Yusuf Ali (Tahrike Tarsile Qur'an, Inc.) Used for all translations in this book, unless otherwise specified as translated by the author. Some spelling and punctuation have been modernized or altered for clarity.

2   Muhammad Abdel Haleem, "Understanding the Quran," Islamicity.com, https://www.islamicity.org/4270/war-and-peace-in-the-quran/ (last viewed November 2016).

3   Muhammad Abdel Haleem, "Understanding the Quran," IslamiCity. com, https://www.islamicity.org/4270/war-and-peace-in-the-quran/ (last viewed November 2016).

4   Open Letter to Dr. Ibrahim Awwad Al-Badri, alias 'Abu Bakr Al-Baghdadi', http://www.lettertobaghdadi.com/14/english-v14.pdf (last viewed July 23, 2018).

5   Open Letter to Dr. Ibrahim Awwad Al-Badri, alias 'Abu Bakr Al-Baghdadi', http://www.lettertobaghdadi.com/14/english-v14.pdf (last viewed July 23, 2018).

6   Open Letter to Dr. Ibrahim Awwad Al-Badri, alias 'Abu Bakr Al-Baghdadi', http://www.lettertobaghdadi.com/14/english-v14.pdf (last viewed July 23, 2018).

7   Muhammad Abdel Haleem, "Understanding the Quran," IslamiCity. com, https://www.islamicity.org/4270/war-and-peace-in-the-quran/ (last viewed November 2016).

8   Asghar Ali Engineer, "Myths about Islam," Islamic Research Foundation, http://www.irfi.org/articles/articles_301_350/myths_about_islam.htm, (Last viewed September 2016).

9   Muhammad Abdel Haleem, "Understanding the Quran," IslamiCity. com, https://www.islamicity.org/4270/war-and-peace-in-the-quran/ (last viewed November 2016).

10 Muhammad Abdel Haleem, "Understanding the Quran," IslamiCity. com, https://www.islamicity.org/4270/war-and-peace-in-the-quran/ (last viewed November 2016).

11   Muhammad Abdel Haleem, "Understanding the Quran," IslamiCity. com, https://www.islamicity.org/4270/war-and-peace-in-the-quran/ (last viewed November 2016).

12   Muhammad ibn Jarir al-Tabari, *Jami' al-Bayan*, verse 29:69 (Beirut: Dar al-Fikr, 1984).

13   Muhammad ibn Jarir al-Tabari, *Jami' al-Bayan*, verse 25:52 (Beirut: Dar al-Fikr, 1984).

14   Ibn Ishaq, *The Life of Muhammad*, ed. Muhammad Hamidullah (Beirut: Dar al-Fikr, 1976), 156.

15   Muhammad ibn Jarir al-Tabari, *Tarikh al-Tabari – Tarikh al-Rosol wal-Molouk* (The history of al-Tabari), ed. Muhammad Abulfazl Ibrahim, vol. 2 (Cairo: Dar al-Ma'arif, 1961); Ali ibn al-Athir, *al-Kamil fi al-Tarikh*, vol 2. (Beirut: Dar al-Sadr, 1979).

16   Muhammad Mubarak, *Nizam al-Islam* (*Hekam al-doulah*) (Beirut: Dar al-Fikr, 1980), 38.

17   Mustafa Huseini Tabatabai, *Islam and the Topic of Violence* (Tehran: Tabatabai, 2017), 8–11.

18   Muhammad Abdel Haleem, "Understanding the Quran," IslamiCity.com, https://www.islamicity.org/4270/war-and-peace-in-the-quran/, (last viewed November 2016).

19   Asghar Ali Engineer,"Myths about Islam," Islamic Research Foundation, http://www.irfi.org/articles/articles_301_350/myths_about_islam.htm, (Last viewed September 2016).

20   Mustafa Huseini Tabatabai, *Bayane Ma'ani Dar Kalame Rabbani*, (Explanation and Meanings of Divine Words) vol. 1–4 (Tehran: Tabatabai, 2017), Translated by the Author, Adil Salahi, Translation and explanation of *Fi Zilal al-Qur'an*, https://www.kalamullah.com/al-quran.html

21   Translated by the author.

22   Muhammad Abdel Haleem, "Understanding the Quran," IslamiCity.com, https://www.islamicity.org/4270/war-and-peace-in-the-quran/, (last viewed November 2016).

23   Muhammad Abdel Haleem, "Understanding the Quran," IslamiCity.com, https://www.islamicity.org/4270/war-and-peace-in-the-quran/, (last viewed November 2016).

24   Translated by the author.

25   Asghar Ali Engineer, "Myths about Islam," Islamic Research Foundation, http://www.irfi.org/articles/articles_301_350/myths_about_islam.htm, (Last viewed September 2016).

26   Muhammad Abdel Haleem. "Understanding the Quran," Islamicity.com, https://www.islamicity.org/4270/war-and-peace-in-the-quran/ (last viewed November 2016).

27   Muhammad Abdel Haleem. "Understanding the Quran," Islamicity.com, https://www.islamicity.org/4270/war-and-peace-in-the-quran/ (last viewed November 2016).

28   Muhammad Abdel Haleem. "Understanding the Quran," Islamicity.com, https://www.islamicity.org/4270/war-and-peace-in-the-quran/ (last viewed November 2016).

29   The Bible: New International Version, https://www.biblegateway.com, (last viewed February 2016).

30   Ya'qoub Abu Yusuf, *Kitab al-Kharaj* (Taxation in Islam) (Cairo: al-Maktab al-Salafi, 1972), 131.

31   Thomas Walker Arnold, *The Preaching of Islam: A History of the Propagation of the Muslim Faith* (Archibald Constable & Co., 1896; Reprinted by Forgotten Books, 2015), 51.

32   Thomas Walker Arnold, *The Preaching of Islam: A History of the Propagation of the Muslim Faith*, 51. (Archibald Constable & Co., 1896; Reprinted by Forgotten Books, 2015), 51.

33   Mustafa Huseini Tabatabai, *Islam and the Topic of Violence* (Tehran: Tabatabai, 2017), 8–11. Translated by the Author

34   Husayn Haykal, *The Life of Mohammad*, 497, vol. 2, translated by Abul Qasem Payandeh to Farsi.

35   Mustafa Huseini Tabatabai, *Tahqiq dar Seerta Nabawi* (Tehran: Tabatabai, 2017). Translated by the Author

36   Ahmad ibn Hanbal, *al-Musnad*, vol. 14 (Lahore: Maktab al-Rahmaniah); Ibn Hisham, *al-Seerat al-Nabawiyyah* (The Prophet's Biography), ed. Ahmad Shams al Deen, vol. 3. (Beirut: Dar al-Maktab al-Hilal, 2009).

37   Ibn Hisham, *al-Seerat al-Nabawiyyah* (The Prophet's Biography), ed. Ahmad Shams al Deen, vol. 3 (Beirut: Dar al-Maktab al-Hilal, 2009).

38   Husayn Heykal, *The Life of Mohammad*, vol. 2, translated by Abul Qasem Payandeh to Farsi.

39   Translated by the author.

40   Muhammad Abdel Haleem, "Understanding the Quran," Islamicity.com, https://www.islamicity.org/4270/war-and-peace-in-the-quran/ (last viewed November 2016).

41   Paul Findley, *Silent No More* (Beltsville, MD: Amana, 2003), 124.

42   Muhammad ibn Jarir al-Tabari, *Tarikh al-Tabari – Tarikh al-Rosol wal-Molouk* (The history of al-Tabari), ed. Muhammad Abulfazl Ibrahim, vol. 5 (Cairo: Dar al-Ma'arif, 1961).

[43] Abu Dawood, *Sunan Abu Dawud*, ed. Sidqi Jamial al-Attar, vol. 2 (Kitab al-jihad) (Beirut: Dar al-Fikr, 2007).

[44] Translated by the author.

[45] Mustafa Huseini Tabatabai, *Islam and the Topic of Violence* (Tehran: Tabatabai, 2017), 8–11.

[46] Raghib al-Isfahani, *al-Mufradat fee Gharib al-Qur'an* (Beirut: Dar al-Marefah, 1946), 282.

[47] Mustafa Huseini Tabatabai, *Islam and the Topic of Violence* (Tehran: Tabatabai, 2017), 12–25. Translated by the Author

[48] Mustafa Huseini Tabatabai, *Islam and the Topic of Violence* (Tehran: Tabatabai, 2017), 12–25. Translated by the Author

[49] Muhammad ibn Umar al-Waqidi, *Kitab al-Maghazi*, ed. Marsden Jones, vol. 2 (Tehran: Danesh Islami, 1985), 821; Ibn Hisham, *al-Seerat al-Nabawiyyah* (The Prophet's Biography), ed. Ahmad Shams al Deen, 407, vol. 2, (Beirut: Dar al-Maktab al-Hilal, 2009), Muhammad ibn Jarir al-Tabari, *Tarikh al-Tabari – Tarikh al-Rosol wal-Molouk* (The history of al-Tabari), ed. Muhammad Abulfazl Ibrahim, vol. 2 (Cairo: Dar al-Ma'arif, 1961), 56.

[50] Muhammad ibn Umar al-Waqidi, *Kitab al-Maghazi*, ed. Marsden Jones, vol. 2 (Tehran: Danesh Islami, 1985), 821; Ibn Hisham, *al-Seerat al-Nabawiyyah* (The Prophet's Biography), ed. Ahmad Shams al Deen, 407, vol. 2, (Beirut: Dar al-Maktab al-Hilal, 2009), Muhammad ibn Jarir al-Tabari, *Tarikh al-Tabari – Tarikh al-Rosol wal-Molouk* (The history of al-Tabari), ed. Muhammad Abulfazl Ibrahim, vol. 2 (Cairo: Dar al-Ma'arif, 1961), 56.

[51] Muhammad ibn Umar al-Waqidi, *Kitab al-Maghazi*, ed. Marsden Jones, vol. 2 (Tehran: Danesh Islami, 1985), 821; Ibn Hisham, *al-Seerat al-Nabawiyyah* (The Prophet's Biography), ed. Ahmad Shams al Deen, 407, vol. 2, (Beirut: Dar al-Maktab al-Hilal, 2009), Muhammad ibn Jarir al-Tabari, *Tarikh al-Tabari – Tarikh al-Rosol wal-Molouk* (The history of al-Tabari), ed. Muhammad Abulfazl Ibrahim, vol. 2 (Cairo: Dar al-Ma'arif, 1961), 56.

[52] Muhammad ibn Umar al-Waqidi, *Kitab al-Maghazi*, ed. Marsden Jones, vol. 2 (Tehran: Danesh Islami, 1985), 821; Ibn Hisham, *al-Seerat al-Nabawiyyah* (The Prophet's Biography), ed. Ahmad Shams al Deen, 407, vol. 2, (Beirut: Dar al-Maktab al-Hilal, 2009), Muhammad ibn Jarir al-Tabari, *Tarikh al-Tabari – Tarikh al-Rosol wal-Molouk* (The history of al-Tabari), ed. Muhammad Abulfazl Ibrahim, vol. 2 (Cairo: Dar al-Ma'arif, 1961), 56.

[53] Ibn Hisham, *al-Seerat al-Nabawiyyah* (The Prophet's Biography), ed. Ahmad Shams al Deen, 412, vol. 2, (Beirut: Dar al-Maktab al-Hilal, 2009), Muhammad ibn Jarir al-Tabari, *Tarikh al-Tabari – Tarikh al-Rosol wal-Molouk* (The history of al-Tabari), ed. Muhammad Abulfazl Ibrahim,61 vol. 2 (Cairo: Dar al-Ma'arif, 1961).

54 Muhammad ibn Umar al-Waqidi, *Kitab al-Maghazi*, ed. Marsden Jones, vol. 2 (Tehran: Danesh Islami, 1985), 835.

55 Muhammad ibn Umar al-Waqidi, *Kitab al-Maghazi*, ed. Marsden Jones, vol. 2 (Tehran: Danesh Islami, 1985), 835.

56 Mustafa Huseini Tabatabai, *Islam and the Topic of Violence* (Tehran: Tabatabai, 2017), 12–25. Translated by the Author

57 Muhammad ibn Umar al-Waqidi, *Kitab al-Maghazi*, ed. Marsden Jones, vol. 2 (Tehran: Danesh Islami, 1985).

58 Muslim ibn al-Hajjaj, *Sahih Muslim*, vol. 4 (Beirut: Dar al-Ahya Turath al-Islami); Eyaz Maghrebi, *Kitab al-Shifa bi-Tarif Huquq al-Mustafa*, vol. 1 (Beirut: Dar Ibn Hazm).

59 Imam Muhammad al-Ghazali, *Ahya al-Uloumuddin*,201, vol. 3 (Dar al-Mesr al-Tab'ah Maktabat, 1998).

60 al-Sharqawi, *Fath al Mubdi*,151, vol 3 (Cairo: Mustafa al-Bub al-Halabi, 1921).

61 Muhammad ibn Umar al-Waqidi, *Kitab al-Maghazi*, ed. Marsden Jones, vol. 1 (Tehran: Danesh Islami, 1985).

62 Muhammad ibn Jarir al-Tabari, *Tarikh al-Tabari – Tarikh al-Rosol wal-Molouk* (The history of al-Tabari), ed. Muhammad Abulfazl Ibrahim, vol. 5, (Cairo: Dar al-Ma'arif, 1961)

63 Ahmad ibn Ya'qub, *Tarikh al- Ya'qubi*, vol. 2 (Beirut: Dar al-Sadr, 1960).

64 Ibn Kathir, *al-Seerat al-Nabawiyyah* (The Life of the Prophet Muhammad), vol. 3 (Beirut: Dar al Fikr,2005)

65 Abu Dawood, *Sunan Abu Dawud*, ed. Sidqi Jamial al-Attar, vol. 2 (Beirut: Dar al-Fikr, 2007).

66 Muhammad ibn Jarir al-Tabari, *Tarikh al-Tabari – Tarikh al-Rosol wal-Molouk* (The history of al-Tabari), ed. Muhammad Abulfazl Ibrahim, vol. 3 (Cairo: Dar al-Ma'arif, 1961); Ibn Hisham, *al-Seerat al-Nabawiyyah* (The Prophet's Biography), ed. Ahmad Shams al Deen, vol. 2 (Beirut: Dar al-Maktab al-Hilal, 2009); Muhammad ibn Umar al-Waqidi, *Kitab al-Maghazi*, ed. Marsden Jones, vol. 2 (Tehran: Danesh Islami, 1985).

67 Abu Dawood, *Sunan Abu Dawud*, ed. Sidqi Jamial al-Attar, vol. 2 (Beirut: Dar al-Fikr, 2007).

68 Mustafa Huseini Tabatabai. *Islam and the Topic of Violence* (Tehran: Tabatabai, 2017), 12–25.

69 Abdul Razzaq San'ani, *al-Musannaf*, vol. 6 (Karachi: al-Majles al-Elmi, 1970).

70 The Bible: New International Version, https://www.biblegateway.com/.

71 André Cresson, *Leo Tolstoy, Russian Stories* (Bulebook, 1948). Translated to Farsi by Kazim Imadi (Tehran: Safi Ali Shah Publishing).

72   Mustafa Huseini Tabatabai, *Islam and the Topic of Violence* (Tehran: Tabatabai, 2017), 2. Translated by the Author

73   John-Jacques Rousseau, *The Social Contract* (New York: Knickerbocker Press, 1893). Translated to Farsi by Inayatallah Shakibapour (Farrokhi Publishing, 1966).

74   Mustafa Huseini Tabatabai. *Islam and the Topic of Violence* (Tehran: Tabatabai, 2017), 2–3. Translated by the Author

75   Charles-Louis Montesquieu, *The Spirit of the Laws* (Cambridge: Cambridge UP, 1989). Translated to Farsi by Ali Akbar Muhtadi (Amir Kabir Publishing, 1984).

76   The Bible: New International Version, https://www.biblegateway.com

77   John Elder, "*History of the American Presbyterian Mission to Iran, 1834–1960*,"38, Literature Committee of the Church Council of Iran-Noor Jahan,Tehran.

78   Tom Anderson, "*Violence More Common in Bible than Qur'an, Text Analysis Reveals*," https://www.independent.co.uk/arts-entertainment/books/violence-more-common-in-bible-than-quran-text-analysis-reveals-a6863381.html, February 9, 2016.

79   M.H. Hart, *The 100: A Ranking of the Most Influential Persons in History* (New York: Citadel Press, 1978), 33.

80   Lamartine, Alphonse de. *Histoire de la Turquie*. Vol. II. (Paris: 1854), 276–277. https://gallica.bnf.fr/ark:/12148/bpt6k29365z/f282.item.r=Page%20276

81   Muhammad ibn Umar al-Waqidi, *Kitab al-Maghazi*, ed. Marsden Jones, vol. 1 (Tehran: Danesh Islami, 1985).

82   Abu Dawood, *Sunan Abu Dawud*, ed. Sidqi Jamial al-Attar, vol. 2 (Beirut: Dar al-Fikr, 2007).

83   Israel Wolfensohn, *Tarikh al-Yahud fi Bilad al-Arab* (History of Jews in Arab Territory) (Egypt: 1927), 142.

84   Ibn Hisham, *al-Seerat al-Nabawiyyah* (The Prophet's Biography), ed. Ahmad Shams al Deen, vol. 1 (Beirut: Dar al-Maktab al-Hilal, 2009).

85   Ibn Hisham, *al-Seerat al-Nabawiyyah* (The Prophet's Biography), ed. Ahmad Shams al Deen, vol. 2 (Beirut: Dar al-Maktab al-Hilal, 2009).

86   Ibn Hisham, *al-Seerat al-Nabawiyyah* (The Prophet's Biography), ed. Ahmad Shams al Deen, vol. 2 (Beirut: Dar al-Maktab al-Hilal, 2009).

87   Abdul Razzaq San'ani, *al-Musannaf*, vol. 6 (Karachi: al-Majlis al-Elmi, 1970).; Muhammad al-Bukhari, *Sahih al-Bukhari*, vol. 4 (Dar Matabea Shuab).

88   Muhammad al-Bukhari, *Sahih al-Bukhari*, vol. 1 (Dar Matabea Shuab).

89 Muhammad ibn Jarir al-Tabari, *Tarikh al-Tabari – Tarikh al-Rosol wal-Molouk* (The history of al-Tabari), ed. Muhammad Abulfazl Ibrahim, vol. 2 (Cairo: Dar al-Ma'arif, 1961); Ibn Hisham, *al-Seerat al-Nabawiyyah* (The Prophet's Biography), ed. Ahmad Shams al Deen, vol. 2 (Beirut: Dar al-Maktab al-Hilal, 2009).

90 Mustafa Huseini Tabatabai, *Tahqiq dar Seerta Nabawi* (Study of the Prophet's Biography) (Tehran: Tabatabai, 2016). Translated by the author.

91 Muhammad ibn Jarir al-Tabari, *Tarikh al-Tabari – Tarikh al-Rosol wal-Molouk* (The history of al-Tabari), ed. Muhammad Abulfazl Ibrahim, vol. 2 (Cairo: Dar al-Ma'arif, 1961); Ibn Hisham, *al-Seerat al-Nabawiyyah* (The Prophet's Biography), ed. Ahmad Shams al Deen, vol. 2 (Beirut: Dar al-Maktab al-Hilal, 2009); Muhammad ibn Umar al-Waqidi, *Kitab al-Maghazi*, ed. Marsden Jones, vol. 1 (Tehran: Danesh Islami, 1985).

92 Muhammad ibn Jarir al-Tabari, *Tarikh al-Tabari – Tarikh al-Rosol wal-Molouk* (The history of al-Tabari), ed. Muhammad Abulfazl Ibrahim, vol. 2 (Cairo: Dar al-Ma'arif, 1961); Ibn Hisham, *al-Seerat al-Nabawiyyah* (The Prophet's Biography), ed. Ahmad Shams al Deen, vol. 2 (Beirut: Dar al-Maktab al-Hilal, 2009); Muhammad ibn Umar al-Waqidi, *Kitab al-Maghazi*, ed. Marsden Jones, vol. 1 (Tehran: Danesh Islami, 1985).

93 Abdul Razzaq San'ani, *al-Musannaf*, vol. 6 (Karachi: al-Majles al-Elmi, 1970).

94 Mustafa Huseini Tabatabai, *Tahqiq dar Seerat Nabawi* (Study of the Prophet's Biography) (Tehran: Tabatabai, 2016), 138–146. Translated by the author.

95 Ibn Hisham, *al-Seerat al-Nabawiyyah* (The Prophet's Biography), ed. Ahmad Shams al Deen, vol. 2 (Beirut: Dar al-Maktab al-Hilal, 2009); Abul Fazi Bayhaqi, *Tarikh-i Bayhaqi*, vol. 3. (Tehran: Hirmand Publishing)

96 Ibn Hisham, *al-Seerat al-Nabawiyyah* (The Prophet's Biography), ed. Ahmad Shams al Deen, vol. 2 (Beirut: Dar al-Maktab al-Hilal, 2009).

97 Suleiman Nadwi, *Seerat Al Nabi*, vol. 1 (in Urdu), narrative from an article by Ustad Sa'd Rustam in Arabic.

98 Mustafa Huseini Tabatabai, *Tahqiq dar Seerat Nabawi* (Study of Prophet's Biography) (Tehran: Tabatabai, 2017), 160–161. Translated by the author.

99 *Sahih Muslim, Kitab al-jihad, bab al-imdad ghazwat al-Badr, no. 1763*

100 Abu Dawood, *Al jihad*, no.2747; Ibn Sa'd, *al-Tabaqat al-Kabir*, vol 2. (Laydan Press, Muassisa al Nasr, 1902)

101 Ibn Hisham, *al-Seerat al-Nabawiyyah* (The Prophet's Biography), ed. Ahmad Shams al Deen, vol. 2 (Beirut: Dar al-Maktab al-Hilal, 2009).

102 Ali ibn Abdel-Malik al-Hindi, *Kanz al-Ummal fi Sunan al-Aqwal wal af'al* (Treasure of Doers of Good Deeds), ed. Mahmud Umar al-Dumyati, vol. 2. (Beirut: Dar al-Kotob al-Ilmiyah, 1998).

[103] Mustafa Huseini Tabatabai, *Tahqiq dar Seerat Nabawi* (Study of Prophet's Biography) (Tehran: Tabatabai, 2016), 160–161. Translated by the author.

[104] Ibn Hisham, *al-Seerat al-Nabawiyyah* (The Prophet's Biography), ed. Ahmad Shams al Deen, vol. 2 (Beirut: Dar al-Maktab al-Hilal, 2009).

[105] al- Bayhaqi, *Dalail -un- Nubuwwah*, vol 3; Ibn Hisham, *al-Seerat al-Nabawiyyah* (The Prophet's Biography), ed. Ahmad Shams al Deen, vol. 2 (Beirut: Dar al-Maktab al-Hilal, 2009).

[106] Muhammad ibn Umar al-Waqidi, *Kitab al-Maghazi*, ed. Marsden Jones, vol. 1 (Tehran: Danesh Islami, 1985).

[107] Ibn Hisham, *al-Seerat al-Nabawiyyah* (The Prophet's Biography), ed. Ahmad Shams al Deen, 501, vol. 1 (Beirut: Dar al-Maktab al-Hilal, 2009); *al Amwal*, 184, (maktab al Kuliat, al Azhariah-Cairo); *Sahih Bukhari*, book 3 (49), book 58 (10 and 17), book 78 (23), book 96 (6); *Sahih Muslim,* book 20 (17), book 44 (50); Ahmad ibn Hanbal, *al-Musnad,* 79,119,122,127, vol 1, 178,180, vol.2, 221, vol 3,141, vol.4 (Lahore: Maktab al-Rahmaniah).

[108] Translated by the author

[109] Muhammad ibn Umar al-Waqidi, *Kitab al-Maghazi*, ed. Marsden Jones, vol. 1 (Tehran: Danesh Islami, 1985).

[110] Mustafa Huseini Tabatabai, *Tahqiq dar Seerat Nabawi* (Study of the Prophet's Biography) (Tehran: Tabatabai, 2016), 164–166. Translated by the author.

[111] Dr. Israel Wolfensohn, *Tarikh al-Yahud fi Bilad al-Arab* (History of Jews in Arab Territory) (Egypt: 1927), 142.

[112] Muhammad ibn Umar al-Waqidi, *Kitab al-Maghazi*, ed. Marsden Jones, vol. 1 (Tehran: Danesh Islami, 1985).

[113] Ahmad bin Zaini Dahlan Makki, *Seerat al-Nabawiyyah*, vol. 1.

[114] Mustafa Huseini Tabatabai, *Tahqiq dar Seerat Nabawi* (Study of the Prophet's Biography) (Tehran: Tabatabai, 2016) 239–240, Translated by the author

[115] Mustafa Huseini Tabatabai, *Tahqiq dar Seerat Nabawi* (Study of the Prophet's Biography) (Tehran: Tabatabai, 2016) 240–246, Translated by the author.

[116] Muhammad ibn Umar al-Waqidi, *Kitab al-Maghazi*, ed. Marsden Jones, vol. 1 (Tehran: Danesh Islami, 1985).

[117] Ibn Hisham, *al-Seerat al-Nabawiyyah* (The Prophet's Biography), ed. Ahmad Shams al Deen, vol. 3 (Beirut: Dar al-Maktab al-Hilal, 2009).

[118] Muhammad ibn Umar al-Waqidi, *Kitab al-Maghazi*, ed. Marsden Jones, vol. 1 (Tehran: Danesh Islami, 1985).

[119] Mustafa Huseini Tabatabai, *Tahqiq dar Seerat Nabawi* (Study of the Prophet's Biography) (Tehran: Tabatabai, 2016, Translated by the author.

[120] Mustafa Huseini Tabatabai, *Bayane Ma'ani Dar Kalame Rabbani* (Explanation and Meanings of Divine Words) vol. 1–4 (Tehran: Tabatabai, 2017): Adil

Salahi, Translation and explanation of *Fi Zilal al-Qur'an* : https://www.kalamullah.com/al-quran.html

[121] What Makes Islam So Different (accessed January 2017): https://www.thereligionofpeace.com/pages/quran/violence.aspx; 164 Jihad Verses in the Koran (accessed January 2017): https://www.answering-islam.org/Quran/Themes/jihad_passages.html

[122] Translated by the author.

[123] Mustafa Huseini Tabatabai. *Islam and the Topic of Violence* (Tehran: Tabatabai, 2017), 35–38. Translated by the Author

[124] Mustafa Huseini Tabatabai. *Islam and the Topic of Violence* (Tehran: Tabatabai, 2017), 35–38, Translated by the author

[125] al-Malik ibn Anas, *Al Muwatta,* (Egypt: al-Makatb al-Tijariah al-Kubra; English version: Norwich, United Kingdom: Diwan Press, 1984)

[126] Ahmad ibn Hanbal, *al-Musnad,* vol 1 (Lahore: Maktab al-Rahmaniah)

[127] Mustafa Huseini Tabatabai. *Islam and the Topic of Violence* (Tehran: Tabatabai, 2017), 38. Translated by the Author

[128] Translated by the author.

[129] What Makes Islam So Different: https://www.thereligionofpeace.com/pages/quran/violence.aspx

[130] Translated by the author.

[131] Muhammad ibn Jarir al-Tabari, *Jami' al-Bayan,* vol. 10 (Beirut: Dar al-Fikr, 1984), 61–63.

[132] Translated by the author.

[133] Translated by the author.

[134] Muhammad ibn Jarir al-Tabari, *Jami' al-Bayan,* vol. 10 (Beirut: Dar al-Fikr, 1984), 61–65

[135] Translated by the author.

[136] What Makes Islam So Different: https://www.thereligionofpeace.com/pages/quran/violence.aspx

[137] Translated by the author.

[138] Muhammad ibn Jarir al-Tabari, *Jami' al-Bayan,* vol. 10 (Beirut: Dar al-Fikr, 1984), 70-72

[139] What Makes Islam So Different: https://www.thereligionofpeace.com/pages/quran/violence.aspx

[140] Translated by the author.

[141] Translated by the author.

[142] Translated by the author.

[143] Translated by the author.

[144] Translated by the author.

[145] Translated by the author.

[146] Translated by the author.

[147] Translated by the author.

[148] Translated by the author.

[149] Translated by the author.

[150] Gustave Le Bon, *La Civilisation des Arabes* (1884); The World of Islamic Civilization (New York: Tudor, 1974).

[151] Adil Salahi, Translation and explanation of *Fi Zilal al-Qur'an,* 93–94 vol.8 (surah_9) https://www.kalamullah.com/al-quran.html

[152] Paul Findley, *Silent No More* (Beltsville, MD: Amana, 2003), 66.

[153] Translated by the author.

[154] Ibn Ishaq, *The Life of Muhammad*, ed. Muhammad Hamidullah (Beirut: Dar al-Fikr, 1976), 156; Muhammad ibn Umar al-Waqidi, *Kitab al-Maghazi*, ed. Marsden Jones, vol. 1 (Tehran: Danesh Islami, 1985).

[155] What Makes Islam So Different: https://www.thereligionofpeace.com/pages/quran/violence.aspx

[156] Beyhaqi, *Dala'il an-Nubuwwa*, 206, vol 5.

[157] What Makes Islam So Different: https://www.thereligionofpeace.com/pages/quran/violence.aspx

[158] Translated by the author.

[159] Translated by the author.

[160] What Makes Islam So Different: https://www.thereligionofpeace.com/pages/quran/violence.aspx

[161] What Makes Islam So Different: https://www.thereligionofpeace.com/pages/quran/violence.aspx

[162] Translated by the author.

[163] Hillary Mayell, "Thousands of Women Killed for Family Honor," *National Geographic News*, Published February 12, 2002, accessed 2017 https://news.nationalgeographic.com/news/2002/02/0212_020212_honorkilling.html

[164] John Esposito, *What Everyone Needs to Know About Islam* (New York: Oxford University Press, 2011), 177.

[165] Jonathan A.C. Brown, *Misquoting Muhammad: The Challenge and Choices of Interpreting the Prophet's Legacy* (London: One World Publications, 2014), 180.

[166] Hillary Mayell, "Thousands of Women Killed for Family Honor," *National Geographic News*, Published February 12, 2002, accessed 2017 https://news.nationalgeographic.com/news/2002/02/0212_020212_honorkilling.html

[167] Greg Woolf, *Ancient Civilizations: The Illustrated Guide to Belief, Mythology and Art* (San Diego: Thunder Bay Press, 2005), 386.

168   Tom Holmberg, "The Civil Code: An Overview," The Napoleon Series. http://www.napoleon-series.org.

169   Tom Holmberg, "France: Penal Code of 1810," The Napoleon Series. http:// www.napoleon-series.org, April 2007.

170   Danielle M. Becknell, "Gender Based Violence in Jordan: Domestic Violence and Honor Crimes," Secular Islam, http://www.centerforinquiry. net; http://digitalcollections.sit.edu/cgi/viewcontent.cgi?article=1427& context=isp_collection

171   What Makes Islam So Different: https://www.thereligionofpeace.com/ pages/quran/violence.aspx

172   What Makes Islam So Different: https://www.thereligionofpeace.com/ pages/quran/violence.aspx

173   What Makes Islam So Different: https://www.thereligionofpeace.com/ pages/quran/violence.aspx

174   Translated by author.

175   What Makes Islam So Different: https://www.thereligionofpeace.com/ pages/quran/violence.aspx

176   Husayn Haykal, *The Life of Mohammad*, 376, vol. 2, translated by Abul Qasem Payandeh to Farsi.

177   Muhammad ibn Umar al-Waqidi, *Kitab al-Maghazi*, ed. Marsden Jones, vol. 2 (Tehran: Danesh Islami, 1985); Ibn Sa'd, *al-Tabaqat al-Kabir,* vol 2. (Laydan Press, Muassisa al Nasr, 1902)

178   Translated by the author.

Index of Qur'an Verses

Subject Index

Author's Biography

Naqi Elmi has been engaged in Islamic studies for over 20 years, including extensive research on the Qur'an. As an active member of his community, he conducts outreach and educational programs for non-Muslims and recent converts to Islam. He has also written several op-eds on the common misconceptions of Islam in the media. He holds masters degrees in engineering and business administration.

Printed in the United States
By Bookmasters